You know you watch too much anime when . . .

You plan to be an astronaut just so you can visit the Moon Kingdom.

You dive your face into a Chinese book and scream ,"Tamahome, I'm coming!!!"

You see a fight breaking out and you start to get a mic to begin singing that your boyfriend is a pilot in order to stop the fight and bring peace to all.

You find a golden bowling ball with a star on it, and you are convinced Vegeta is nearby.

You attempt to find *Vision of Escaflowne* songs in a hymn book during church services.

You capture mice and stick their tails into electric sockets hoping that they will become like Pikachu.

You research travel guides about information on Chinese springs because you desire an instant and painless sex change.

You catalog all the phone numbers listed with the name "Goddess" or "Belldandy" and start calling.

You get blueprints of your school and look for an upside-down floating castle in the sky or ruins that act as a gate to an alternative world.

You attempt to send things through "Kiki's Delivery Service" because you think it's faster than UPS.

If you are a man in love with a male friend, you believe it's because you were a dead moon woman in your past life.

You think the Christmas song "Angels We Have Heard on High" is actually an *Evangelion* prophecy.

You are an engineering major and you send your application to the Gundam Department of NASA.

You are a girl who applies to get into the Greenwood Dorm just to see how long it takes for all your dormmates to realize that you're not a boy.

You try to find the video store Gokuraku and insist on a lifetime membership.

You watch *Otaku no Video* . . . and forget to laugh.

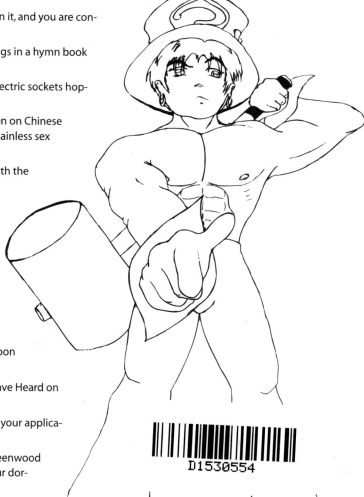

Who said "too much anime"?!

RYAN OMEGA

Anime Trivia Quizbook
From Easy to Otaku Obscure

EPISODE 1

Stone Bridge Press • Berkeley, California

Published by
Stone Bridge Press
P.O. Box 8208, Berkeley, CA 94707
TEL 510-524-8732 • FAX 510-524-8711
sbp@stonebridge.com • www.stonebridge.com

Printed in the United States of America.

10   9   8   7   6   5   4   3   2   1
2004 2003 2002 2001 2000

ISBN 1-880656-44-2

Contents

Introduction

Okay, boys and girls, *shōnen* and *shōjo*, looking for a challenge? Try climbing Mt. Fuji! Looking for fun? Go to Disneyland! In Tokyo! But if you have been watching Japanese animation for countless hours and think that—when it comes to anime—you're somewhat of an expert, you've come to the right place!

It's my job to prove you wrong<^.^>

If you think I'm going to ask you what color Pikachu is or which character in *Ranma 1/2* changes from a guy to a girl, you are sadly mistaken. This book is not for the anime wimp. But to see how the book got this way, here's the little history behind this book. (Don't wanna read it? Tough!)

It started as a game show for the anime convention, Fanimecon, in San Jose, with my partners in crime, Scott Rux and Matt Stocksiek (sorry for being so comma-happy in that last sentence!). Actually, Scott wanted to go with the format that you see now; he has a shrine made for the computer game *You Don't Know Jack*. I wanted to use any game show with a lightning round and use real lightning if the contestants got a wrong answer. But we could not fit it into our budget so we settled for throwing Koosh balls instead. Oh, and Matt did not get a say. Scott and I were busy kidnapping him into our writing team and forcing him to write with a Koosh ball held to his face.

By the time Fanimecon rolled around, we were all devoid of sleep, but as long as Scott got his coffee, we knew no furniture would be harmed. A crowd of seven people swarmed in. We brought three people up to the table: our first victims. Well, I did not mean to put it that way, but they were slaughtered when that whole group of contestants could answer only 5 of our 25 questions. That's when I realized our questions were not for the ill-informed anime fan whose claim to fandom consisted entirely of watching *Sailor Moon* on TV and *Akira*.

So what happens if you are able to answer all the questions in this book?

Fame and glory? Riches beyond your wildest dreams? An unexpected phone call from a Goddess granting any wish you want? Pah! Get real! But at least you'll know why *Pokemon* is called "Pocket Monster" in Japan, why Ken from *Street Fighter* has the last name "Masters," and what Sailor Moon's blood type is (in case you need a blood transfusion, of course).

If you are a rather new anime fan, please don't be discouraged. I'm sure there's going to be some anime here that you've never heard about before, and I hope this encourages you to go find those tapes. Anime is not just giant robots and magical girls; it definitely has a lot more to offer.

If you are a self-proclaimed *otaku* (a person obsessed with anime), then your otakuness is at stake! The average fan should be able to answer 50% of the questions. Since you otaku consider yourselves a higher standard of anime fan (or lower standard, depending who you ask), your target rate should be 80%.

However, there is one obstacle; if you are a *Macross* freak and know everything there is to know about *Macross*, it can't help you here! This book covers a lot of different kinds of anime, from your basic shōnen (boys') and shōjo (not *shojo*, which means "virgin") anime to merchandise, translations, and even gender confused (which is not technically correct since the anime characters know what gender they are even if the audience doesn't). Then I throw in a couple of random categories for questions that did not necessarily fit anywhere (i.e., I just got lazy).

Of course, there is a bias to these questions. I know some anime better than some others (obviously, you do too). At first I was ambitious and tried to achieve a balance with the questions, but later I pretty much said, "Screw it!" and just wrote them out. So there's going to be anime that I left out of here and some that I mention too much. Hey, if you want fair, go to a courthouse. Not here. Some questions won't be for you. But the categories in this book are generally arranged in order of difficulty, with, for example, the questions on video games preceding those for the less-better-known voice actors. But there are difficult questions within each category as well.

Scattered throughout are some sidebars and images. More puzzles!

If you need answers, check the reverse of the question page you're on (except for answers to questions in sidebars). You should be able to figure that out on your own, but I'm being nice here.

How to use this book

Okay, on the off-chance that you actually try to use this book to test out the anime knowledge of your friends or a group, here are some tips:

1. You can do it informally. Just have someone read the questions and have everyone else answer them. It would probably be better letting people take turns being the quizmaster. Share the wealth.

2. Divide into teams and have a neutral person ask the questions. You can use buzzers or sledgehammers, just something to indicate who has the right to answer first. Personally, we like throwing a koosh ball at the host.

3. Questions get harder toward the end of each question category. Give each set of five questions a different value. For example, the first five questions might be worth a hundred points. The next set of five might be two hundred and so on.

4. Keep track of your answers—indicated in the text by the symbol ■ —using the chart at the back of the book. I've talked to the publisher, and he hereby grants you permission to copy the answer chart as often as you need to. Generous!

5. Snappy banter is included with the answers. Use it at your own risk.

6. Give the winner either a trip to Hawaii or a used lottery ticket. Your choice.

7. The point is basically to have fun.

Romanization and titles

Romanization, or the system of writing Japanese words in English, can be a bit tricky. So here's a guide to how I romanized Japanese words in this book:

1. The letters ō and ū indicate extended or "long" vowel sounds. Long vowel signs are not used in Japanese words or in proper names that have come into general use in English (like Tokyo, Osaka) or when the anime itself uses a particular spelling for its English-language edition (like "Mousse" and "Ryoga" instead of the more "correct" Mūsu and Ryōga). Yes, I know this creates some consistency problems, but I swear I've done my best to keep this all straight!

2. Anime are referred to by their most familiar titles (or what I think is their most familiar titles) in the U.S. For example, I will refer to *You're Under Arrest!* instead of *Taihō Shitchau Zo!* But I may in some cases give both names, as in *Yū Yū Hakusho* (Poltergeist Report).

3. An anime not officially released in the U.S. that has only a Japanese title will be referred to by its Japanese name and a translation of that name as in *Kareshi to Kanojo no Jijō* (His and Her Circumstances). Be aware that when the anime is eventually released overseas, its English name may be different from what I've provided here.

4. I am going with the sticky Western convention of given name first and family name last for Japanese names. Most anime are released in the U.S. with press materials and credits giving the names in Western style, so it makes sense to follow that same practice here. But I don't know .... hmmm, I guess "Schodt Fred" would look kind of odd.

Acknowledgments

People I would like to thank:

Gilles Poitras, who gave me the opportunity to show how much useless information I know regarding the hobby I love.

Scott Rux and Matt Stocksiek, my aforementioned partners-in-crime, who did more than their fair share for the game show.

Mabel at Vallejo Comics and Baseball, whose store has such a great selection of anime that she made it inevitable that I become a fan.

Niko, whose constant enthusiasm reminds me why I am an anime fan in the first place.

Mike Siu, who claims to be a jaded fan but puts his heart and soul into everything.

The crew at Fanimecon, especially Tomoko and Yoko, who work hard and play harder!

All my sensei at Berkeley, where I learned the word *jimaku* (subtitles).

Professor Miryam Sas, Kirsten, and the Japanese Cinema class, from whom I learned that I actually had a lot to say and a lot to learn about anime.

Actionace.com for paying me for my hobby <^.^>. Especially John Wong and Renee Adams for helping me keep on track.

My buddies at Cal Animage Alpha at U.C. Berkeley, especially:

Soung Lee, the *seiyū* guru and all-around good guy.

Mara Cheng, my favorite cat-girl and the one who dragged me into the club.

Eileen "Kaki" Hu, my best friend and the all-around perkiest girl in a short skirt (I had to mention it, don't kill me!).

Her sister, Emily "Ami-chan" Hu, for all the fun companionship where we can just get silly sometimes.

Monica "Akira-chan" Shin, Miss Anime Fangirl, who I have to bow down to for her vast knowledge and massive collection, as well as a good friendship.

Brian "Chairman" Mao, for being the guy that has to deal with the administration so we can show all this anime.

Craig Nishida, for getting all those tapes!!! Banzai!

Egan Loo, for all those updates and yummy rumors.

"If I left anyone out, don't hate me<*.*>"

And last but not least, I have to thank Ranma Saotome, Subaru Sumeragi, Makino Tsukushi, Kyōsuke Kasuga, Kamui Shirow, Chichiri, Hotaru Tomoe, Issei Nishikiyori, Kaede Rukawa, Shinji Ikari, Utena Tenjou, Sana Kurata, Himeko Nonohara, Yū Matsuura, Sakura Kinomoto, Nausicaä, Ashitaka and San, Faye Valentine and Spike, and everyone else. None of them are real, but all of them live in my own world.

Puffball

These are the easy questions. However, what I might consider easy might not be easy for someone else, so these questions deal exclusively with the anime that are well known among American fans. Enjoy!

1. I Choose You!

In order to be a Pokemon master, you have to collect Pokemon. The problem is, some people are so addicted to collecting Pokemon they act more like Pokemon slaves!

Everyone knows that when Ash got to Professor Oak's lab, he was given Pikachu as his first Pokemon. However, which Pokemon did Ash originally intend to choose?

- Charmander
- Bulbasaur
- Squirtle
- Ryo-Ohki

2. Sailor Salaries

Even though the Sailor Scouts fight to save Earth from the Negaverse, they aren't paid for it, so they need jobs on the side. Most of the girls will be okay in that respect, but Serena has got to list more on her resume than stuffing her face with food, although she definitely has experience with that.

Which Sailor Scout likes to "play nurse?"

- Sailor Venus
- Sailor Jupiter
- Sailor Mercury
- Sailor Hotpants

3. Son of a . . .

Dragonball characters have got to be the strongest people in the universe. So why aren't they in the Mr. Universe pageant? How much dignity do you think Piccolo can have wearing a pair of skimpy briefs and being paraded out on stage?

How are Son Goku and Son Gohan in *Dragonball Z* related?

- Brothers
- Cousins
- Father and son
- Cow and dairymaid

4. Your ad here!

There was a time when race cars simply had numbers and not all those advertisements stuck on them. I figure while the cars are going around the race track about 400 times, you better give the audience something to read.

What is painted on the side of Speed Racer's car?

- A number
- A symbol
- A large X
- A bucket of dancing chickens from Bubba's Barbecue Grill and Chicken Hut

5. Instant Dye

Only true *Ranma* fans would take a dip in the Spring of Drowned Man or Woman just to change the color of their hair! It also changes which restroom you have to go to, but that is another matter.

What color is Ranma-chan's hair in the manga?

- Red
- Black
- Blue
- Plaid

1. I Choose You!

- **Charmander**. Although Ash would never have to worry about making instant toast, it's not the right answer.

- **Bulbasaur**. This Pokemon would be useful if the Pokemon trainer was Indiana Jones, but Ash isn't exactly as nimble, nor is he pursuing the Holy Grail; so this isn't the right answer either.

- ■ **Squirtle**. Well, I'm impressed. If nothing else, you have at least watched the first episode of *Pokemon*. And you have a good memory as well!

- **Ryo-Ohki**. Well now, this isn't good. Ryo-Ohki isn't even a Pokemon. She's not even in the *Pokemon* series! What kind of *Pokemon* fan are you anyway?

Pikachu is so popular that is inevitable that stuffed animals are made of this Pokemon. What I did not expect was a warning that said "Do not stick tail into electric socket" on its tag!

2. Sailor Salaries

- ■ **Sailor Venus**. Good! You know your Sailor Scouts!

- **Sailor Jupiter**. Nope. She would make a better chef than a nurse.

- **Sailor Mercury**. Uh-uh. Sailor Mercury is destined not only to be a protector of the Moon Princess, but you can play doctor with her. Although she can immediately give you an ice blast if you get too out of control.

- **Sailor Hotpants**. Yes, Sailor Hotpants, the least known Sailor Scout, loves to play nurse. But she's an even better dominatrix.

Sailor Venus may be a well-intentioned nurse, but I don't want to be target practice with a well-intentioned nurse when syringes are around.

3. Son of a . . .

- **Brothers**. Yes, the mother believed in having her kids very far apart so that she doesn't have to hire a babysitter the second time around. I don't think so.

- **Cousins**. "Cousins, they're identical cousins . . ." except one is really scrawny and the other looks like he's on steroids. Nope.

- ■ **Father and son**. Precisely. Son Goku and Son Gohan are indeed father and son. You were good enough that the name "Son" did not confuse you, as it did one confused person who wondered why their first names were alike and if their last names were different, how they could be related?

- **Cow and dairymaid**. Um, no.

The main moral found in *Dragonball* is that if you work hard enough, you can accomplish anything. Which doesn't explain why their hair looks like that.

4. Your ad here!

- ■ **A number**. That's right. "5" is the number on the side and the car is known as the infamous Mach 5, although I have yet to see it go that fast.

- **A symbol**. Who do you think he is? Prince? Uh-uh.

- **A large X**. This is the Mach 5, not the car from the Dukes of Hazzard!

- **A bucket of dancing chickens from Bubba's Barbecue Grill and Chicken Hut**. Are my questions really that straining on you?

At this moment, I really can't think of any appropriate advertisements on Speed's car except for Sesame Street, brought to you today by the number "5."

5. Instant Dye

- **Red**. Hey blind eyes! Didn't you remember to read the word "manga?" Hint, hint.

- ■ **Black**. Correct. The answer is simple, isn't it? Manga are printed in black and white, so Ranma's hair has got to be black, even if Ranma has Clairol hair colors in the manga.

- **Blue**. Um. Why would it be blue? I don't remember Ranma going through a blue hair phase (although Akane is still in hers in the anime).

- **Plaid**. It is completely possible for Ranma to have plaid hair in the manga, but why have a hair color that fashion editors dictate will always be in or out of season?

Drowned springs . . . safer than chemicals! Although there are still side-effects . . .

1. You'd have to be dim as a bulb not to know this one . . .

Who knew that sweet little Pikachu could be a serial killer? Although the judge and jury were especially harsh on him by giving him the death sentence, the judge was too taken with Pikachu's cuteness that he let Pikachu decide how wanted to die. What would be Pikachu's most logical choice of all the execution systems currently in existence?

- ANSWER: _____

2. She's too cute to be a Ghost King

Some snobby people like to say that they are descended from kings. Of course, the closest they have actually come to kings is in a casino playing video poker while begging for change.

Which of these animals cannot claim to be a relative of the *Tenchi Muyō* mascot, Ryo-Ohki?

- Bugs Bunny
- Garfield
- Felix
- Mr. Ed

3. Life is like a box of chocolates . . .

Sometimes if you have to explain something, it is best to use an analogy. We use analogies all the time, like "Life is like a box of chocolates; you have to see a dentist eventually."

In *Dragonball*, which of these things is the closest to what a "Dragonball" looks like?

- A gold tennis ball with stars on it
- A bead the size of a marble
- A bowling ball with a snake trapped inside it
- A crystal ball with the decapitated head of Sailor Moon

4. Odd woman out

Due to budgeting cuts, Sailor Moon has to drop one of her Sailor Senshi (yeah, yeah, I know about this being contrary to an earlier question, but who cares?). Sailor Moon, in a strange burst of intelligence, decides that only ASTRONOMICAL inner planets can stay.

Which Senshi gets canned and writes a tell-all book on Sailor Moon?

- Sailor Mercury
- Sailor Mars
- Sailor Venus
- Sailor Jupiter

5. I can just eat you up

Have you have heard someone go, "Ooh, you are so cute, I can just eat you up?" Isn't that just a little disturbing?

Judging from Mokona's appearance in *Magic Knight Rayearth*, it would most likely be an ingredient for a:

- PB&J
- S'mores
- BLT
- Falafel

Mitsuru from *Here Is Greenwood* shows off his big sword. In this scene, who is on the other end of this sword?

(a) Shinobu (b) Kazuya (c) Shun (d) Aoki

1. You have to be dim as a bulb not to know this one . . .

- ■ **Electric chair**. Hey, if I gave you a selection, the answer would be too easy! At least, it would be too easy unless you were hiding under a rock for the past 20 years. Or you're such a pacifist that you dropped electric chairs from your selective memory.

2. She's too cute to be a Ghost King

- **Bugs Bunny**. Sorry. Bugs Bunny can claim to come from the rabbit side of Ryo-Ohki's family. But Bugs Bunny doesn't really need Ryo-Ohki's help. He just needs to sell licensing rights of himself in Japan.

- **Garfield**. Nope. Garfield can claim to come from the cat side of Ryo-Ohki's family. Although Ryo-Ohki isn't as fat as Garfield, she definitely has the child-breeding hips!

- **Felix**. Uh-uh. So Felix from the cat side of Ryo-Ohki's side of the family is going to be httting Ryo-Ohki for some money. And Ryo-Ohki can turn into a spaceship and ram him out of existence.

- ■ **Mr. Ed**. Yes, Mr. Ed is not any part of a cabbit (cat + rabbit), which is what Ryo-Ohki is. Well, at least he'll still be in retirement eating peanut butter.

By the way, the name "Ryo-Ohki" translates into "Ghost King" which does not match Ryo-Ohki at all as far as I'm concerned. But "Bunny-Kitty" is too cute a name and if she wears it, she'll be more annoying than Barney.

3. Life is like a box of chocolates . . .

- ■ **A gold tennis ball with stars on it**. Yes, this is a close description of what the dragonballs are, although people can argue on the size rather easily. I've never had any, so I can't say for myself how big they actually are.

- **A bead the size of a marble**. Nope. That's too small for the size of a Dragonball, unless you are farsighted.

- **A bowling ball with a snake trapped inside it**. Nice try, but it shows that you've guessed at the most obvious answer. And by the way, how are your SAT scores?

- **A crystal ball with the decapitated head of Sailor Moon**. Ewwwww. . . .

Dragonballs would make nice earrings . . . if you like the idea of eventually stretching your ears to your ankles.

4. Odd woman out

- **Sailor Mercury**. Um, no. That can't be right. According to that rule, then ALL of the Sailor Senshi would be unemployed. Maybe Sailor Moon is thinking of a solo career.

- **Sailor Mars**. Yes, they may hate each other very much and maybe they might agree to wrestle each other for money but this is not the correct answer.

- **Sailor Venus**. Yeah, it might be tempting to become the only blonde among the inner senshi, but Sailor Moon needs to keep her around so that possibly, she wouldn't look so dumb.

- ■ **Sailor Jupiter**. Correct. Jupiter actually belongs to the outer planets but is with the inner senshi. But Jupiter's revenge would not be too hard. All she has to do is melt chocolate Ex-lax and then . . .

But don't worry, this will never happen. Sailor Moon isn't that brilliant.

5. I can just eat you up

- **PB&J**. No, Mokona would neither be peanut butter nor jelly. Not in solid form anyway.

- ■ **S'mores**. Correct. Since Mokona looks most like a marshmallow, he would seem great squeezed between two graham crackers and chocolate.

- **BLT**. Nope. Mokona is neither bacon, lettuce, nor tomato, nor any of the four basic food groups.

- **Falafel**. This looks more like Mokona's dung, rather than Mokona. Although they are delicious (I'm talking about the falafel and NOT the dung, of course).

Never take Mokona camping. If people run out of food, Mokona will give campers too many ideas.

■ *Answer to picture puzzle:* (b) Kazuya. Who isn't happy that his sword isn't as big as Mitsuru's.

1. At least she can boil water

If it wasn't for fast food, I would die. I don't know how to cook. Let me put it this way: I'm so bad at cooking that it takes an hour for me to cook minute rice. I live with the comfort that I'm not the only one who cannot cook either.

What is the first thing that Akane attempted to cook for Ranma in the *Ranma 1/2* anime series?

- Miso soup
- Curry
- Cookies
- Sukiyaki

2. Tricky finger

Yūsuke from *Yū Yū Hakusho* (Poltergeist Report) joins the yakuza and does something dishonorable. The punishment is to lose a finger. Because he needs this finger to use his power, which one does he refuse to cut off?

- Thumb
- Index finger
- Middle finger
- Pinky finger

3. Is that a hickey?

Hotohori from *Fushigi Yūgi* was very popular with the ladies (and one particular guy) in the emperor's court. One morning he woke up and found that someone had given him a hickey where he normally has his mark of Suzaku. What should he wear to cover this embarrassing blemish?

- Long pants
- A turtleneck
- A headband
- A pair of briefs

4. And even more angels hit the fan

Let's assume God's in his Heaven and All's right in the world and Gendō decided to adopt all the Eva pilots in *Neon Genesis Evangelion*, from First Children to Fifth Children. Who would be suffering from middle-"Children" syndrome?

- Kaworu
- Rei
- Asuka
- Shinji

5. All she wants is . . .

A woman departs into the Slayers world looking for a one-night stand and she does not want to have to think about it the next day. Who is both good-looking and stupid enough to attract the attraction of this lusty young wench?

- Gourry
- Zelgadis
- Xelloss
- Lina Inverse

1. At least she can boil water

- **Miso soup**. Sorry. This is the one thing that Akane could cook when the Spring of Life is around. But even if you poisoned the Spring of Life, it still might be safer than Akane's cooking.

- ■ **Curry**. Exactly. I'm surprised that Akane did not kill him because when curry is cooked badly, curry is REALLY bad. I guess he must love her after all, and be blessed with a cast-iron stomach.

- **Cookies**. Uh-uh. Akane's cookies are kinda good, according to Ranma. But some poisons taste like bitter almonds, which explains why he looked like he was going to die the next day.

- **Sukiyaki**. Akane and meat? No way!!!

I'd like to see Akane as a chef someday . . . for enemy armies. They will surrender before you can say "Bathroom Halls of Montezuma!"

2. Tricky Finger

- **Thumb**. No. Otherwise, he can't pick up stuff. Like women. Not like he does anyway.

- ■ **Index finger**. Right, his index finger! Otherwise, how else is he going to use his "rei gun"? But just once, I want to see him fight like these enemies who shoot things from their behinds. "Get a whiff of this!"

- **Middle finger**. It might be tough, but as long as he is not driving in L.A., he should be able to eventually adapt to it.

- **Pinky finger**. Well, if he loses his pinky finger, he can finally join Bugs Bunny, Bart Simpson, and the rest of the four-fingered American cartoons.

Losing a finger has got to be tough but look on the bright side: one less fingernail to clip.

3. Is that a hickey?

- **Long pants**. No. Even if Hotohori doesn't wear pants, he doesn't have to worry about the hickey because it won't be exposed. But something else might . . .

- ■ **A turtleneck**. Precisely. Hotohori's mark is on his neck so a turtleneck will do just fine. However, I don't remember seeing any turtlenecks in ancient China, so he's out of luck.

- **A headband**. Good guess, but Tamahome is the one who has to worry about wearing a headband with the sign of *oni* (demon) on his forehead. Reminded me of a guy in an anime convention who wore

"Watashi wa etchi da" (I am a pervert) on his head; he's asking for trouble. . . .

- **A pair of briefs**. If someone has left a hickey in that region, you have to wonder what Nuriko was doing the night that happened.

Clothes make the man. I wonder how Nuriko feels about that statement?

4. And even more angels hit the fan

- **Kaworu**. As the Fifth Child (or "Fifth Children" in Japanese), he would be treated as the baby in the family. Can you imagine Kaworu in diapers? The strange thing is that I can . . .

- **Rei**. As the First Child ("First Children"), she is supposed to be the privileged one. Privileged to be Gendō's doll, I guess.

- **Asuka**. As the Second Child ("Second Children"), she is supposed to look up to her older sister, Rei, from whom she can learn the virtues of self-control and emotionlessness.

- ■ **Shinji**. Wow. As the Third Child ("Third Children"), Shinji just gets the brunt of suffering, doesn't he? The guy must be wearing the fan!

To get out of the syndrome, all Shinji has to do is to knock off any of his siblings. I would say more, but I don't want to spoil things. . . .

5. All she wants is . . .

- ■ **Gourry**. Well-built blonde guy with an IQ of spinach? Gourry's your man! Although I would advise the woman to tell him that even though it's called "sleeping together," there is no actual sleeping going on.

- **Zelgadis**. Well, he could use a chisel in the face department, but although women find him attractive, he's not as dumb as a brick.

- **Xelloss**. This twisted little man may be handsome but he is not as dumb as a russet potato.

- **Lina Inverse**. I don't know, if pressed, Lina would try new things, but she is definitely not as dumb as a rock. Maybe if there was more money involved. . . .

There are so many ways to complete "dumb as a ____" as long as you choose an inanimate object. Rule of thumb, if you stub your toe on it and swear at an inanimate object, you can use it, although personally I've never stubbed my toe on a russet potato.

1. Groovy sitcoms

Ranma 1/2 has reformatted its show so that the intro looks like the intro to the *Brady Bunch*. According to this setup, who is most likely going to be in the center square?

- Ranma
- Akane
- Kunō
- Kasumi

2. Good morning, Miss Macross!

One of the keys to winning the Miss Macross pageant is a sense of style, a pretty face, and . . . the ability to get it written into the script.

What did Lynn Minmei wear at the Miss Macross City pageant?

- A Greek Goddess–like dress
- A Chinese dress
- A military-style vest with chiffon long skirt
- A Playboy Bunny suit

3. There's no place like home . . .

Through a very strange turn of events (you'll see just how strange in a moment), the three girls of *Magic Knight Rayearth* are confronted with William Tell. He challenges them to a contest and if they win, they get to return home without having to worry about saving Cephiro or whatever the name of the place is. Who is the best person to represent them in the contest?

- Hikaru
- Umi
- Fū

4. For mature audiences . . .

The Fushigi Yūgi Sukazu group all get drunk at a bar and begin to tell intimate stories about themselves. They play a little truth or dare, but just before things go on from there, which member of the group is kicked out because, as the youngest member, they are afraid that what they'll do next will corrupt his little mind?

- ANSWER: _____

5. That special place

The special place that I'm referring to here is the place where you and your loved one met for the first time. It can be anywhere from an accidental encounter to a pick-up at a bar. Although being able to find someone driving a pick-up through a bar is very unlikely.

Where does Relena first meet Heero in *Gundam Wing*?

- At school
- At a party
- At the beach
- At a shooting range

This is Subaru and Seishirō from *Tokyo Babylon*, and Subaru is unhappy with the outfit he's wearing. Who is he going to blame?

(a) Hotaru (b) Himeko (c) Hanako (d) Hokuto

1. Groovy sitcoms

- **Ranma**. Sorry. It makes sense, doesn't it, to put the star in the center square. But this isn't *Hollywood Squares*, it's the *Brady Bunch* and there's a special reason why Ranma isn't in the center.

- **Akane**. Akane is another good guess because she is essentially the target of Ranma's affections, right? But that's also incorrect.

- **Kunō**. Uh-uh. If Kunō had his way, this show would be called *Kunō 1/2*. Why the "1/2?" The show would focus on him trying to decide between Akane and the pigtailed girl!

- ■ **Kasumi**. Yup. You remember who was in the center square in *Brady Bunch*? It was none other than Alice, the loyal housekeeper who keeps everything stable in the Brady household. Well, I don't know if Kasumi's household is what you'd call stable, but at least she keeps it clean.

Home is where the heart is. And with all the antics that go on in the Tendō household, I'm surprised that Kasumi is not suffering from heart failure.

2. Good morning, Miss Macross!

- **A Greek Goddess-like dress**. No. Although it would not look bad on her though.

- ■ **A Chinese dress**. Right. Lynn Minmei came out with a beautiful Chinese dress and sent hordes of people into a frenzy. Fortunately, not like Woodstock '99.

- **A military-style vest with chiffon long skirt**. Stylish as this may be, it wasn't stylin' enough for Lynn Minmei to wear.

- **A Playboy Bunny suit**. <*.*> No. She's going for the title of Miss Macross, not Playmate of the Year!

Announcer: "Miss Minmei, you have just won the Miss Macross pageant. What are you going to do next?"
Minmei: "I'm going to sing that my boyfriend is a pilot!"
Announcer: . . .

3. There's no place like home . . .

- **Hikaru**. Wrong. She would be way too hyper to shoot with a bow and arrow. She is just about as accurate in aim as Cupid is!

- **Umi**. Nope. The only bows she knows how to use will clip onto her hair!

- ■ **Fū**. Good guess, because it's right! Fū is the member of the trio who knows archery, and it makes sense for her to challenge William Tell, a legendary archer.

And the challenge: Shoot an apple from William Tell's son's head. If Fū misses, she'll just have to complete the quest and be accused of third-degree murder. No pressure.

4. For mature audiences . . .

- ■ **Chiriko**. Again, I did not put the answer up because it would be way too easy. The boy is obviously prepubescent and could not get a drink at a bar even with a fake ID.

But the real question is, if the Suzaku group is composed of all guys, what were they going to do that was inappropriate to do in front of Chiriko at the bar?

5. That special place

- **At school**. Well, school is where they officially learn each other's names, but they actually meet earlier than this.

- **At a party**. With the laconic Heero around, how do you get him to mix at a party? Exchange death threats?

- ■ **At the beach**. Yes, Relena finds an unconscious Heero on the beach and he runs away as soon as he wakes up. How . . . romantic.

- **At a shooting range**. Nothing says lovin' like a shot on the buttocks. But just not for Heero or Relena.

And if Heero were indeed shot on the buttocks, that would totally redefine "that special place."

■ *Answer to picture puzzle:* (d) Hokuto, Subaru's twin sister. The outfit is okay, but the lace panties don't agree with him.

1. We do chicken right!

Colonel Sanders was magically transported to the world of *Final Fantasy VII*. He stumbles across a ranch of huge birds that were often used in transportation and racing. However, Col. Sanders also found in a pinch that he liked them with his original recipe. Since he was nowhere near Kentucky and just used the name of the bird, what did he call his new chain of restaurants?

- Chickadee Fried Chicken
- Chocobo Fried Chicken
- Chug-A-Lug Fried Chicken
- Here a chick, there a chick, everywhere a chick-chick Fried Chicken

2. Nice Japanese songs named after beef stew

You and your friends go out to a karaoke bar. After singing the mandatory karaoke songs like "Sukiyaki," "Sobakasu," and "It's the End of the World As We Know It" some smart aleck goes up to the mic and sings the Jigglypuff song. Well actually, he isn't that smart, because he still needs to read the lyrics from the karaoke screen, but if he were really Jigglypuff, what would have happened?

- Everyone would be dancing uncontrollably
- Everyone would be hypnotized into doing the next thing you say
- Everyone would be taking off their clothes
- Everyone would be falling asleep

3. Do you believe in life after love?

You are a faithful believer in true love. So when your significant other drugs himself or herself and dies, this person will suddenly come back from the dead. You have also been watching the *Yū Yū Hakusho* (Poltergeist Report) and when you go to the open-casket funeral, you see that the body has turned golden. Forgetting that this is a cruel trick of the stained glass window and sunlight, what do you immediately do to resurrect your loved one?

- You scream loudly in the ear for the corpse to wake up
- You gently squeeze the corpse's right hand and lift it to your forehead
- You kiss the corpse on the lips
- You grab the corpse between the legs and make a crude remark

4. Ranma: the girly playboy

A girl decides to foolishly pursue Ranma along with the long list of fiancées that he already has because she is intrigued by the fact that he can change into a girl, and she is willing to experiment. Anyway, besides that point, she decides to treat Ranma to a movie and he was screaming the entire time because it struck his innermost fear. What movie were they probably watching?

- *Scream 7*: The boyfriend did it again
- *Mortal Kombat 6*: Where are the fatalities?
- *Nightmare on Elm Street 17*: Why you should stay away from cheese pizza
- *Hello Kitty 4*: Hello Kitty finds a ball of yarn

5. Look out villains, I'm Sailor . . . what is that thing?

Someone has just acquired the license to make *Sailor Moon* T-shirts, and although the T-shirts themselves look nice, many people were not buying them because they say that the design is incorrect. The T-shirt maker complains, "It's a moon, isn't it?" To which the fans replied, "Duh! But the moon behind her is supposed to be shaped like a _____ moon! Baka!" What kind of moon?

- Full
- New
- Half
- Crescent

1. We do chicken right!

- **Chickadee Fried Chicken**. Wrong, my little Chickadee!

■ **Chocobo Fried Chicken**. Correct! I heard the thigh was the best part!

- **Chug-A-Lug Fried Chicken**. This is the Final Fantasy World, not a college town!

- **Here a chick, there a chick, everywhere a chick-chick Fried Chicken**. Old McDonald had a farm, E-I-E-I-O, and on this farm there was a dumb cluck reading a trivia book!

I like the original recipe, but the extra crispy chocobos are to die for!

2. Nice Japanese songs named after beef stew

- **Everyone would be dancing uncontrollably**. Can you imagine Jigglypuff at a rave? I guess if you're high enough. . . .

- **Everyone would be hypnotized into doing the next thing you say**. "Jig-gle-ly-puff, Jig-gle-ly-puff . . ." Now you will buy more of these books. It is much better than *Cats*. You will read it again and again!

- **Everyone would be taking off their clothes**. Oh yes! Jigglypuff was responsible for Sodom and Gomorrah! I don't think so.

■ **Everyone would be falling asleep**. Yes, Jigglypuff's power of singing causes everyone to fall sleep. Anvilania!

So the next time you see people falling asleep when you sing, check to make sure that a Jigglypuff was not a direct ancestor of yours! Then again, that would imply that one of your relatives got really drunk with a Jigglypuff and . . .

3. Do you believe in life after love?

- **You scream loudly in the ear for the corpse to wake up**. In the middle of church services? What kind of inconsiderate louse are you anyway?

- **You gently squeeze the corpse's right hand and lift it to your forehead**. Nope. That gesture will not work here.

■ **You kiss the corpse on the lips**. Good job! And of course, after the corpse wakes up, expect a good many heart attacks. But that's good if you didn't care for your future in-laws in the first place.

- **You grab the corpse between the legs and make a crude remark**. Ugh! You necrophile!

Love conquers everything. It works in theory, but I don't remember love lifting up the Pentagon building the first time they tried it.

4. Ranma, the girly playboy

- **Scream 7: The boyfriend did it again**. Ranma would probably fall asleep on this one. Not enough action and no possibility of martial arts.

- **Mortal Kombat 6: Where are the fatalities?** Nope. Ranma might even heavily get into the movie, saying he can beat them all!

- **Nightmare on Elm Street 17: Why you should stay away from cheese pizza**. This would not scare Ranma; this would just make him hungry.

■ **Hello Kitty 4: Hello Kitty finds a ball of yarn**. Ranma would not be able to sit still as he is forced to watch a cat in action due to his immense fear of cats. I guess he's fairly unpopular at the Sanrio store.

At least the girl was not thinking of taking Ranma to a musical. He would never like *Cats*.

5. Look out villains, I'm Sailor . . . what is that thing?

- **Full**. Ooh! Sailor Moon mooning her fans like that? Uh-uh.

- **New**. Uh . . . that would be like no moon at all. Then Sailor Moon would be standing all alone. Wouldn't that look silly?

- **Half**. Nope sorry.

■ **Crescent**. Yes! A crescent moon shown behind Sailor Moon. If it were a crescent roll, she would have eaten it already.

If Sailor Moon is fighting evil by moonlight, then why do most of her battles occur during the day?

Shōnen Anime

"Shōnen anime," or boys' anime, has long been in existence in America and often features young boys getting into a lot of adventure . . . or mischief. How well do you know your shōnen anime?

1. You call this training?

Part of King Kai's training is to run around until you catch Bubbles, the chimp. Which of these characters in *Dragonball Z* did this with almost no effort?

- Son Goku
- Krillin
- Piccolo
- Michael Jackson

2. It's a cover up!

When FUNimation bought *Dragonball Z*, they censored a lot of things by the use of what is commonly known as "digital underwear." So which of these things was NOT subject to these restrictive little briefs?

- Butts
- Cigarettes
- Tears
- All of the above

3. Chinese cuisine

If Shampoo was trapped on a deserted island with the rest of the *Ranma 1/2* cast and got hungry, which of these dishes can she NOT prepare?

- Szechuan steamed duck
- Cantonese cat stew
- Pork fried rice
- Panda sandwiches

4. You make bathtime so much fun!

In the "Tendō Family Christmas Scramble" episode in the *Ranma 1/2* OAVs, Mousse and Ryōga were sitting naked in a hot bath. What causes them to jump out and run into the kitchen?

- A crab
- Soy sauce
- A "Baby Ruth"
- Ryōga's probing hand

5. Mr. Universe in some other universe

Fujisawa-sensei from is competing for the world's strongest man title in *El Hazard*. What needs to be kept away from him?

- A pair of scissors
- Anything made of gold
- A bottle of nail polish remover
- Electrical batteries

This young man named Tsubawaki from *Utena* is a fierce and dedicated young man. Who is he fighting in this scene?

(a) Nanami (b) Tōya (c) Saionji (d) A boxing kangaroo

1. You call this training?

- **Son Goku**. Uh-uh. Goku has to work hard at everything he does.
- **Krillin**. Nope, with baldy chasing Bubbles, Bubbles could see the glare a mile away!
- ■ **Piccolo**. Piccolo is the man. Well, he's a green man with snail antennae but a man nonetheless.
- **Michael Jackson**. I'm not going there.

2. It's a cover up!

- **Butts**. Nope, the censors are paranoid about a person's behind, even if several cartoons have featured them already.
- **Cigarettes**. Smoke . . . bad. Censor . . . stop.
- **Tears**. Why did they censor tears? Probably it's the idea that boys are not supposed to cry. Even when Daddy's dead. How harsh.
- ■ **All of the above**. From reading the previous three answers, you find out that everything is fair in the censor game in *Dragonball*.

3. Chinese cuisine

- **Szechuan steamed duck**. I guess that's one way to stop him from pursuing you. . . .
- ■ **Cantonese cat stew**. Correct. Why? Although Shampoo can transform into a cat, she can't cook herself! Besides, why do that when pork is tastier?

- **Pork fried rice**. Yup, poor Ryōga. Sweet and Sour Ryōga does not seem too appetizing right now.
- **Panda Sandwiches**. At least the cast of *Ranma 1/2* can survive a year on those sandwiches!

4. You make bathtime so much fun!

- **A crab**. Ouch. At least, I would think that if this actually happened, but it didn't.
- ■ **Soy sauce**. And because of that soy sauce, girls can get one of the few fanservice shots made for women in the entire history of the *Ranma 1/2* series.
- **A "Baby Ruth."** Ewwww! These grown men should be able to control themselves in the tub!
- **Ryōga's probing hand**. Don't go there. Ryōga's hand didn't.

5. Mr. Universe in some other universe

- **A pair of scissors**. Who do you think he is, Samson?
- **Anything made of gold**. Nope. Sorry, that's wrong, too.
- ■ **A bottle of nail polish remover**. Yup. Alcohol is what makes Fujisawa-sensei lose his powers. And since nail polish has alcohol, it might be a good idea to lock up the beauty shop until the contest is over.
- **Electrical batteries**. To power up the hydraulic lifts in his arms? Nope.

■ *Answer to picture puzzle:* (d) A boxing kangaroo. Sometimes a funny bit from the Looney Tunes cartoons is worth repeating.

Wait a Minute . . . That's Not a Girl?

Many anime feature young male characters who are so pretty that they can be mistaken for young girls. Before you conclude that Japanese men are effeminate (have you seen any samurai movies?), you should know a little history. These characters, called *bishōnen* (pretty boys) or *biseinen* (pretty men), may today be used to titillate the fantasies of young girls, but they can be traced all the way back to an older Japanese art form: Kabuki theater.

In 1692, women were banned from Kabuki because it was believed that women in theater troupes were used in prostitution. Subsequently, in *wakashu kabuki* (young boy's Kabuki), young boys took on the women's roles, but this also led to protitution and was banned. Eventually came *yaro kabuki* (men's Kabuki), where

1. The moral of the story Is . . .

In *Urusei Yatsura*, Ataru tells the legend of Kintarō to a kindergarten class. (No, not the legend of Kintarō Ōe from *Goldenboy* and his love for toilets!) What lesson do the kids learn from the tale?

- If you are strong enough, you can wrestle bears
- Even the smallest person can chop the largest tree
- Be kind to animals. They can help you in times of need
- Your life will go no higher than middle management

2. Briefs on boxers

Kosaku, from *One Pound Gospel*, has a boxing idol whose name he uses in the anime. . . . If he wanted to be just like his boxing idol, what should he do in the ring?

- Brag that he is the "Thrilla from Manila"
- Call himself the "Goldenboy"
- Scream "I pity the foo' who wears mo' gold chains than me!"
- When all else fails, snack on someone's ear

3. "Omake" does not rhyme with cake"

"Omake" is pronounced *oh-ma-kay* and it is like a freebee of sorts. And remember, friends don't let friends rhyme "Akane" with "rain."

In "Video Girl Ai," which of these was not an "omake" of the show?

- Explaining Ai-chan as a dinosaur
- A fashion show with Ai-chan
- Redoing the show with non-standard Japanese dialects
- A video of Ai-chan singing with split personalities

4. Smarty pants

In *Goldenboy*, how far did Kintarō Ōe go in terms of his education?

- High school
- College
- Law school
- Ramen shop apprentice

5. Weak Spot needs to be put to sleep

In *Yū Yū Hakusho* (Poltergeist Report), Kuwabara has a weakness for:

- Kittens
- Puppies
- Stuffed animals
- Frilly dresses

adult males played the female roles. Actors specializing in female roles were called *onnagata*; dressing as women even outside the theater, some became so popular that they were instantly recognized wherever they went. *Onnagata* were men, but they became the feminine standard that many Japanese women aspired to.

That *onnagata* in Kabuki dress and talk like women does not indicate their sexual preferences; many *onnagata* do become married men. Gay men who dress in drag and have overtly feminine behavior are known as *okama*. This term does not apply to all gay men; Nuriko from *Fushigi Yūgi* would be considered an *okama* while Daley Wong from *Bubblegum Crisis*, who just has a romantic interest in men, would not.

If you also happen to be a fan of J-pop (Japanese pop music), this *bishōnen* concept may explain why some women go wild for male musicians who look like gorgeous women. And it's not just for the makeup tips!

1. The moral of the story Is . . .

- **If you are strong enough, you can wrestle bears**. And if you are dumb enough, you would wrestle bears.

- **Even the smallest person can chop the largest tree**. But without an axe, he can't do very much.

- **Be kind to animals. They can help you in times of need**. And if you feed a lion, he'll eat out of your hand. In fact, he'll eat out your enitre arm!

- ■ **Your life will go no higher than middle management**. Yes, what a sad thought that children cannot always rise to the top. Okay, I'm depressed now. Next!

2. Briefs on boxers

- **Brag that he is the "Thrilla from Manila."** Nope, it's not Muhammad Ali. It's not Imelda Marcos, either.

- **Call himself the "Goldenboy."** No it's not Oscar De La Hoya. It's not Kintarō Ōe, either! The only thing Kosaku does with toilets is vomit in them.

- **Scream "I pity the foo' who wears mo' gold chains than me!"** No. You're thinking of Mr. T, the Village People reject.

- ■ **When all else fails, snack on someone's ear**. Correct. Mike Tyson is Koasku's boxing idol. And the reason why some boxers wear earmuffs with their mouthguards.

I thought nibbling on a person's ear is supposed to be romantic. I didn't know it could be tasty, too!

3. "Omake" does not rhyme with "cake"

- **Explaining Ai-chan as a dinosaur**. Nope, this was the first "omake" in **Video Girl Ai**. It's a wonder how you can compare a cute girl to Godzilla and not insult her!

- **A fashion show with Ai-chan**. Hey, if you remember Ai-chan with a whip, then you remember the fashion show!

- **Redoing the show with non-standard Japanese dialects**. Yup, this happened too.

- ■ **A video of Ai-chan singing with split personalities**. This is the only one that did not occur. This ain't *Ranma 1/2*, you know.

4. Smarty pants

- **High school**. He may look like a high school student riding his bike, but no.

- **College**. He may look like a student of U.C. Davis riding his bike, but no.

- ■ **Law school**. Yup, Kintarō Ōe is no dummy. But right now, he is enrolled in the school of life. Try explaining that to a corporation where you are trying to get a middle management job!

- **Ramen shop apprentice**. Well, if this were true, at least he won't starve.

5. Weak Spot needs to be put to sleep

- ■ **Kittens**. Correct! You can't blame a man for loving his pussy (ouch, that was bad . . .).

- **Puppies**. Nope. Think feline.

- **Stuffed animals**. What man is going to admit that he has a Hello Kitty plush pillow? Other than me, of course. . . .

- **Frilly dresses**. He was cured of this when he found that lace panties gave him the same satisfaction and were less conspicuous.

1. If they only had salt

In one of the *Slayers* movies, Naga uses her Golem to fight against a giant metallic snail. What happens initially when they both meet to fight?

- The snail wins
- The golem wins
- Neither win; both are destroyed
- They fall in love, skip along the city streets and destroy everything in their path

2. Hey, where's the hunchback?

In "Sanctuary," who is the virile American President with the hot secretary?

- President Clanton
- President Clint
- President Clefton
- President Jesse "The Body" Ventura

3. Da plane! Da plane!

Okay, you must think that there must be a "tattoo" related theme here. And of course, you're right! You're brilliant!

Which part of "Crying Freeman's" body can a person say for sure is not covered with a tattoo?

- His pee-pee
- His butt
- His lower back
- His face

4. Sweet dreams are made of this

In *My Dear Marie*, when Marie starts to have dreams, which of the following did NOT happen in them?

- The tennis ball talks to her
- A wolf gets her into bed
- She kisses another girl that looks just like her
- She throws her creator to the ground, intending to have her way with him

5. More possessive than apostrophes

What is the demon's name that possesses Akira to make him "Devilman"?

- Ramses
- Erasmus
- Amon
- Athena

© GAINAX/Project Eva • TV Tokyo

"Hi, I'm Shinji Ikari from *Neon Genesis Evangelion*, and I'm ... naked! Arrrrrrrrrrrrrrrrrrrrrrrgh! Stop taking pictures! I said stop, Kaworu!"—Evangelion™ film, for those special moments. Where did Kaworu confess his love to Shinji?

(a) In a closet (b) In an eva (c) In a bath (d) In bed

1. If they only had salt

- **The snail wins**. No.
- **The golem wins**. No.
- **Neither win; both are destroyed**. No.
- ■ **They fall in love, skip along the city streets and destroy everything in their path**. Yup. With Slayers, you have to go with the most ridiculous answer at all times.

2. Hey, where's the hunchback?

- **President Clanton**. Nope.
- ■ **President Clint**. Yup. Thanks to Eugene Kim for this question.
- **President Clefton**. Nope.
- **President Jesse "The Body" Ventura**. Ummm . . . he may have his eyes set on the White House, but he's not there yet. . . .

Thanks to Eugene Kim for this question.

3. Da plane! Da plane!

- **His pee-pee**. The operative word is "for sure." (Actually, that's two words). That part is always censored out, even in up-close shots.
- **His butt**. I forget. Is it on one or both of his buttcheeks that he has tattoos?
- **His lower back**. Nope, that is definitely where the dragon left its mark.
- ■ **His face**. You can't ruin a pretty face like that! How else is he going to attract them? His body? Oh yeah.. . . I guess you can get a muscular workout with clay pots. . . .

4. Sweet dreams are made of this

- **The tennis ball talks to her**. Yup, what a trip. . . .
- ■ **A wolf gets her into bed**. He tries to, but it fails. I guess she's already read "Little Red Riding Hood."
- **She kisses another girl that looks just like her**. Fanservice! Fanservice!
- **She throws her creator to the ground, intending to have her way with him**. Fanservice! Fanservice! (Especially when the creator looks like a geek. I guess it gives fanboys a little glimmer of hope).

5. More possessive than apostrophes

- **Ramses**. Well, if a legendary pharaoh who fathered more than a hundred children is a demon, then I guess he's one pretty lucky demon!
- **Erasmus**. Nope. Sorry about that. Actually, I'm not sorry, I just don't want you feel bad. Wanna cookie?
- ■ **Amon**. Yup. That's it. What? You want me to say more?
- **Athena**. Since when was this goddess of wisdom evil? I guess since she turned into an idol star for the King of Fighters tournament . . .

■ *Answer to picture puzzle:* (c) In a bath. Kaworu certainly moves fast. . . .

1. Destructive heavy metal

In *Bastard!!* what is Dark Schneider's Ultimate Destruction Spell?

- Gunsenro
- Anthrax
- Megadeath
- Halloween

2. Watch where you point that thing!

In *Those Who Hunt Elves*, what is the "Miracle Cannon?"

- A smokestack that also acts like a wand
- A large armored tank
- A satellite in the sky that seems to blast things randomly
- Junpei's nickname for the bulge in his pants

3. To know you is to love you

In *Slam Dunk*, how did Haruko know Rukawa before he came to her high school?

- From a mutual friend
- From watching him play basketball at the junior high level
- They were next to each other when they tested for the school
- From the underwear ads Rukawa used to do

4. Why can't I just get nosebleeds?

In *DNA²*, Momonari-kun does not get nosebleeds when he gets sexually stimulated. What happens instead?

- He burps disgustingly
- He farts uncontrollably
- He throws up
- He gets a Lincoln Log the size of Guam

5. Win a personal servant for life!

In Flame of Recca, Recca originally intends to serve as a personal ninja to whoever:

- Defeats him in a fight
- Wins over his heart
- Can guess where his flame-shaped birthmark is
- Knows why this series looks a lot like *Yū Yū Hakusho*

1. Destructive Heavy Metal

- **Gunsenro**. Short for "Guns 'N' Roses," this attack involves a bazooka and an appearance by Tuxedo Mask. Uh-uh, I don't think so.

- **Anthrax**. This attack involves a . . . okay, considering Desert Storm, we won't go there.

- **Megadeath**. It's such an obvious answer! Which is why it is automatically wrong!

- ■ **Halloween**. This attack originally involved Michael Myers, but he was busy doing Austin Powers.

Thank you to a member of Cal-Animage for this question. Ugh! I don't remember who you are! I owe you dinner.

2. Watch where you point that thing!

- **A smokestack that also acts like a wand**. I guess anything is possible in anime . . . except this one.

- ■ **A large armored tank**. Correct. But why they did not call it a "Miracle Tank" is beyond me . . .

- **A satellite in the sky that seems to blast things randomly**. And this answer was a random guess for you, wasn't it?

- **Junpei's nickname for the bulge in his pants**. Look at this miracle! It rises by itself! Nope.

3. To know you is to love you

- **From a mutual friend**. How? Rukawa doesn't have any friends!

- ■ **From watching him play basketball at the junior high level**. Correct. She was a big admirer of him when he played basketball at junior high. I guess you can call her a "basketball otaku."

- **They were next to each other when they tested for the school**. Uh-uh. That's not it.

- **From the underwear ads Rukawa used to do**. Um . . . . I doubt it. Rukawa is pretty much "free" in that area, to the nervousness of his teammates.

4. Why can't I just get nosebleeds?

- **He burps disgustingly**. Nothing says love like a good belch. . . .

- **He farts uncontrollably**. Nothing says love like a . . . uh, no one could love the aftermath of having chili for lunch!

- ■ **He throws up**. Yup, poor guy. He makes Stan of *South Park* seem normal.

- **He gets a Lincoln Log the size of Guam**. I wonder how Guam can deal with a solar eclipse one-third of a day?

5. Win a personal servant for life!

- ■ **Defeats him in a fight**. That's the original intention. If you can defeat him in a fight, you have a personal ninja.

- **Wins over his heart**. Even though it's not what he intended, it's actually what happened. Fickle, isn't he?

- **Can guess where his flame-shaped birthmark is**. If he took showers in gym class, he'd be in big trouble wouldn't he?

- **Knows why this series looks a lot like *Yū Yū Hakusho***. And to this day, Recca never had to serve for that purpose.

1. Glasses menagerie

In Detective Conan, what is unusual about Conan's glasses?

- They are X-Ray glasses
- They are infrared glasses
- They change your eye color
- They have no lenses

2. Nice guys finish dead last

In *Jojo's Bizarre Adventure*, who was the first "good guy" to die?

- Iggy
- Kakyouin
- Jotarō
- Abdul

3. Touch me!

In the anime *Touch*, when Tatsuya imitates his twin brother, Kazuya, at a baseball game after Kazuya accidentally breaks his arm, what is the only word Tatsuya says to fool the rest of the team?

- Hai!
- Un!
- Yo!
- Us! (pronounced "Ooce")

4. Vs. The Wizard of Oz

In *Berserk*, why was Gatts able to defeat the fat tin man?

- Luck
- He tripped him first and stabbed him in the back
- He shot him in the eyes to blind him first
- The tin man rusted quickly and there was no oil can around

5. Dark fiddler

What do *Bastard!!* and the *Violinist of Hamelin* have in common?

- They star the same actor
- They're both set in a weird alternate universe medieval period
- The main hero is rude and obnoxious
- All of the above

Kuwabara from *Yū Yū Hakusho* (Poltergeist Report) may have quite the ugly mug, but he's a softie when it comes to kitties. What is the name of this boy's kitty?

(a) Eikichi (b) Emi (c) Miko (d) Meowth

1. Glasses menagerie

- **They are X-Ray glasses**. If this were true, he can find out easily which man and women are padding themselves with socks and then attempt to blackmail them. Well, at least I would.
- **They are infrared glasses**. Nope, they're not those type of glasses.
- **They change your eye color**. And if they are tinted lenses, they change your skin color as well.
- ■ **They have no lenses**. Precisely. I guess in his spare time, he probably has a "Sixth Sense" with dead spirits.

2. Nice guys finish dead last

- **Iggy**. Uh-uh.
- **Kakyouin**. Uh-uh.
- **Jotarō**. Uh-uh.
- ■ **Abdul**. Uh-huh.

Next!

3. Touch me!

- **Hai!** lie.
- **Un!** lie.
- **Yo!** lie.
- ■ **Us! (pronounced "Ooce")** Hai! Tatsuya was able to fool them until he actually had to step up to bat and play. Someone should have told him that, unlke in bowling, strikes are not a good thing.

Sugi!

4. Vs. The Wizard of Oz

- ■ **Luck**. One could have said talent, but the fact that he was narrowly missed and the weapon managed to get the tub of lard by a freak occurrence cannot be completely skill.
- **He tripped him first and stabbed him in the back**. Nope. That didn't happen.
- **He shot him in the eyes to blind him first**. Good strategy. Wrong weapon.
- **The tin man rusted quickly and there was no oil can around**. How anticlimactic. And wrong.

5. Dark fiddler

- **They star the same actor**. Sorry. Both shows star Yao Kazuki (at least, the movie version of *Violinist of Hamelin* starred this guy), and he also played Starscream in *Beast Wars* and Fei Long in *Street Fighter II V*).
- **They're both set in a weird alternate universe medieval period**. Hey, I qualify using heavy metal bands' names as the names of spells weird enough.
- **The main hero is rude and obnoxious**. True, but it's part of his charm....
- ■ **All of the above**. Correct. Which goes to show that if a concept did well, why not do it again?

Shōjo Anime

What about the girls? There was virtually no appreciation for shōjo anime ("girls' anime") until *Sailor Moon* landed on the U.S. airwaves. Now because of moon prism power, anime fans can now appreciate what this type of anime has to offer.

---

1. Hey, no sailor outfits!

In the *Sailor Moon* manga, Mamoru (Darien) is a lot more fashion conscious than in the anime. Which of these does Mamoru have in the manga?

- A pierced ear
- A tattoo
- A pierced nipple
- A "Prince Albert"

2. Ghostbusters

In *Here Is Greenwood*, Misato haunts Mitsuru because

- He is cute
- He got her pregnant
- He killed her
- He owes her 78 yen

3. What is the sound of one hand clapping?

Ryōga from *Ranma 1/2* gets a toughened body in the "Breaking Point" episode when his body is constantly hit by boulders. If that is the case, then what part of Anthy Himemiya's body from *Revolutionary Girl Utena* would be really tough?

- Her butt
- Her breasts
- Her arms
- Her cheeks

4. Girls whose names sound like Hello Kitty characters

When did Pretty Sammy make her first appearance in the Tenchi Muyō anime universe?

- Saving a school from a wicked fire
- Saving a village from a flood
- In an alternative universe created by Washū's dimension warping machine
- As a new mascot just outside McDonald's

5. Get out!

In *Fushigi Yūgi*, the Genbu Seishi gave Miaka a test to prove that she really is the Suzaku no Miko. What is it?

- They trap her in a mirror and she needs to get out
- They freeze her in water and she needs to get out
- They put her in a pit of fire and she needs to get out
- They lock her in a Port-a-Potty and she needs to get out

1. Hey! No sailor outfits!

■ **A pierced ear**. Yup. Look on one of the covers of the Japanese **Sailor Moon** Manga and there you'll see Mamoru with a pierced ear. Cool huh?

• **A tattoo**. Can you imagine Usagi looking at the tattooed name on Mamoru's arm and going "Who the Hell is Serena?!" and dumping him for Rei?

• **A pierced nipple**. If he had one, he better either keep his shirt on or take off the ring before he fights! No sense your enemy an ideal target.

• **A "Prince Albert."** If you're not cringing right now, then you don't know what this is . . .

2. Ghostbusters

■ **He is cute**. Yup. That's the only reason she is haunting him. Isn't that the only reason to hurt anybody?

• **He got her pregnant**. Nope. I don't remember Misako wearing a maternity dress when she came to haunt him.

• **He killed her**. He killed her with his good looks. That's all he's guilty of.

• **He owes her 78 yen**. If that were true, that would be quite pathetic. But not totally unexpected in anime.

3. What is the sound of one hand slapping?

• **Her butt**. Um . . . wrong cheeks.

• **Her breasts**. I heard from a girl that hitting there would be like kicking a man in the groin. All's fair in love and body parts. Let's leave that alone.

• **Her arms**. Why don't we try toughening up your butt for that incorrect answer?

■ **Her cheeks**. Correct!

Poor Anthy! That girl has been slapped so many times, I'm surprised her teeth didn't fall out! Of course, if they did, she must have had really bad brushing habits to have dentures that early.

4. Girls whose names sound like Hello Kitty characters

• **Saving a school from a wicked fire**. Nope. She's a hero of love and justice. She can't put out fires.

• **Saving a village from a flood**. Nope. She's a hero of love and justice. She can't put stop floods.

■ **In an alternative universe created by Washū's dimension warping machine**. Yup! Sailor Moon, eat your heart out!

• **As a new mascot just outside McDonald's**. Ugh . . . how embarrassing. She's a hero of love and justice . . . and polysaturated foodstuffs!

5. Get out!

• **They trap her in a mirror and she needs to get out**. Nope. This was done earlier in the series.

■ **They freeze her in water and she needs to get out**. Yup. She was frozen in her underwear but I doubt Tamahome would be turned on by making it with a popsicle.

• **They put her in a pit of fire and she needs to get out**. Nope. This is Miaka, not Joan of Arc!

• **They lock her in a Port-a-Potty and she needs to get out**. There were no port-a-potties in this time period. Haven't you ever heard of squatting?

Sugar and Spice, Snails and Tails

It is known that boys and girls have their own little play places, play things, and restrooms, but how about their own little anime as well?

Shōnen anime (boys' anime) generally has a male main character who is the hero of the story. The anime is action oriented and the struggles tend to be external (fighting and war). The plot tends to be linear (the storyline might concentrate more on the adventure of saving the damsel in distress rather than the relationship of the hero and the damsel). Power is found in physical prowess, so the men tend to be superhuman by skill (like martial arts) or strength. The prime example of shōnen anime in America is *Dragonball Z*.

Shōjo anime (girls' anime) generally has a female protagonist. It relies more on emotion than action, so the struggles tend to be more internal ("Does he love me or doesn't he?"). A love story can take place in both shōjo and shōnen anime, but the shōjo is more likely to dwell on the relationship. Power is found in magic more than skill, even though there are plenty of anime women who are skilled with the sword. The prime example of shōjo anime in America is *Sailor Moon*.

1. There are no small parts . . .

. . . Unless you are a male lifeguard on *Baywatch*. Ouch . . . .

Yukie Nasu plays a small part in the *Here Is Greenwood* anime, the anime based on her manga of the same name. What does she play?

- A cute schoolgirl
- The ferryman's wife in Aoki's movie
- A gang thug from a girl gang
- A manga artist

2. Can I make world peace my third wish? (SPOILER QUESTION! OK TO SKIP!)

In *Fushigi Yūgi*, Yui makes three wishes to the god, Seiryū. Which of these is not one of the wishes that she makes?

- Yui gives Miaka the ability to call Suzaku
- Nakago becomes a deity
- Yui takes away Suzaku warriors' powers
- Yui sends Miaka to her own world

3. That's why the Lady is a vamp

In *Vampire Princess Miyu* OAV, the doll vampire seduces a pretty boy into being her next victim. But what was unusual about him?

- He was actually a boyish-looking girl
- He already was a vampire
- He was anemic and therefore, naturally warded off vampires
- He knew she was a vampire and he sought her out

4. Past lives

In *Please Save My Earth*, what is Rin's own explanation as to why he is younger than the rest of the reincarnated moon people?

- He says it's in the studio contract. Look it up!
- He says that he was hit by a car in the first reincarnation
- He says his psychic powers stopped him from growing
- He is a "late bloomer," if you get what I mean. . . .

5. Past lives (part 2)

Here's an additional question: What's the REAL reason Rin is younger than the rest of the reincarnated moon people?

- He actually died much later than the others
- The Goddess had punished him for his deeds
- A freak science experiment
- No freak science experiment . . . Rin himself is just a freak

1. There are no small parts . . .

- **A cute schoolgirl**. Why should a manga creator have

All the above nothwithstanding, the real test of shōnen vs. shōjo is how the anime is marketed. If advertisements for the anime pop up in boys' magazines and manga, it's shōnen anime. If it is marketed to girls, it's shōjo anime.

Yū Watase, creator of the shōjo manga *Fushigi Yūgi*, was very happy that she had a large male audience in America. She said that she did not write her manga to target a particular gender; it just happened to be marketed that way.

Can you separate the He-man anime from the She-ras? Classify the following anime as either shōnen or shōjo:

A: *Revolutionary Girl Utena*	F: *CLAMP School*
B: *Please Save My Earth*	G: *Eat Man*
C: *Ninja Scroll*	H: *Golgo 13*
D: *Record of Lodoss Wars*	I: *Fake*
E: *Hakkenden*	J: *My Dear Marie*
	K: *Cutey Honey*
	L: *Cutey Honey Flash.*

ANSWERS

A: shōjo, B: shōjo, C: shōnen, D: shōnen, E: shōnen, F: shōjo, G: shōnen, H: shōnen, I: shōjo, J: shōjo, K: shōnen, L: shōjo.

to be limited to playing the role of "Schoolgirl C?"

- **The ferryman's wife in Aoki's movie.** Good guess but wrong answer.

- **A gang thug from a girl gang.** There are girl gangs in Japan? Naw . . .

- ■ **A manga artist.** Yup. Yukie Nasu pretty much played herself in the anime. No wonder she seemed like a natural!

2. Can I make world peace my third wish? (SPOILER QUESTION! OK TO SKIP!)

- **Yui gives Miaka the ability to call Suzaku.** Through her long-distance plan. Only 10¢ a minute except on weekends and weekdays.

- ■ **Nakago becomes a deity.** If Nakago became a deity, it would be all over . . . (All over the Nakago fan web pages with the utmost joy and celebration.)

- **Yui takes away Suzaku warriors' powers.** Great! Now they have to use remote controls like normal people.

- **Yui sends Miaka to her own world.** Well, ditzy Miaka can sometimes be in her own little world, so this is in fact a wasted wish.

You can pretty much figure out which wish is which but no more on this subject! I don't want you to kill me! (More than you already want to.)

3. That's why the Lady is a Vamp

- **He was actually a boyish-looking girl.** And what would be original about this concept if this were true?

- **He already was a vampire.** Nope, that's not it.

- **He was anemic and therefore, naturally warded off vampires.** What caused you to believe that crock of . . .

- ■ **He knew she was a vampire and he sought her out.** Correct. He wanted to live forever. And it's freaky what happens when he does. And because I like this show, I won't spoil it for you.

4. Past lives

- **He says it's in the studio contract. Look it up!** Of

course, he also has lawyers more dangerous than he is in order to enforce it.

- ■ **He says that he was hit by a car in the first reincarnation.** Correct. And he says it without even batting an eye.

- **He says his psychic powers stopped him from growing.** Which explains Yoda, in general.

- **He is a "late bloomer," if you get what I mean.** . . . Nope.

5. Past lives (part 2)

- ■ **He actually died much later than the others.** And if you watch the series, you'll know what a difference seven years makes . . .

- **The Goddess had punished him for his deeds.** And The Goddess will punish you for this incorrect answer!

- **A freak science experiment.** Nope. Not this answer. Sorry.

- **No freak science experiment . . . Rin himself is just a freak.** He's a little too young to get it on with the ladies, don't you think?

1. Chess: a civilized sport about war

One of my favorite classic movies has got to be *History of the World, Part I*. It is lewd and tacky but it is so much fun to watch. It kind of reminds me of another anime: *Miyuki-chan in Wonderland*, and they have one thing in common:

If the life sized chess board in the *History of the World, Part I* was anything like the chess board in *Miyuki-chan in Wonderland*, what happens after a player screams "Knight jumps Queen?"

- The Queen gets slapped and loses her clothes
- The Queen erotically dances for the player
- The Queen and the Knight disappear from sight and you hear moaning
- The Queen just lies still because the Knight has ten other Queens to jump over in the 100m Queen Hurdle Dash

2. Miyuki-chan in Otherland

Miyuki-chan is not only limited to Wonderland; she appears in several other places as well. In fact, which CLAMP anime does Miyuki-chan appear in, trying to find her man-hating ferret?

- *CLAMP School*
- *Magic Knight Rayearth*
- *Card Captor Sakura*
- *X*

3. Not more CLAMP!!!

Yup, here's another CLAMP question. Hey don't blame me! CLAMP dominates this shōjo anime category like the Queen of Hearts!

What outfit was Sakura wearing in Card Captor Sakura when she captured her first card?

- Her well-known pink battle outfit
- A battle outfit that looked like a jester outfit
- A battle outfit that looked like a teddy bear costume
- A battle outfit that appeared to be nothing more than her pajamas

4. Transformation = strange body

In Japanese, the word for transformation is *henshin*. The *hen* in *henshin* also means "strange." Not the chicken. Unless you are talking about turning a live chicken into someone's lunch. In *Mahō Tsukai Tai* OAV what does Sae turn the huge enemy alien structure in the last episode into?

- A big teddy bear
- A big cherry blossom tree
- A big fishcake
- A block of tofu

5. T & A

Ha ha! This question is about Tsuyoshi and Akito from *Kodomo no Omocha* (Child's Toy). What kind of question did you think this was? <^.^>

In *Kodomo no Omocha*, why does Akito Hayama smirk after Tsuyoshi gets a girlfriend?

- Tsuyoshi stops chasing after Hayama
- Hayama knows Tsuyoshi did some dirty things to get his girlfriend
- Tsuyoshi's girlfriend is a psycho and he can't say anything about it
- With Tsuyoshi out of the way, Hayama gets Sana all to himself

Here in *My Dear Marie*, who is Marie looking at?

(a) Tanaka   (b) Hiroshi   (c) Mari   (d) Hibiki

1. Chess: a civilized sport about war

■ **The Queen gets slapped and loses her clothes**. Correct. Every time a chess piece is defeated, she loses her clothes. Something like this could have saved "Melrose Place" from cancellation.

• **The Queen erotically dances for the player**. No. But it will at least prove which of the chess pieces are non-eunuch men!

• **The Queen and the Knight disappear from sight and you hear moaning**. Do you know why the Queen is moaning? Because your answer is wrong!

• **The Queen just lies still because the Knight has ten other Queens to jump over in the 100m Queen Hurdle Dash**. This scene was edited for *History of the World, Part 2*, but I'm STILL waiting for that to come out, darn it!

2. Miyuki-chan in Otherland

■ **CLAMP School**. Well the ferret hates everyone but Nokoru. I wonder what that says about Nokoru? Hmmm...

• **Magic Knight Rayearth**. I guess she must be the fourth Magic Knight...not! (Ick. That "not" at the end is kind of old, isn't it?)

• **Card Captor Sakura**. Nope. Although it would be interesting for Miyuki-chan to be one of the cards and when her power is used, a bunch of women dressed in bunny suits will follow her wherever she goes...

• **X**. Forever Love! Forever Dream! Forever Dream on, pal, because it's not going to happen!

3. Not more CLAMP!!!

• **Her well-known pink battle outfit**. Nope. That famous outfit will come in later in the series.

• **A battle outfit that looked like a jester outfit**. Nope. She used that outfit when she was fighting the Clow Card, Watery.

• **A battle outfit that looked like a teddy bear costume**. Even Tomoyo would not be so cruel as to dress up her best friend in that kind of outfit!

■ **A battle outfit that appeared to be nothing more than her pajamas**. Well actually, it was only in her pajamas. And before you get any weird ideas, Sakura is only ten and her pajamas are not going to distract anyone.

4. Transformation = strange body

• **A big teddy bear**. Nope. She managed to cause a large teddy bear to appear very early in the OVA, but it's not the answer.

■ **A big cherry blossom tree**. Yes. Only a magical girl show can think of this...

• **A big fishcake**. Hmmm...fishcakes...Nope.

• **A block of tofu**. What is this? Resident Evil? Uh-uh.

5. T & A

• **Tsuyoshi stops chasing after Hayama**. Nope. Tsuyoshi stopped doing that a long time ago.

• **Hayama knows Tsuyoshi did some dirty things to get his girlfriend**. Uh-uh. Tsuyoshi ain't that kind of boy.

• **Tsuyoshi's girlfriend is a psycho and he can't say anything about it**....No.

■ **With Tsuyoshi out of the way, Hayama gets Sana all to himself**. Correct. Whoever said love is kind! Love has got to be pretty selfish in order to work! (Not psycho-selfish, though. There is a difference between mere jealousy and *Basic Instinct*.)

■ *Answer to picture puzzle:* (b) Hiroshi. Couldn't you tell by the bowl cut on that person's head?

1. Does this thing wet itself?

In *Akazukin Cha-cha* (Red Riding Hood Cha-Cha), what is so freaky about Seravy carrying around his doll Elizabeth?

- The doll would sometimes talk to itself
- The doll liked to steal things for Seravy
- It's a mini-version of his rival that he used to be in love with
- Its head spun in circles and spit pea soup

2. After these messages . . .

In *Marmalade Boy*, why does Yū never want to do commercials ever again?

- It almost broke up him and Miki
- He had no free time for himself
- His mom made him dress up in drag
- He had to model in his underwear

3. Not just four boys

Pretty boys get all the glamour in anime. Girls like them, boys want to be like them, and in some cases, boys want to date them because they are prettier than the girls in the show. I mean, don't you think Hotohori would make a much better-looking babe than Miaka?

In *Hana Yori Dango*, the F4 controls the school. What does the F4 stand for?

- The 4 Fly Boys
- The 4 Flowery Boys
- The 4 Fine Boys
- The 4 F***able Boys

4. Transformation = strange body (part 2)

In *Hime-chan no Ribon* (Hime's Ribbon), what are the magic words that she uses to transform into another person?

- Parallel, parallel
- Nice and lovely change now
- Mix and match, mix and match
- Ribbon, mummify!

5. X does not mark this spot

In *Nurse Angel Ririka SOS*, what mark do all members of the group Dark Joker have on their right hand?

- A star
- A spade
- A Chinese character
- A Hello Kitty Tattoo

1. Does this thing wet itself?

- **The doll would sometimes talk to itself**. "Red drum ... red drum ... red drum ..." Nope.

- **The doll liked to steal things for Seravy**. Nope. That's like saying Mr. Hat in **South Park** is a pervert. Well, it's Mr. Garrison who has his hand shoved up Mr. Hat's....

- ■ **It's a mini-version of his rival that he used to be in love with**. Correct. Elizabeth is the mini version of his rival, Dorothy, when she was young and cute. What's a guy doing with a doll anyway? Hmmm ... I might be afraid to ask.

- **Its head spun in circles and spit pea soup**. And on Fridays, it spits minestrone. On Saturdays, clam chowder.

2. After these messages . . .

- **It almost broke up him and Miki**. In this anime, EVERYTHING almost breaks up Yū and Miki.

- **He had no free time for himself**. Of course, when you are popular, you never do have time for yourself. Such is the price of fame.

- ■ **His mom made him dress up in drag**. Correct. One of the few characters that proved that he was such a pretty boy, that he can also be a pretty girl too! Ironically, he played a "Queen" in the commercial.

- **He had to model in his underwear**. I don't think that would have been much of a problem compared with what he actually had to do....

3. Not just four boys

- **The 4 Fly Boys**. These aren't Air Force pilots. They're pretty boys. They would be beaten up by Air Force pilots.

- ■ **The 4 Flowery Boys**. Even Tsukushi-chan would say that this is lame. It's correct, though.

- **The 4 Fine Boys**. Uh, no.

- **The 4 F***able Boys**. Even if they were, no self-respecting group of boys would call themselves this.

4. Transformation = strange body (part 2)

- ■ **Parallel, parallel**. Yup. These are the words that Hime-chan says to transform into anyone she chooses. Then I kind of wondered if it ever occurred to her to transform into the guy she likes, Daichi, and then start taking off "his" clothes? (Hee hee, only I tend to think like that ...)

- **Nice and lovely change now**. Ugh. I know sometimes the Japanese use some strange English but this is too sickeningly sweet....

- **Mix and match, mix and match**. This sounds like she's going to have a head of a lizard, body of a turtle, and feet like a duck! Nope.

- **Ribbon, mummify!** Who do you think this is? Mummra from Thundercats?

5. X does not mark this spot

- **A star**. Nope, it's not a star.

- ■ **A spade**. Correct. All Dark Joker members are marked with a spade. I guess a heart seemed too nice to put there. And overdone.

- **A Chinese character**. Nope. This ain't *Fushigi Yūgi*, you know.

- **A Hello Kitty Tattoo**. And this would be even nicer than the heart. But if there is a Hello Kitty wedding dress, what can't there be Hello Kitty tattoos?

For You Anime Convention Virgins . . .

Anime conventions are a lot of fun, and if you attend the right convention you'll find there is much to do there. If you have never been to a convention before, don't assume you can just dress up as Nuriko and begin flirting with everyone in the room (this advice can apply to either sex). Here are a few tips for you.

Start small. Before going to a large-scale anime convention like Anime Expo or Otakon, go to a small-sized convention first to get a taste of what the fan and convention scenes are like. You definitely do not want to be overwhelmed your first time out. Even going to a small convention can be intimidating; so what do you think a larger one would be like?

Two things to bring: lots of money and patience. The money is for spending at the dealer's room for those *Card Captor Sakura* dolls, and you'll occasionally come across the cool, rare item. But be prepared to pay for it. The patience is for the constant waiting in line.

1. Is this the right address?

When Sailor Saturn takes a form of a little girl in *Sailor Moon Stars*, how does she address Sailor Saturn at her mansion?

- Haruka-san
- Haruka-sama
- Haruka-senshi
- Haruka-papa

2. A word for the intellectual shōnenai fan

In the world of *Zetsuai*, what does "Cathexis" refer to?

- The name of Kōji's band
- The moment when Kōji confesses his love to Izumi
- The word tattooed on his hip as punishment
- A bunch of rock videos sung by Kōji

3. Where else can we advertise?

No one actually knows that when the Magical Thief, St. Tail says her fighting motto, she is actually promoting a company. Recently, the company dropped their account with her and a rival company took its place. Now every time St. Tail attempts to steal something, she says:

- "It's Memorex!"
- "It's Cinemax!"
- "It's OfficeMax!"
- "It's Microsoft!"

4. Engagement rings not worn on the finger

In *Ai no Kusabi* (translated as "Love's Wedge"), where does Riki wear his pet ring?

- His pinky finger
- On his neck
- On his big toe
- On his "other big toe"

5. Congratulations! You gave birth to a bouncing baby sword!

What is the translation of the Hebrew script imprinted on Kamui's blade in *X*?

- "Vengeance is that of the Lord, only of the Lord, and no one else but the Lord."
- "Praised are You, Lord our God, King of the Universe at whose word all things come into being."
- "The Lord giveth and the Lord taketh away. That is the will of our Lord."
- "Beware the false prophet. Only the True Lord will reign."

Sometimes you'll be bored to tears. At least you'll have your Sakura doll to play with.

Plan ahead. Check the program guide; chances are that you'll want to go to several events, film showings, panels, and so on, some of which will clash time-wise. Decide early what you want to do so you won't be left hanging.

Hook up. Anime fans are pretty easygoing to talk to, especially when you are waiting in line. Being at the convention proves that both of you like anime, right? There's your conversation starter. You can't play with your Sakura doll all the time, can you?

Most important, have fun. And remember, if you're not having fun, you can always go home. And watch more anime.

1. Is this the right address?

- **Haruka-san**. Nope. Too generic.

- **Haruka-sama**. Nope. Too formal.

- **Haruka-senshi**. Nope. Too . . . weird, since Saturn is technically a senshi as well. And to my knowledge, no such title exists.

- ■ **Haruka-papa**. Correct. Unless Sailor Uranus decides to adopt, she may never hear those words again. Awwww . . .

2. A word for the intellectual shōnenai fan

- **The name of Kōji's band**. Nope. That's not it.

- **The moment when Kōji confesses his love to Izumi**. The moment does not have a name. Why would it?

- **The word tattooed on his hip as punishment**. Hmmm . . . that's actually a pretty cool word to tattoo; I can think of worse words. Like "Colostemy bag enters here."

- ■ **A bunch of rock videos sung by Kōji**. Correct. The collection of videos is called "Cathexis" because it sounds a lot better than "a bunch of videos that Kōji made and now we have to sell these. . . . "

3. Where else can we advertise?

- **"It's Memorex!"** It's not live. It's anime.

- ■ **"It's Cinemax!"** Yes. You have to remember that St. Tail says, "It's Showtime!" So what would be similar? Cinemax! "Playboy Channel" would have also been acceptable here.

- **"It's OfficeMax!"** What do you think St. Tail says? "Staples?"

- **"It's Microsoft!"** Hmmm . . . who would Microsoft's competition be? Eventually everybody?

4. Engagement rings not worn on the finger

- **His pinky finger**. It's a little too innocent for a correct answer, don't you think?

- **On his neck**. Uh-uh. Sure, the pet ring can be a controlling device, but that's not what Iason wanted to control.

- **On his big toe**. Nope. See below.

- ■ **On his "other big toe."** I felt that I had to phrase it this way. If I said "He put a ring on the ding-a-ling," it would have sounded tacky, wouldn't it?

5. Congratulations! You gave birth to a bouncing baby sword!

- **"Vengeance is that of the Lord, only of the Lord, and no one else but the Lord."** Good guess, but it's incorrect.

- ■ **"Praised are You, Lord our God, King of the Universe at whose word all things come into being."** Correct. How would I know this? I didn't. My friend, Mara, said she got this from Mark who had someone slow down the tape while someone who understood Hebrew translated the Hebrew script on the sword. Great piece of trivia, isn't it?

- **"The Lord giveth and the Lord taketh away. That is the will of our Lord."** Another good guess, but also not correct.

- **"Beware the false prophet. Only the True Lord will reign."** Didn't this just tell you to beware the false stuff?

Thanks to Mara, Mark, and the CLAMP mailing list for this question.

Video Games

Video games are a rather important part of anime. It's partly because of video games that the spread of anime has become worldwide. So, have you played enough video games to come up with the answers to these questions?

1. Who's your daddy?

You gotta love Dan, the fighter in the pink gi. Only Capcom would be twisted enough to actually come up with a weak character and then promote off the fact that's he's weak! Maybe they should give Andy Bogard a call . . .

In *Puzzle Fighter* and *Pocket Fighter* (Gem Fighter), Dan's gems always come out what color?

- Red
- Yellow
- Blue
- Puce

2. Who's da man?

Bust-A-Groove is one of the few games where you gotta have rhythm to play. But just because you have the timing to know when to hit the buttons doesn't mean you can grab yourself and dance like Michael Jackson. LaToya Jackson, maybe.

In *Bust-A-Groove*, who's the "Natural Playboy of Town?"

- Gas-O
- Hamm
- Hiro-kun
- Burger Dog

3. Color theory

Think hard. Think impatience. Think "Darn it! How long is it gonna take before I get one?" I'm not talking about a pass to a supermodel's dressing room, I'm thinking more along the lines of a fantasy: *Final Fantasy*.

In *Final Fantasy VII*, blue + green =

- Purple
- Black
- Yellow
- Blue-green, duh . . .

4. Video game guest stars

One of the cool things in a video game is when a character pops up to make a cameo appearance in another video game. The game can still suck, but it's like a treat: After you digest it, you hope that you're not left with crap.

In *Final Fantasy Tactics*, Cloud appears as a special character in the game. Who was he looking for before he joins your party? And spell it . . .

- ANSWER: _____

5. Breaths of Fire NOT caused by extra spicy curry

I love curry, but there are three things you should know about it. 1. If you've never had curry before, don't ask for extra spicy. You will regret it. 2. If you are cold, curry will warm you up. Perfect if you have no central heating. 3. Do not eat curry by Akane Tendō unless you have a death wish. I mean it.

In *Breath of Fire III*, when the child, Ryu (the Hero) attacks someone at the beginning of the game, what does he usually do as he attacks?

- He screams angrily at the enemy
- He accidentally burps fire
- He throws rocks from afar
- He cries like a baby

1. Who's your daddy?

■ **Red**. If you said "Red," then you're the Man! (Or Woman! We can't be politically incorrect all the time, you know). Although I'm not sure you want to be compared to Dan, though.

- **Yellow**. Someone has not been playing *Pocket Fighter* or *Puzzle Fighter*, we see . . .

- **Blue**. This must the color of the bruise on your head when Dan knocked you senseless for giving this answer!

- **Puce**. This is *Pocket Fighter*, not *Martha Stewart's Living*!

Only REAL men cry for their daddies . . .

2. Who's da man?

- **Gas-O**. He could be "da man" if he stopped eating chili dogs, but nope. He's not the natural playboy.

- **Hamm**. Uh-uh. No guy with a gut full of burger goodness is going to be a playboy anytime soon.

- ■ **Hiro-kun**. Yeah! You can't be a playboy without those bellbottoms sweeping the dust off the dance floor. I think the hairy chest is where the "Natural" part comes in.

- **Burger Dog**. Burger Dog can't be "da man." He's not even of the same species!

Many people will play this game and yet will have no courage to go out on the dance floor. At least many ladies can rest easy knowing they can wear open-toed shoes to the dance floor without fear.

3. Color theory

- **Purple**. You'll turn purple when you realize this isn't the right answer. Actually, you'll turn purple if you color yourself with red and blue markers.

- ■ **Black**. Correct! You must know the pain of breeding Chocobo to get this answer, don't' you?

- **Yellow**. Uh, no.

- **Blue-Green**. Nope. Things in video games are not always determined by logic. Duh . . .

Sigh. Getting a blue Chocobo to breed with a green Chocobo takes forever! Where's the Viagra when you need it?

4. Video game guest stars

■ **S-E-P-H-I-R-O-S**

The answer is actually supposed to be "Sephiroth" from the famous Cloud vs. Sephiroth rivalry of *Final Fantasy VII*, but I think the producers might have been too cheap to add an extra letter to the name so they adjusted accordingly.

5. Breaths of Fire NOT caused by extra spicy curry

- **He screams angrily at the enemy**. Watch enemies cower in fear as Ryu screams "You poopyhead!" over at the enemy. Even RPGs aren't THAT pathetic.

- **He accidentally burps fire**. Hey, didn't I just say to lay off the extra spicy curry? Sorry, wrong answer.

- **He throws rocks from afar**. One of those rocks must have hit your head because that isn't the right answer.

- ■ He cries like a baby. Correct. But don't underestimate the guy, small puppies will be big dogs someday. Or in this case, big dragons!

Curry advice number 4: Do not eat curry by Akane Tendō unless you have a death wish. Any good piece of advice is worth repeating. As long as the curry does not repeat on you.

1. Butterflies are free . . . but *Jade Cocoon* costs money

If you ever wanted to know what it's like to play Nausicaä or Princess Mononoke, *Jade Cocoon* is the next best thing. It has all the classic struggles of man coexisting with nature. And I'm not talking about men who need to relieve themselves in the forest when there's nothing but poison ivy to wipe with. . . .

If you knew that Mahbu's birthday was coming up in the game *Jade Cocoon* and she was self-conscious about what is happening to her as she purifies cocoons, what would be the most appropriate gift?

- A pair of sunglasses
- A robe
- A hunting knife
- Tickets to the Ice Capades

2. East of the sun and west of the . . .

Which *King of Fighters* character moons his opponents before he fights?

- Terry Bogard
- Joe Higashi
- Sie Kensou
- Chris

3. How to win a girl's heart. While she's still alive.

Ah, the things people do for love. They say they will climb the highest mountains or swim the widest seas. Of course, people who do these things are not only romantic, but voluntarily contribute to population control.

If you had to win over a girl like the main character had to win Cheryl's heart in *Azure Dreams*, what are you most likely going to do?

- Heal her of a debilitating disease
- Buy everything off the menu at a restaurant
- Compliment her dancing
- Take her bowling

4. Hmmm . . . I guess tobacco companies do lurk everyhwere . . .

It's a fact of life that people smoke. But if your breath gets so bad that you can win fighting matches with it, I better get stock from the company that manufactures Listerine.

In *Samurai Shodown*, there is a character who fights with cigar smoke. What is his name?

- Cigarette
- Nicotine
- Carcinogen
- Joe Camel

5. MAD about the plumber

Every time I see Mario, he is always saving the Princess from his enemy, Bowser. He jumps and squashes, throws fireballs, and pounds his enemies with hammers but I have yet to see a plunger or a toilet in a Mario game. . . .

When *MAD* spoofed Nintendo mascots Mario and Luigi on their cover, what mistake did they make with the character designs?

- They gave Mario a mustache but left Luigi without one
- They made Mario the taller and thinner one and Luigi the shorter and rounder one
- They switched the "L" and "M" on their hats
- The lengths on their skirts were not short enough

1. Butterflies are free . . . but *Jade Cocoon* costs money

- **A pair of sunglasses.** Hee hee. You are obviously so blind that you can't see the right answer! I know. Lame joke. So shoot me.

- ■ **A robe.** Correct. Poor Mahbu gets cursed markings all over her skin when she purifies cocoons in the game. And to think that you thought acne was a problem when you were a teenager like her. Tsk, tsk, tsk . . .

- **A hunting knife.** If someone is self-conscious, why would you want to give her something sharp and pointy to make her paranoid as well?

- **Two tickets to the Ice Capades.** Yes, I'd like to see Dorothy Hamill suddenly skate through this village and give her a mascot costume to solve her self-consciousness problem. What is this, "Wise Blood?" (If you got this reference, you are ultimately cool.)

So where is the mystical laser surgeon when you need him?

2. East of the sun and west of the . . .

- **Terry Bogard.** Just because he can kick @$$ doesn't mean he has to show his!

- ■ **Joe Higashi.** Yup. This immodest little fighter not only wears the least amount of clothing among all the fighters, but he can prove that he'll wear even less!

- **Sie Kensou.** Well, his pants slip off once in a while, but he's not really mooning anyone. The boy just needs a belt (in the head for not getting clothes to fit him right in the first place.)

- **Chris.** Chris may be cute, but he's not "cheeky."

I have never understood why mooning is considered a taunt. If someone mooned me in a fight, I wouldn't consider it an insult at all. I'd think of it as free target practice.

3. How to win a girl's heart. While she's still alive.

- ■ **Heal her of a debilitating disease.** Correct. The main character saves Cheryl's life by getting a rare healing herb in the monster tower. When you save someone's life, for some reason, you start looking pretty good to them.

- **Buy everything off the menu at a restaurant.**

Nope. Who'd want a golddigger like that anyway?

- **Compliment her dancing.** No. This is how you win Vivian's heart and not Cheryl's. And she dances alone so you don't have to embarrass yourself with your third-rate version of the funky chicken.

- **Take her bowling.** You are as romantic as a cold fish that is thawing and attracting flies. But there might be people into that sort of thing so you'll be okay.

In *Azure Dreams*, you aim to win the hearts of seven young girls while trying to reach the top of the monster tower. And I thought Hiro-kun was the natural playboy of town . . .

4. Hmmm . . . I guess tobacco companies do lurk everywhere . . .

- **Cigarette.** Well, no. Besides, such a feminine name is unbecoming an old man with teeth like sticks of butter.

- ■ **Nicotine.** Correct. I heard that if you get one kiss from him, you'll need a patch to recover from it.

- **Carcinogen.** Nope. Not even close.

- **Joe Camel.** That would actually be quite scary. Dang, those tobacco companies don't give up, don't they?

After all that smoking, Nicotine would be one of those guys whose senior high school picture would be hard to forget. He actually did look like a senior in high school. So much like a senior that the principal mistook him for the school janitor.

5. MAD about the plumber

- **They gave Mario a mustache but left Luigi without one.** I guess Luigi could not find that caterpillar to sit still long enough to take that picture. Wrong answer.

- **They made Mario the taller and thinner one and Luigi the shorter and rounder one.** Hey, who knows? Maybe they were at a funhouse mirror! Maybe not.

- ■ **They switched the "L" and "M" on their hats.** Yup. You would not believe how many scathing letters **MAD** received just on this mistake. But then again, how much of a life do you actually have to take time to write the letter, buy a postage stamp, and send the letter just to tell **MAD** that they are wrong?

- **The lengths on their skirts were not short enough.** I guess Mario and Luigi were tired of saving princesses so they decided to become queens instead . . .

1. No wonder you look like crap . . .

Which video game character is quoted as saying "I won't rest until this girl is finally happy?"

- Donovan from *Darkstalkers*
- Ken from *Street Fighter*
- Andy Bogard from *Fatal Fury*
- Galford from *Samurai Shodown*

2. On stage Persona

I actually wrote my senior thesis using this game, *Persona*. I am quite serious. At least I did not have to explain the talking toilets that you have to battle in the game. How come Mario is never around for this?

In the game *Persona*, the characters themselves are playing a game called *Persona*. It's a different version of what kind of game?

- Marco Polo
- Twenty Questions
- Truth or Dare
- Bloody Mary

3. Hair for your enjoyment at my expense

You decide to get your hair styled like Tony from *Bushido Blade 2* because you think that it will attract a lot of attention. But instead, you end up being teased and you can never face your friends again. What name did they most likely taunt you with?

- Mophead
- Q-tip
- Mr. Clean
- Rooster Boy

4. Materia ™

In *Final Fantasy VII*, there is a materia that has the longest animation sequence when you use it. The problem is someone is suing for copyright infringement over the use of the name of the materia. Who is most likely to milk the claim for as much money as he can from the *Final Fantasy* franchise?

- King Arthur
- The swordsmaker, Masamune
- Alexander the Great
- George Lucas

5. "What!"

Fighting taunts are pretty interesting, although the only reason they are there is just to look cool. But anything is better than just screaming or grunting. Yet not always. For example:

In *Samurai Shodown*, before Charlotte fights a match, she always proclaims "Am I _____ or what?"

- Hot
- Cool
- A babe
- Chopped liver

© 1995 Yuzo Takada/Takeshobo · BS Project · TV Tokyo · NAS

Ah, a romantic pic of Kaede and Mamoru from *Blue Seed*! What? You don't know who Kaede and Mamoru are? Then you are probably thinking of two other famous Kaede and Mamoru. What are their last names?

(a) Fujisawa and Jinnai (b) Kiseragi and Kusanagi (c) Rukawa and Chiba (d) Kinomoto and Tsukino

1. No wonder you look like crap . . .

- ■ **Donovan from *Darkstalkers***. Correct. And with the somber girl, Anita, always tagging at his side, it looks like he won't be making pit stops any time soon.

- **Ken from *Street Fighter***. I've never actually seen Ken with Eliza much, so I don't know how he is supposed to make her happy. In fact, I see Ken more with Ryu than anyone else. Hmmm. . . .

- **Andy Bogard from *Fatal Fury***. I don't think it takes much to keep Mai Shiranui happy. But I won't go into details as to how to keep her that way. . . .

- **Galford from *Samurai Shodown***. If Galford is referring to his dog companion . . . and depending on how you define "happy" . . . I don't even want to think about it.

Hey Donovan, just remember: "A smile is only a frown upside-down." So, just pick up Anita by the feet and . . .

2. On stage Persona

- **Marco Polo**. Unlike other RPG's, this game is not spent getting lost. . . .

- **Twenty Questions**. Nope. This is *Persona*, not *Jeopardy*!

- **Truth or Dare**. *Persona* may be many things, but an adult game is not one of them!

- ■ **Bloody Mary**. Yup. In the game *Persona*, the gang says "Persona, Persona, please come to us" in a dark room to get a ghost to appear in front of them.

Why do people in a dark room always want to summon ghosts? Haven't they watched enough horror movies to know that ghosts can do bad things?

3. Hair for your enjoyment at my expense.

- **Mophead**. Nope. This is not Raggedy Ann or Andy (hmmm . . . are you old enough to remember them?) Tony does not have dreadlocks crown his lovely head.

- ■ **Q-tip**. Yup. Tony is man enough to look good with an Afro on his head. Although those bellbottoms have got to go.

- **Mr. Clean**. No. Tony does not suffer from being "Follicly-challenged."

- **Rooster Boy**. Anyone who wears a mohawk these days deserves to be laughed at.

"Q-tip" may not be much of an insult, until you realize what people actually do with those things.

4. Materia™

- ■ **King Arthur**. Correct. "Knights of the Round Table" is King Arthur's original idea. If King Arthur were a really wise king, he would have trademarked the name Camelot and make his money off of the Kennedys!

- **The swordmaker, Masamune**. Although Masamune's sword is always in the game, it was never Materia to begin with.

- **Alexander the Great**. Nope. Even though there is a Materia bearing his name "Alexander" the animation using that materia cannot be used as a timer to boil eggs.

- **George Lucas**. Although Jar Jar Binks appears nowhere in *Final Fantasy VII* (thank goodness), he can lay claim to Vicks (Biggs) and Wedge, two characters from *Star Wars* that always appear in the *Final Fantasy* series of games.

If Hershey's or Nestlé can somehow link Chocolate with Chocobo, Squaresoft will be in some real trouble here.

5. "What!"

- ■ **Hot**. Correct. I guess in that armor, if she were in Calcutta, she'd be boiling!

- **Cool**. Any girl who struts around saying this about herself just . . . isn't.

- **A babe**. (See above.)

- **Chopped liver**. Liver paté is more like what you will become if you told this to Charlotte in person.

I don't know about you, but bulky French armor and an epée of death pointing at me does not lead me to think of anyone as "sexy."

■ ***Answer to picture puzzle:*** (c) Rukawa and Chiba. Kaede Rukawa is from *Slam Dunk*. Mamoru Chiba is from *Sailor Moon*.

1. Day-jobs for gaming heroes

Ivanov from the role-playing game *Suikoden* is out of work and goes to the nearest employment office. If you worked at the employment agency, what would the most suitable job available?

- House painter
- Carpenter
- Electrician
- Exotic male dancer

2. As long as it's bulletproof . . .

You have enlisted in one of the most challenging police academies in existence. In fact, it is so challenging that there is a course in bullet dodging. If you were Tabasa (also known as Tessa or Tabitha) in *Pocket Fighter*, what would you instinctively use to protect yourself from harm?

- A cat
- A big baseball glove
- A large wooden block
- Your assistant, Tao

3. The dangers of time machines

You know you are an otaku if you solely use a time machine to go back and come up with *Sailor Moon* and *Dragonball* before Naoko Takeuchi and Akira Toriyama did and make tons of yen to buy all the manga in existence. Well, it's not a bad idea, really . . . but bad things can happen as well.

You go back in time, carelessly leave a banana peel on the street and cause Mary Shelley to kick the bucket. If Mary Shelley never existed, which of these fighting games would be affected?

- *Street Fighter*
- *X-Men*
- *King of Fighters*
- *Darkstalkers*

4. What's "normal?"

Why is it that in a video game, especially an RPG, using magic is "normal" while not being able to use it means there's something wrong with you? I guess this means David Copperfield is the most normal person on earth. Hmmm . . . why doesn't that sound right?

In *Chrono Trigger*, why can't Ayla use magic?

- She lacks the intelligence to use it
- Magic was not created by the time she was born
- She is not connected enough with nature to use it
- She opted for chest enhancements rather than the ability to summon fire

5. Fighters®, now available in travel size!

Why are little tubes of toothpaste and small bottles of mouthwash called "travel size" instead of "mini size?" If I were Gilligan stranded on a strange island, that bottle of deodorant better last for more than two weeks, dangit!

Which of these fighting games does NOT have an SD (Super Deformed) puzzle fighting game made of the game?

- *Tekken*
- *Street Fighter*
- *Battle Arena Toshinden*
- *Psychic Force*

1. Day-jobs for gaming heroes

- ■ **House painter**. Correct. Although he is used to painting murals on walls, it's never a bad thing to have a Mona Lisa painted on the side of your house.
- **Carpenter**. If I had a hammer, I would hammer in the morning, I would hammer in the evening, and I would hammer your head for this wrong answer.
- **Electrician**. You didn't get this right. What a shock . . .
- **Exotic male dancer**. Unless Ivanov has been working out, I would not suggest this one.

There's never a classified ad for "Hero" in real life. Thank goodness video game characters aren't real. The idea of video game characters asking for spare change is . . . pathetic.

2. As long as it's bulletproof . . .

- **A cat**. Can we say ASPCA?
- **A big baseball glove**. I don't think trying to catch bullets is such a good idea.
- **A large wooden block**. When bullets are flying at you, the last thing you want to do is be playing with a bunch of legos!
- ■ **Your assistant, Tao**. In *Pocket Fighter*, Tabasa instinctively uses Tao to block attacks. I hope Tao gets paid extra for this!

Why wear something as tacky as a bulletproof vest when having a really, really, really, really, really good friend will do?

3. The dangers of time machines

- **Street Fighter**. Nope. Someone would have to come up with a fighting game eventually. Which is ANOTHER good idea if you decide to go back in time and try to get royalties for all the *Street Fighter* games ever produced.
- **X-Men**. Nope. *X-Men* is in no danger of being erased if Mary Shelley was gone. People will mutate anyway, although it's more likely that they'll get an extra toe than cause lightning storms.
- **King of Fighters**. Um, no.
- ■ **Darkstalkers**. Great! You obviously know that Mary Shelley wrote *Frankenstein* and if it weren't for her, there would be no "Victor" who shows up as the Frankenstein monster's equivalent in the game.

4. What's "normal?"

- **She lacks the intelligence to use it**. She may not be wise, but she can beat your @$$ with a stick!
- ■ **Magic was not created by the time she was born**. Correct. But if you can spar with a dinosaur and kick its butt effectively, why do you need magic?
- **She is not connected enough with nature to use it**. Well Ayla is a cavewoman so if she's not connected enough to nature, then Harry Houdini must have been Tarzan in a past life!
- **She opted for chest enhancements rather than the ability to summon fire**. Well, I guess she could compromise and have fire come out of her [CENSORED].

Ayla proves that you can be as beautiful as Miss Universe and as strong as Mr. Universe. If she looked like Mr. Universe and was as strong as Miss Universe, I'd tell her to lay off the steroids. . . .

5. Fighters®, now available in travel size!

- ■ **Tekken**. Correct. Although the idea of Xiaoyu kicking balloons at her opponents has a strange appeal to it.
- **Street Fighter**. You have got to be kidding! You don't remember *Puzzle Fighter* at all? It is in the very first question!!!
- **Battle Arena Toshinden**. Yes there is an SD puzzle version of this game. But trying to explain why a child-like Sofia wears that leather suit, carries a whip, and looks like she is padding herself with gym socks will be too difficult to get past the censors.
- **Psychic Force**. Yes, there is an SD puzzle version of this game too.

I hear Mokujin refused to do an SD puzzle game because no one would take him seriously. Hmmm . . . I guess fighting with a tree stump does not sound like much of a challenge, does it?

1. Extra! Extra! Bart falls into a black hole! Read all about it!

Bart from *Xenogears* in a strange event (for lack of a better idea, there was a black hole somewhere and he happened to fall in) is suddenly transported to the *Five Star Stories* universe. Although he is a stranger, once men learn his name, they start to pander to him. What do they want him to do?

- Write a Headliner
- Read a Headliner
- Control a Headliner
- Wear a Headliner

2. Love is in the air, but it's better than hay fever

You have a girlfriend or a boyfriend (hypothetically for some of you). You are also a video game freak. You decide to propose at the same place where Sakura and Ichirō from *Sakura Taisen* first met. Where are you going to give your loved one that zirconium ring?

- Tokyo Tower
- Ueno Park
- At a small café in Kyoto
- In a love hotel in the red-light district

3. Raising your daughter to be a "princess"

In English, sometimes calling a girl a "princess" means calling her a spoiled brat. Which explains they were are so many Princess slim phones in 90210.

In *Princess Maker III*, which of these can you NOT put onto your daughter's schedule?

- Church
- Dancing
- Tea making
- Dieting

4. Code name: "Friendly"

"The guy who is friends with everyone will have no enemies. And he who is friends with everyone will have no lovers, either."—Anonymous

In *Tokimeki Memorial*, what happens if you give yourself "Minna Nakayoshi" as a character name?

- You will know all the girls and their phone numbers
- You will know all the girls' phone numbers, but you actually will not know any of the girls
- You will be very popular in the game but also have high stress levels
- All the girls will think of you as a "good, good friend" and you won't be able to date any of them

5. "Yes, master . . ."

Well, most people think the 13th Amendment to the U.S. Constitution outlawed slavery until they realized what kind of paycheck they are taking home. . . . In *Street Fighter*, why is Ken called "Ken Masters?"

- It suggests he is the master of his own destiny
- He did not want to be confused with Ken of Barbie and Ken
- The character is based on a real person of the same name
- The name reflects his preferences in an S/M relationship

1. Extra! Extra! Bart falls into a black hole! Read all about it!

- **Write a Headliner**. Extra! Extra! Read all about it! "YOU GOT THE WRONG ANSWER!" Read all about it!

- **Read a Headliner**. Whoop-dee-doo . . . Bart reads a newspaper and saves the world. How impressive.

- ■ **Control a Headliner**. Yup! In *Five-Star Stories*, Fatimas are needed to control Headliners, which are giant robots. And ever since Bartholomew Fatima arrived in this world, men have been asking him to control their robots. And that isn't a metaphor for anything inappropriate.

- **Wear a Headliner**. If a Headliner is some sort of a can-can dress, then imagining the tough guy Bart from *Xenogears* wearing this would be a strange fetish to say the least.

I'm sure you thought this question was about the Bart Simpson falling down the well episode. Hee hee, you simple folk . . .

2. Love is in the air, but it's better than hay fever

- **Tokyo Tower**. Hmmm . . . every anime uses Tokyo Tower! Except this one, because at the time Sakura first met Ōgami, Tokyo Tower had not yet been built.

- ■ **Ueno Park**. Correct. Ueno Park is quite a pretty place, especially when the sakura are in bloom. And I don't mean Sakura going through puberty you horntoad! I mean sakura as in "cherry blossoms."

- **At a small café in Kyoto**. Who wants to go there for a proposal? (I meant the small café, not Kyoto.)

- **In a love hotel in the red-light district**. If a cheap motel with the sounds of other people going at it like rabbits is your ideal take on where to pop the question, I hate to think of what your wedding would be like . . .

3. Raising your daughter to be a "princess"

- **Church**. Nope. This is where your daughter in the game learns about religion and morality. And learning to sleep while looking like she's paying attention from the pew.

- **Dancing**. Sorry, all princesses have to learn how to dance. Princesses as a rule should never have to dance the funky chicken at the court ball.

- **Tea making**. Precisely. No princess should have to make tea when servants can do that for her.

- **Dieting**. Believe it or not, this is part of the game, too. In the game, she just sits there and starves. But as a video game character, can't she just shave a few extra pixels off her tummy?

4. Code name: "Friendly"

- ■ **You will know all the girls and their phone numbers**. If you did not already know, "Minna Nakayoshi" means "Good friends with everyone" in Japanese.

- **You will know all the girls' phone numbers, but you actually will not know any of the girls**. Nope. Wouldn't that look a little dorky just collecting girls' numbers anyway? What are you going to do with them, scrawl them across the boys' bathroom walls?

- **You will be very popular in the game but also have high stress levels**. Oh yeah. Popular people have it so tough. <*.*>

- **All the girls will think of you as a "good, good friend" and you won't be able to date any of them**. What a bittersweet reality. However, that's "reality"; video game rules do not apply. In a video game, if you can be hero of the universe, you can definitely be a stud among women. You can also be a monkey with five @$$e$, but that's beside the point.

5. "Yes, master . . . "

- **It suggests he is the master of his own destiny**. Ugh. That's too corny, even for me!!!

- ■ **He did not want to be confused with Ken of Barbie and Ken**. All right, you got it! When Mattel created *Street Fighter* action figures, they already had the popular Ken from the Ken and Barbie dolls. So Street Fighter Ken was given a last name to clear up confusion.

- **The character is based on a real person of the same name**. Uh-uh. And shell out royalties whenever a *Street Fighter* game is played? I don't think so.

- **The name reflects his preferences in an S/M relationship**. I would crack the whip on you for giving me the wrong answer, but I'm afraid you might like it too much.

Mascots

They are cute, cuddly, and totally merchandisable! They are the mascots, characters that are supposed to add comic relief in any anime.

---

1. How much is that duckie in the window?

It seems that Ryōga is off on another trip and Akane still has not made the connection that he is P-chan. However, Ryōga is gone for so long that she decides on another pet: a Chinese duck with rather big spectacles. Based on the way P-chan got his name, what is Akane going to name this new found duck?

- A-chan
- D-chan
- M-chan
- Dinner for two

2. Battle of the binge

Ryo-Ohki is hungry and goes on an eating binge for days and days just eating her favorite food. She eats so much that she actually changes into the color of the food she ate. So what color crayon does Sasami mistake her for when drawing a picture of Tenchi?

- Orange
- Red
- Green
- Blue

3. Luna-tic

What is on the top of Luna's forehead?

- A jewel
- A scar
- A moon
- A bullseye target

4. Ring around the rosies

In *Pokemon*, Pikachu always looks like he has rosy cheeks. On Pikachu, what are they called?

- Mating blushes
- Electric sacks
- Air jowels
- Clown makeup

5. No, pigs can't fly, but they can . . .

The talking pig in *Dragonball* and *Dragonball Z* is named after a particular kind of what?

- Vegetable
- Snail
- Tea
- Underwear

© 1995 Tatusya Egawa/Shueisha/KSS

In *Goldenboy*, why does Kintarō obsess with this particular toilet?

(a) Because it is self-cleaning (b) Because he discovered the joys of a bidet (c) Because it backs up easily (d) Because women have used it

1. How much is that duckie in the window?

- **A-chan**. Nope. It's not Ahiru-chan ("Ahiru" is the Japanese word for "duck")

- ■ **D-chan**. Correct. Since Ryōga transforms into a pig, he is called P-chan. A duck would logically be D-chan. I guess you can call Ranma H-chan (H for Human), but the idea of naming anything H-chan (H is an abbreviation for sex) would be ... odd.

- **M-chan**. Nope. The duck would not be called M-chan (or Mousse-chan). Although Mousse would love it if Shampoo called him that.

- **Dinner for two**. Ummm ... yeah ... but what are you going to do when you put him in boiling water and he turns back into a man?

2. Battle of the binge

- ■ **Orange**. Yup. Ryo-Ohki's favorite food is carrots, and actually, if you eat enough of them, you actually won't turn orange, you'll turn yellow. If you want to turn orange, add some tomato juice to your diet!

- **Red**. Red? I'm red from embarrassment that you don't know this answer!

- **Green**. I'm green with envy that I'm not as naïve as you are....

- **Blue**. I'm blue that you did not watch *Tenchi Muyō* long enough to know this...

3. Luna-tic

- **A jewel**. This is a cat, not a cabbit! Sorry!

- **A scar**. You must be thinking of the lobotomy scar on your own head! Wrong!

- ■ **A moon**. Hee hee. This was a no-brainer. If you did not get this one, you have no brains!

- **A bullseye target**. Hmmm.... I'm sure this had been done for fan art, but it's not a correct answer.

4. Ring around the rosies

- **Mating blushes**. Do you think with censors editing out Gohan's pee-pee in *Dragonball Z* that they would show Pikachu mating? I don't think so ...

- ■ **Electric sacks**. Correct. Those rosy cheeks are called his electric sacks.

- **Air jowels**. Sorry ... jowels don't look attractive on anyone ...

- **Clown makeup**. Well no, but it would be easier for a Pikachu to run away to join the circus. It won't need makeup!

5. No, pigs can't fly, but they can ...

- **Vegetable**. This might apply to someone like Raditz (named after the Radish), but not to a talking pig

- **Snail**. Hmmm ... the only snails I know are the ones you can eat and the ones you can't eat. I can't imagine that the name of the talking pig is "Don't eat this one, it's dirty!"

- ■ **Tea**. Right! The name of the talking pig is Oolong, just like Oolong tea, which is fermented tea, and things like alcohol are fermented, so does that mean that if you managed to cook the character, Oolong, that you would be drunk on his pork rinds?

- **Underwear**. Trunks fits into this category (actually "trunks" is Japanese boys' gym shorts, but close enough), but the answer is incorrect.

■ *Answer to picture puzzle:* (d) Because women have used it. Yes, anime caters to every fetish.

1. Upstaged by a flock of feathers

Everyone who plays *Final Fantasy* knows what a Chocobo is. However, what *Squaresoft* mascot that came from the *Final Fantasy* games looks like a white stuffed animal with attitude? And is always upstaged by Chocobo wherever he goes?

- Nog
- Pog
- Mog
- Jan Brady

2. Anime traffic laws

You are driving down the newly paved streets of Cephiro when suddenly without warning, you see Mokona at the side of the street. Mistaking Mokona's jewel on its forehead for a traffic light, what would you tend to do (assuming that you are observing basic traffic laws)?

- You screech to a halt
- You speed before the light changes
- You go normal speed, which is four times the speed limit
- You attempt to ram into Mokona, citing that traffic lights infringe upon your civil liberties

3. You called?

If you called the cat in *Fushigi Yūgi* that hangs around Mitsukake by name, which of Miaka's guardian's might actually turn around because he would mistake you calling his name?

- Tamahome
- Chiriko
- Tasuki
- Nuriko

4. Spelling bee

In *Kiki's Delivery Service*, what is the name of the cat that rides along with Kiki on her broom? And spell it . . .

- ANSWER: _____

5. Monster in my pocket

In *Bust-A-Groove* (or *Bust-A-Move* in Japan), Shorty's pet in her pocket gets sick but she does not have the confidence to dance alone. So she manages to stuff a character of the same name into her pocket and falls down as soon as she attempts to dance. What kind of person has she stuffed in her front pocket?

- The discoverer of America
- The woman holding a torch at the beginning of that studio's movie
- A bulky Russian metal mutant from the *X-Men*
- A seemingly bumbling and cockeyed detective

1. Upstaged by a flock of feathers

- **Nog**. What's a "nog" anyway. Isn't that short for "nog-gin," as in "What's wrong with your noggin that you chose this answer?"

- **Pog**. If a Chocobo was upstaged by a bottlecap, that would be sad. Very sad.

- ■ **Mog**. Correct. And he hates Chocobo with a passion. With a Kentucky Fried Passion

- **Jan Brady**. Marcia, Marcia Marcia! What am I doing here?

2. Anime traffic laws

- ■ **You screech to a halt**. You see "red," you stop. Unfortunately, I was a passenger in a car of a driver who believed, "You see red, you go really fast so you don't hit anything."

- **You speed before the light changes**. You must be the guy that I rode with.

- **You go normal speed, which is four times the speed limit**. I still think you are the guy that I rode with.

- **You attempt to ram into Mokona, citing that traffic lights infringe upon your civil liberties**. Now I am SURE that you are the guy that I rode with!

3. You called?

- ■ **Tamahome**. Correct. The name of the cat is "Tama." "Tama" is also slang for "balls," but I don't think Miaka has that in mind when she calls Tamahome. At least, I don't think so.

- **Chiriko**. Nope.

- **Tasuki**. Uh-uh

- **Nuriko**. See above.

4. Spelling bee

- ■ **J-I-J-I**

Believe it or not, I know a lot people who spell it "Gigi" and they are convinced that they are right. Actually it's not a lot of people, it's one person in particular. I'm writing this for posterity so you all can back me up when I say that the cat's name is spelled J-I-J-I!

5. Monster in my pocket

- **The discoverer of America**. Columbus? Why would she want an Italian explorer in her pocket? (Hmmm . . . use your imagination and make your jokes accordingly)

- **The woman holding a torch at the beginning of that studio's movie**. Uh-uh. It's not Columbia either. And of course, even if Shorty did agree to this substitute, that torch better go!

- **A bulky Russian metal mutant from the X-Men**. Nope. It's not Colossus. Besides, how could she stuff that in her overalls, huh?

- ■ **A seemingly bumbling and cockeyed detective**. Yup. "Colombo" is not only the name of Shorty's pet, but the name of a certain famous detective on TV that makes Sherlock Holmes look like Michael Jordan. Hmmm? Let's just say that Colombo needs a little work in the "coolness" department.

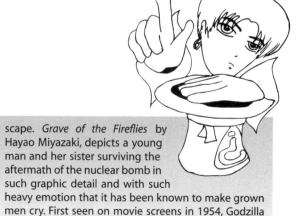

The Ultimate Ghost Story: World War II

The biggest influence on anime in Japan was an event that took place before anime was even recognized as a distinct form of entertainment: World War II. In many anime features, such as *Nausicaä, Neon Genesis Evangelion,* and *Akira,* for example, the nuclear bomb and total destruction are the source of themes and imagery, such as the recognizable atomic mushroom cloud or the crumbling of entire buildings in the urban landscape. *Grave of the Fireflies* by Hayao Miyazaki, depicts a young man and her sister surviving the aftermath of the nuclear bomb in such graphic detail and with such heavy emotion that it has been known to make grown men cry. First seen on movie screens in 1954, Godzilla (the predecessor of many live-action monsters and anime monsters) is often interpreted as a projection of the Japanese fear of the nuclear bomb and radiation.

1. At least he's a quiet roommate

You are looking for a roommate and you find an application from Pen-Pen from *Evangelion* at your door. What is one adjustment you would have to make at your domicile?

- He needs his own fridge
- He needs his own computer
- He needs his own phone line
- He needs to make sure that he can have drinking parties late at night to attract the ladies

2. It's all Greek to me

In *Card Captor Sakura*, it is rumored that Kero-chan's pure form, Kereberos, isn't that pure at all because if it was, it would scare the heck out of Sakura and she would never touch another Clow card again. If his namesake is anything like Greek mythology, which of these would be true of Kero-chan?

- He would sprout out nine heads
- He would turn you to stone
- He would cause you to be forever hungry
- He would sprout three heads and breathe out flames

3. Doll factory

You watch *Princess Mononoke* and you love the Kodama in the movie so much you decide to make a toy out of them. When you make the prototype, what would be good to use as a preliminary head?

- A golf ball

- A small pumpkin
- A rattle
- The face of George Washington on a quarter

4. Beasts of burden

In *El-Hazard*, Makoto prepares to go into battle, but the armored animal, Ura, is missing. Based on the fact that Ura and this animal are the same type of animal, who does he use as a breastplate and dies within three seconds of battle?

- Snoopy
- Snagglepuss
- Garfield
- Crocodile Dundee

5. Inconvenient pet

In the game *Azure Dreams*, the hero has a pet named "Kewne" that follows him wherever he goes, and he is finding that this is not popular with the seven girls he wants to date because they want to be alone. So what is the best way to take care of "Kewne?"

- Tie up his wings so he can't fly
- Bind up his feet so he can't walk
- Attach chains to his lower body so he can't crawl
- Gag his mouth because despite his advice, you actually think it is possible to date seven women at once and get away with it

In a country that has been demilitarized since 1945 (consitutionally, Japan cannot have its own military but can maintain a Self-Defense Force), many of the older generation in Japan believe that the youth of today have no comprehension of war. Older generations learned military history from their own experience of the war or because the war was still fresh on everyone's mind. Japanese kids, however, have had no such opportunity . And yet video games like the *Final Fantasy* series and anime like *Neon Genesis Evangelion* are popular among Japanese young people. There is no explanation why Japanese youth find experiencing "virtual war" through playing video games or watching anime so fascinating. But perhaps the people of the older generation and the young students of Japan are looking for the same thing: resolution of the war that ended a half century ago, before the first anime ever hit the market.

1. At least he's a quiet roommate

■ **He needs his own fridge**. Correct. Pen-Pen lives in a specially made fridge, except when he goes to take a bath. Then he lives in the bathtub.

• **He needs his own computer**. What would a penguin need with a computer other than to surf the net for "Playmate Penguins?"

• **He needs his own phone line**. What would a penguin need with a phone line other than hook up to a computer to surf the net for "Playmate Penguins?"

• **He needs to make sure that he can have drinking parties late at night to attract the ladies**. Yup, Pen-Pen's a party penguin! Not the right answer, but watching a penguin hanging over a toilet is a sight that you would not want to see again.

2. It's all Greek to me

• **He would sprout nine heads**. Nope, he is not a hydra that sprouts nine heads. Kero-chan would not be cute anymore if he did that.

• **He would turn you to stone**. Nope. You're thinking of a gorgon like Medusa. And Kero-chan ain't that ugly.

• **He would cause you to be forever hungry**. Hey, if Kero-chan worked me as hard as he does Sakura in order to get those Clow cards, I'd be forever hungry anyway.

■ **He would sprout three heads and breathe out flames**. Correct. Kerebos is the Greek term for the more familiar "Cerebus," which has three heads and breathes flames. But that would look rather uncute, you think?

3. Doll factory

• **A golf ball**. Nope, you shouldn't use this. It would be too tempting to whack it on the head with a golf club.

• **A small pumpkin**. Anything that can splatter into a rather messy pile should be avoided when making toys.

■ **A rattle**. There you go! How can a Kodama be a Kodama if its head doesn't rattle?

• **The face of George Washington on a quarter**. A Kodama is supposed to be cute, not presidential!

4. Beasts of burden

• **Snoopy**. If Snoopy goes to war, he would make a better pilot than someone's shield.

• **Snagglepuss**. Tell the answer to exit stage right! And not to come back!

■ **Garfield**. Correct. Like Ura, he is a cat. Unlike Ura, he is not designed for battle, unless you count his fat as some sort of shield.

• **Crocodile Dundee**. This Aussie is going to be no one's shield; unless you pay him enough.

5. Inconvenient pet

■ **Tie up his wings so he can't fly**. Correct. If you have Kewne possession, he flies with you everywhere you go. Which makes bathroom times rather inconvenient.

• **Bind up his feet so he can't walk**. Binding his feet might slow him down but he might have pretty powerful wings so you might want to try something else.

• **Attach chains to his lower body so he can't crawl**. (See above).

• **Gag his mouth because despite his advice, you actually think it is possible to date seven women at once and get away with it**. He'll still follow you . . . he'll stalk you until you're with one woman! But then again you are with one woman; one woman at a time, that is . . .

1. Name dropping

When the *Kodomo no Omocha* (Child's Toy) series aired, there was a character that narrated throughout the series but did not have a name until six episodes into the series. Why not?

- The character was originally meant to be decoration only
- His name would have given away part of the plot
- He was originally nameless, but many people demanded to know his name
- There was a contest to name him, and it had not finished yet when it started

2. Tickling the ribbons

In *Hime-chan no Ribon* (Hime's Ribbon), how did Hime come to know Pokota?

- He was her favorite toy come to life
- She accidentally opened a book and he appeared
- She found him as a stray and he opened up her powers
- She used a demon ritual and a demon in the form of a stuffed animal appeared

3. I was a teenage possessed cat

In *Kimagure Orange Road*, there was a time when Kyōsuke possessed the body of Jingoro, the cat. What almost happened before he returned to his body?

- He was almost run over
- He was almost kissed
- He was almost eaten
- He was almost about to mate with a dingy stray cat from a back alley

4. Magical girl toys

In *Mahō Tsukai Tai*, Jeff-kun is a cute bear that Sae always likes to keep at her side. What is Jeff's true form?

- A wizard, as in *Dungeons and Dragons*
- An elf, as in one of Santa's helpers
- A dwarf, as in *Austin Powers*'s Mini-Me
- A bard, as in "It's a bard, it's a plane, it's Shakespeare on a stealth bomber!"

5. Everyone wants to get into the act

If Chu-Chu from *Utena* were a pokemon like Pikachu, what kind of pokemon would Chu-Chu be classified under in the Pokedex?

- Mouse Pokemon
- Monkey Pokemon
- Teddy Bear Pokemon
- Pirate Pokemon

© GAINAX/Project Eva • TV Tokyo

"It's me again, Shinji Ikari, and when I listen to music, I use Evangelion™ tape players. Evangelion™ tape players, great when you're alone, but better in stereo." With whom did Shinji have to learn a synchronization attack on an Angel?

(a) Rei (b) Asuka (c) Misato (d) Pen-Pen

1. Name dropping

- **The character was originally meant to be decoration only**. Which means that if no one talked about it at all, everyone would have mistook it for a rabbit rather than a bat.

- **His name would have given away part of the plot**. As in what? A Babbit Conspiracy? The idea that every item made in *Kodomo no Omocha* has Babbit on it and therefore he controls the world? Hmmm … not a bad idea.

- **He was originally nameless, but many people demanded to know his name**. Something like that can't be nameless. No way that anything that cute could be called "It" for long.

- ■ **There was a contest to name him, and it had not finished yet when it started**. Correct. There was a naming contest to name this particular mascot. Hmmm … wouldn't "Omega" have been a nicer name? Hmmm?

2. Tickling the ribbons

- ■ **He was her favorite toy come to life** . Correct. Hime-chan's stuffed lion, Pokota, came to life with the help of the magical ribbon. Which is kind of unsettling because if you take him hostage and talk, you can get Hime-chan's secrets from him!

- **She accidentally opened a book and he appeared**. Nope, this isn't *Card Captor Sakura*. You must be thinking of Kero-chan, who somewhat appeared this way.

- **She found him as a stray and he opened up her powers**. Wrong again. This is how Luna opened up Serena (Usagi's) powers in *Sailor Moon*.

- **She used a demon ritual and a demon in the form of a stuffed animal appeared**. I don't even want to figure out what kind of anime that story detail came from!

3. I was a teenage possessed cat

- **He was almost run over**. If my driving friend had been in the anime, this surely would have happened.

- **He was almost kissed**. He narrowly missed being kissed. Of course, being kissed as a cat and no one knowing that you were a cat can't do much for your ego, can it?

- **He was almost eaten**. Yum! Cat food! Uh … no.

- **He was almost about to mate with a dingy stray cat from a back alley**. Hmmm … even Kosuke is not that desperate, or sick.

4. Magical girl toys

- ■ **A wizard, as in *Dungeons and Dragons***. Of course it would have to be a wizard! This is a show about magic! Duh!

- **An elf, as in one of Santa's helpers**. I always thought elves were supposed to be tall and beautiful and magical adepts. I guess the idea of Santa's gnomes wasn't promoted very well by the Gnome Association of Middle Earth.

- **A dwarf, as in *Austin Powers*'s Mini-Me**. I have seen Mini-Me in person, and dang! He is short! I mean, he is REALLY short! It's not the trick of a camera. He is SHORT! Oh, by the way, your answer is wrong.

- **A bard, as in "It's a bard, it's a plane, it's Shakespeare on a stealth bomber!"** No.

5. Everyone wants to get into the act

- **Mouse Pokemon**. Nope that spot is already taken by Pikachu and if Chu-Chu were to take it, I'm sure Pikachu's legal team would sue him for every penny he's got!

- ■ **Monkey Pokemon**. Yup! Chu-Chu is a monkey. Yeah, I know what he looks like. I can't explain it either.

- **Teddy Bear Pokemon**. I know Pokemon are supposed to be cute, but there is such a thing as excessive cuteness, you know.

- **Pirate Pokemon**. Only because he has one large pierced ear (of all the mascots, I think this is the only one that has this type of jewelry). But he has no eyepatch, no sword, and no scruffy voice to threaten the landlubbers.

■ ***Answer to picture puzzle:*** (b) Asuka. Now if Shinji only had his Evangelion™ swim-trunks. . . .

1. Kappa chameleon

In *Marmalade Boy*, Yū gets a cute UFO catcher doll and gives it to Miki. However, if the cute kappa becomes a real monster, Miki would be in plenty of trouble. What is the first thing she should do to keep the monster from attacking her?

- Transform into the Moon Princess and hit it with a tiara
- Put a wooden stake in its heart
- Stop, drop, and roll
- Politely bow to him

2. He's a small mascot and I ain't lion

Nadia has a small pet lion and today, he did not get his fill of food. The lion was so hungry that he began to eat chess pieces. He ate the chess piece that matched his name but Jean was there to spank it out of the lion before he ate the other pieces. What piece is covered in lion grime?

- King
- Bishop
- Knight
- Rook

3. I did not know body parts could apply for sainthood

In *Kaitō St. Tail* (Magical Thief St. Tail), a criminal purchased the hedgehog Ruby for a specific purpose. If someone used you the same way they used Ruby, which of these illegal actions would be pretty close?

- You would be pricking people for torture
- You would be crawling through small holes and stealing things
- You would be swallowing cocaine in rubber packages for the drug cartel
- You would be streetwalking and selling your ... stuff

4. D is for dog

Peropero from *Kareshi Kanojo no Jijō* (His and Her Circumstances) is a cute, simple dog to draw. In fact, let's draw one right now! What letter of the alphabet would you use to draw Peropero's eyes?

- O
- I
- U
- X

5. The Nausicaä 5

The Jackson 5 come to visit the Valley of the Wind (okay, suspend your belief systems right now) and perform for the villagers. Unfortunately, one of the Jackson 5 is sick and he is replaced with Nausicaä's pet. Because Nausicaä's mascot's name is so similar to this member of the Jackson 5, which Jackson member now looks even shorter than Michael?

- ANSWER: _____

1. Kappa chameleon

- **Transform into the Moon Princess and hit it with a tiara**. Oh yeah. I can transform into the Moon Princess everyday. I get compliments on my tiara at work. Not too hard. Not hard at all . . .

- **Put a wooden stake in its heart**. Nope. This ain't no vampire!

- **Stop, drop, and roll**. You're dealing with a monster; you're not on fire!

- ■ **Politely bow to him**. According to Japanese legend, the kappa has water on the top of his head and if you politely bow to it, the water will fall out and you can escape safely. Unless you are rather bold and take the kappa's head as a nice flower pot for your mother.

2. He's a small mascot and I ain't lion

- ■ **King**. Yes. King is the name of Nadia's pet lion. He's rather small to be a king, but then he's sort of like the Lion King; he'll grow up and rule the animal kingdom. And then eat them for his dinner.

- **Bishop**. Nope. This lion isn't like the *X-Men* mutant from the future at all.

- **Knight**. Uh-uh. Since when has this lion become anything like the Dark Knight, Batman? Oh, except for the dark gray fur and stuff.

- **Rook**. Nope. Sorry.

3. I did not know body parts could apply for sainthood

- **You would be pricking people for torture**. Yes, hedgehogs are certainly capable of doing that but humans can't do that unless they have fingernails of death.

- **You would be crawling through small holes and stealing things**. Nope. Unless you are Mini-Me, you should not be trying this anyway.

- ■ **You would be swallowing cocaine in rubber packages for the drug cartel**. Yes, in the show, Ruby was originally used to swallow a jewel in order to hide it. And when the thief need to get the jewel out, he was going to "open her up." Just be sure that the same won't happen to you if for some reason you do hide things in your body for a drug cartel <*.*>

- **You would be streetwalking and selling your . . . stuff**. I may be into many things but love with a hedgehog would be . . . painful to say the least.

4. D is for dog

- ■ **O**. Hee hee. Rather obvious, isn't it? Except in this case, Pero-Pero's eyes look like buttons, so the letter O would be the closest approximation.

- **I**. Wow. A dog with no peripheral vision. How terrible.

- **U**. How useful is a dog that doesn't open its eyes?

- **X**. When you use X's for eyes, doesn't that mean that the character's dead?

5. The Nausicaä 5

- ■ Tito

Since the name of the little creature that hangs around Nausicaä is "Teto," he could easily replace "Tito." Although getting an Afro in Teto's size would be rather difficult without having to cut off someone's armpit hair and gluing it to Teto's head (now there's a sentence or thought you don't hear everyday!)

Romance

Ranma and Akane. Miaka and Tamahome. Tenchi and everybody. Romances are very popular in anime. Are you as lovestruck with anime romances as these lovebirds are?

1. If you wanna know if he loves you so, it's in his . . .

When Ranma and Akane did *Romeo and Juliet* in the school play, the plot started off as *Romeo and Juliet* but ended up as:

- *Cinderella*
- *Snow White*
- *Beauty and the Beast*
- *Little Red Riding Hood*

2. Time reveals everything

When did Sailor Moon find out that Darien was Tuxedo Mask?

- After Serena had no choice but to transform in front of him
- He transformed first to rescue Serena in front of her when she was not Sailor Moon
- Serena found his mask in a bag full of his belongings
- He threw roses instead of darts at a local pub

3. I get drunk on Chichis all the time

Son Goku and Chichi had their first kid, Son Gohan (no news there). But what is Chichi so insistent on making her son become?

- As strong as his father
- A very smart man by making him study
- Extremely obedient so he can be a soldier
- A circus performer in hopes that one day, he will marry a bearded lady

4. Older women are ok, but she's older than your grandma!

Brock falls in love with every woman he meets. But one time, Brock and James fall in love with a ghost of the same woman. How long ago did she die?

- ANSWER: _____ years ago

5. Picture this . . .

Kunō and Nabiki are the perfect couple, simply because he has a lot of money and she likes to spend it. But before that, Nabiki was a working woman. What is the first thing that Nabiki ever sold to Kunō in the anime series?

- Semi-nude pictures of Akane
- Semi-nude pictures of Nabiki herself
- Semi-nude pictures of Ranma as a girl
- Semi-nude pictures of Ranma as a guy

1. If you wanna know if he loves you so, it's in his . . .

- *Cinderella*. Only if Ranma has a foot fetish . . .

- ■ *Snow White*. Correct. First they were on a balcony and then Juliet laid unconscious and could not be awoken until Romeo kissed her. I guess they really did not want any drugs in school.

- *Beauty and the Beast*. Nah . . . Akane isn't tomboyish enough to leave her legs unshaved for this part.

- *Little Red Riding Hood*. What is Ranma supposed to do with Akane? Eat her?

Oh yes, sake is not a drug! It's a dew of love!

2. Time reveals everything

- ■ **After Serena had no choice but to transform in front of him.** Yup. If she did not transform into Sailor Moon, they both surely would have died. And Tuxedo Mask gets a peep show if all that dammed glitter wasn't in the way.

- **He transformed first to rescue Serena in front of her when she was not Sailor Moon.** Nope. And can I be more grammatically confusing than this? You bet your bippy!

- **Serena found his mask in a bag full of his belongings.** And what is she doing in his bag? And who is that woman? And what is this condom doing here?

- **He threw roses instead of darts at a local pub.** It may look strange, but then again, Sailor Moon throws her tiara like a frisbee. Think of these as anime's version of extreme sports.

3. I get drunk on Chichis all the time

- **As strong as his father.** Can you imagine Gohan gobbling Weightgainer 2000 to become as massive as his father? Beefcake!

- ■ **A very smart man by making him study.** Hey there is nothing wrong with studying and becoming a smart man. Then you can figure out why the heck some sadist picked a number like 5,280 and made that the number of feet in a mile.

- **Extremely obedient so he can be a soldier.** He is already a nice kid. Don't ruin him by making him obedient.

- **A circus performer in hopes that one day, he will marry a bearded lady.** I don't think so.

4. Older women are ok, but she's older than your grandma!

- ■ 2000 years ago

And despite all the lingustic changes that have occurred in the past 2,000 years, she can speak to them perfectly.

5. Picture This . . .

- **Semi-nude pictures of Akane.** Akane would not debase herself for those kind of pictures.

- **Semi-nude pictures of Nabiki herself.** And let the possibility of blackmail come Kunō's way? Not a chance.

- ■ **Semi-nude pictures of Ranma as a girl.** Yup. And when Kunō saw a picture of Ranma-chan with her shirt off and back to the camera, you have to hear the noise he makes as he holds on to the picture! I think he needed a cigarette afterwards.

- **Semi-nude pictures of Ranma as a guy.** Hey there's nothing wrong with that if Kunō wants to see what he's up against. Unless boy-type Ranma is what he would like to be "up against."

Japanese Honorific Suffixes: A Quicklist

-San is a generic polite honorific suffix.

-Kun is applied to (1) young boys or young men or (2) a colleague who is the same status as or lower (if you want to give them respect) than the speaker.

-Chan is for (1) young girls and sometimes young women that are cute, (2) close friends, (3) boyfriends and girlfriends, (4) children.

-Sama is used (rarely) to show deference to a person higher in status than yourself (it is also used, sometimes mockingly, in "kissing up").

-Sensei is for a teacher (or in some cases a tutor), a doctor, or for any eminent expert or authority, such as an artist or writer.

-Senpai is used to address an upperclassmen or senior in school or at work

1. If you wanna know if he loves you so, it's in his . . . (part 2)

Which of these characters in *Fushigi Yūgi* have NOT kissed Tamahome in the anime series?

- Yui
- Nuriko
- Nakago
- Tamahome's mother

2. Why working VCRs rock!

Suppose that Yōta in *Video Girl Ai* had a VCR that worked properly! Which of these things would have surely happened since the VCR wasn't broken?

- Ai-chan would have been a lot taller
- Ai-chan would be a lot more effeminate
- Ai-chan would have looked older
- Ai-chan's chest wouldn't deflate so much

3. I'll kill you! I mean it!

In *Gundam Wing*, what did Heero do just before he uttered the ever-so-famous words to Relena, *Omae o korosu* (I will kill you)?

- He served Relena a letter
- He tripped embarrassingly in front of the entire school
- He wiped a tear from Relena's face
- He lost a bet and was forced to do a lap dance for her

4. I can't tell if she likes it or not

Shinji from *Evangelion* accidentally swallows some Spanish Fly when he tries to kill himself and now he can't control himself anymore. Which of these people is going to be the least vocal (or will not vocally complain) when Shinji attempts to become their daddy?

- Rei
- Misato
- Asuka
- Ritsuko

5. 911

In *Ah! My Goddess* or *Oh! My Goddess* (however you call it), what was Keiichi intent on doing to the phone before he accidentally called Belldandy on the Goddess Help Line?

- Calling the police for help
- Giving his mom a call
- Ordering food for delivery
- Something that involves "heavy breathing"

OTHER LESS-COMMON HONORIFICS

-Kaichō is for the president or leader of a club or an association.

-Kōchō is for a school principal.

-Shachō is for the president of a company.

-Hakase seems to be an equivalent of *-sensei* but is generally used for professors and doctors of a higher, Ph.D-level.

-Senshu is applied to athletes, almost any athlete, and in theory could be applied to someone like Speed Racer. (Sumo wrestlers are given the surtitle *-zeki*.)

-Dono is an honorific even more respectful than *-sama*. It means "lord" and is rarely used today.

When a title is not used when addressing another person, it can mean a number of things: (1) The speaker and the addressee are young or have been childhood friends. (2) They are very close friends or even lovers. (3) The speaker is a leader or commander addressing a subordinate. (4) The speaker does not respect the addressee or considers him an enemy or a criminal.

1. If you wanna know if he loves you so, it's in his . . . (part 2)

- **Yui**. Well, Yui took complete advantage of Tamahome when he was drugged. I suppose that means that he was unwilling. . . .

- **Nuriko**. Nuriko just kissed Tamahome out of the blue. And this was when Tamahome thought that Nuriko was a girl!

- **Nakago**. An effective strategy when fighting an opponent is to confuse him or to freak them out of his mind, which Nakago managed to do by kissing him.

- ■ **Tamahome's mother**. This was a pretty tricky question because Tamahome's mother was never in the series! But then, would you kiss your mom the same way you'd kiss a lover? Ewwww . . . .

2. Why working VCRs rock!

- **Ai-chan would have been a lot taller**. No, this isn't a Paula Abdul video! Who's Paula Abdul? I don't know. Do you?

- **Ai-chan would be a lot more effeminate**. A lot more effeminate, but not as much fun.

- **Ai-chan would have looked older**. The point of capturing things on a tape is so that they stay young forever. This isn't the picture of Dorian Grey, you know.

- ■ **Ai-chan's chest wouldn't deflate so much**. Correct! This is the case of Ai-chan and the shrinking breasts. I guess someone used Preparation H in the wrong places!

3. I'll kill you! I mean it!

- **He served Relena a letter**. If Heero is going to be a threat, I seriously doubt that it would look like a subpoena for court.

- **He tripped embarrassingly in front of the entire school**. Heero is a lot tougher than that. He'd probably kick everyone who laughed at him and maybe even more.

- ■ **He wiped a tear from Relena's face**. Correct. This scene is well remembered for its irony. It's not like rain on your wedding day or the free ride that you've already paid for. . . .

- **He lost a bet and was forced to do a lap dance for her**. And if Heero is wearing his usual spandex shorts, Relena can automatically tell if he's enjoying it.

4. I can't tell if she likes it or not

- ■ **Rei**. Rei will just lie there like the inflatable, clonable doll she is.

- **Misato**. Misato would slap him.

- **Asuka**. Asuka would slap him.

- **Ritsuko**. Ritsuko would mention something about her mother's genius on computers, then slap him.

5. 911

- **Calling the police for help**. Help! I need someone to give me help in finding the right answer!

- **Giving his mom a call**. Think about this carefully; are you going to say, "I want you to be with me forever," to your mom? There's nothing wrong with that, though (within reason).

- ■ **Ordering food for delivery**. Correct. Who knew that the Goddess Help Line and Domino's Pizza were one digit away from each other?

- **Something that involves "heavy breathing."** I don't think talking to someone after you've crossed the Saharan Desert is such a good idea.

1. Pink-y promise

In *Tokyo Babylon*, according to Seishirō's explanation to a very young Subaru, why are sakura (cherry blossoms) pink?

- Because they are a symbol of a woman's tears
- Because there is a living heart in a sakura tree
- Because Hello Kitty said so
- Because sakura trees drink the blood of corpses beneath them

2. Please save my promise

In *Please Save My Earth*, What is the one thing that Mokuren made Shion promise to her before she died?

- Never take your own life
- Never pass up love if he found another
- Never let them see you sweat
- Never eat beans again, at least not while he's around her

3. What in blazes are you doing?

Even though Yūsuke in *Yū Yū Hakusho* (Poltergeist Report) is tough, he is rather a sweet guy. At one time, he saved Keiko from a burning house by doing something very important by clearing a path in the flames. You were inspired by that scene to become a fireman/firewoman but instead of bringing a hose full of water to a fire, what do you bring, since that was what Yūsuke used to save Keiko?

- A fan
- A blanket
- A bowl of magic ramen
- Eggs

4. How many times can you say "I love you"?

Kazuya from *Here Is Greenwood* loves Miya so much that he tried several ways to get in touch with her even though she avoided him constantly. Which method did he NOT use on the girl of his dreams?

- Phone call
- Love letter
- E-mail
- Visits to her school

5. For everyone else's eyes only

Ataru has eyes for everyone but Lum in *Urusei Yatsura*. But he risks his life for Lum when Lum's fiancé, Rei, comes to Earth and challenges Ataru. The contest looks something like:

- A race across hot lava using only socks
- A knife-throwing contest, except the knives are twice their size
- An electric chair competition without the chairs and using real lightning
- A spanking contest where they get spanked until someone screams "uncle!"

© 1991 Yuike Nasu/Hakusensha/Victor Entertainment, Inc. /Pierrot Project

In this scene from *Here Is Greenwood*, a gang of boys forcibly strip Kazuya of his clothes. So they can do what to him?

(a) Videotape him (b) Spank him (c) Throw eggs at him (d) Have their way with him

1. Pink-y promise

- **Because they are a symbol of a woman's tears.** Since when do anyone's tears turn pink unless you have pinkeye or something?

- **Because there is a living heart in a sakura tree.** Nope. That would be . . . disturbing. But the real answer is even more disturbing.

- **Because Hello Kitty said so.** Yes, Hello Kitty is the high priestess of the anime world. I think not.

- ■ **Because sakura trees drink the blood of corpses beneath them.** Correct. Once you know this, you'll never think of sakura trees the same again.

2. Please save my promise

- ■ **Never take your own life.** Correct. If Shion took his own life, he could not reincarnate.

- **Never pass up love if he found another.** Well, what else is he going to love if everyone else on the moon is dead? His right hand?

- **Never let them see you sweat.** Yes, Mokuren worked for a deodorant commercial on the moon. I imagine it must come in pretty handy since it looked like there were no showers on that moonbase.

- **Never eat beans again, at least not while he's around her.** Sound advice. Ha ha! Get it? SOUND advice!

3. What in blazes are you doing?

- **A fan.** A dinky little fan? I don't think so.

- **A blanket.** That's going to be one huge blanket to put out the fire to that house!

- **A bowl of magic ramen.** You mean the type of ramen that makes you disappear into the bathroom never to be seen again? Nope.

- ■ **Eggs.** Yes, a monster egg was used to clear a path in the flames to save Keiko. Although egging a house would give people the wrong idea of what you are trying to do with the house.

4. How many times can you say "I love you"?

- **Phone call.** I just called to say "I Love You." Aren't Stevie Wonder songs supposed to work like a charm?

- **Love letter.** Love Letter from China! Love Letter from China! Oops, wrong love letter . . .

- ■ **E-mail.** Nope. Kazuya never sent her e-mail. It's just as well; she could easily delete it.

- **Visits to her school.** The dedicated Kazuya visited her at school every day. Now only if he were as dedicated to being as cool as Mitsuru or Shinobu, he would never have to worry about Miya and let the girls flock around him like a babe magnet!

5. For everyone else's eyes only

- **A race across hot lava using only socks.** Socks? Socks are for wimps! And besides, it's wrong!

- **A knife-throwing contest, except the knives are twice their size.** Nope, this is Ataru we are talking about, not Cloud Strife from *Final Fantasy VII*.

- ■ **An electric chair competition without the chairs and using real lightning.** Yes, and Ataru wins the contest! He's the man!

- **A spanking contest where they get spanked until someone screams "uncle!."** And if Ataru was being spanked by a girl, he'd probably scream, "More! More!"

1. Forever bachelor

In *DNA²*, poor Momonari-kun has this terrible curse called the "Lady Allergy." Whenever he gets sexually excited, what is the first thing you need to get him?

- A handkerchief
- An ice pack
- A paper bag
- A chastity belt

2. Let me hear you scream!

In one of the *Kimagure Orange Road* OVAs, Kyōsuke had a dream where he was constantly screaming Madoka's name. When he woke up, his sisters thought he was having an *etchi* dream. Why was he screaming Madoka's name?

- Because Madoka was pushed off a cliff by Hikaru
- Because Madoka broke up with Kyōsuke and walked away
- Because an idol singer revealed his secret to Madoka
- Because Kyōsuke actually had an *etchi* dream

3. Does it count as a kiss when you're nearly unconscious?

In *Princess Mononoke*, there is a scene from the audience's point of view where it looks like Lady San is kissing Ashitaka. What is she actually doing?

- Licking a wound on his face
- Feeding Ashitaka with her mouth
- Sucking out venom on his neck
- Eating the parasites from his jaw

4. I'm gonna make you work, boy!

Yurika may love Akito Tenkawa in the anime *Nadesico*, but she is the captain and he is much lower in rank. Because of his position that he had when he boarded the *Nadesico*, what could Yurika command him to do?

- Scrub out the latrines
- Cook her a Denver omelet
- Make her bed
- Satisfy her in bed

5. Everyone loves Yukito

There are just some characters that are quite well-loved. Yukito from *Card Captor Sakura* happens to be one of them. To which of these characters has Yukito NOT been romantically linked? (Romantically linked does not necessarily mean it's reciprocal. . .)

- Sakura
- Tōya
- Li Shaoran
- Tomoyo

In this scene in *Utena*, Anthy is covering herself when her dress melts in the middle of the ballroom. What melted the dress?

(a) Water (b) Heat (c) Lemon juice (d) Chicken soup

1. Forever bachelor

- **A handkerchief**. All I can say is I wish it were that simple. . . .
- **An ice pack**. Nah. It doesn't apply here.
- ■ **A paper bag**. Yup. Expect a load from Momonari-kun because whenever he gets excited, he blows chunks! Pink ones the size of your head!
- **A chastity belt**. Ooh, how cruel. But what better way to stop the Mega Playboy than to train him early!

2. Let me hear you scream!

- **Because Madoka was pushed off a cliff by Hikaru**. Yeah, you go, Hikaru! Show the girl who's the man! Uh . . . I mean, woman!
- **Because Madoka broke up with Kyōsuke and walked away**. How heartbreaking. And fortunately, incorrect.
- ■ **Because an idol singer revealed his secret to Madoka**. Correct. A male idol singer told the audience of Kyōsuke's psychic power and it freaked Kyōsuke out. Although, why would they be scared of a man who could potentially give them winning lottery numbers?
- **Because Kyōsuke actually had an *etchi* dream**. Kyōsuke is such a nice guy; you don't think he's actually capable of something like that, do you?

3. Does it count as a kiss when you're nearly unconscious?

- **Licking a wound on his face**. This is Lady San, not a puppy!
- ■ **Feeding Ashitaka with her mouth**. Oh so that's what you call it nowadays, hmmm? Just kidding. It's the correct answer.
- **Sucking out venom on his neck**. A great excuse for a hickey but not the right answer.
- **Eating the parasites from his jaw**. Hmm . . . she really is a monster, isn't she?

4. I'm gonna make you work, boy!

- **Scrub out the latrines**. What is this? The army? No.
- ■ **Cook her a Denver omelet**. Correct. Akito is employed as a cook when he boards the ship. Sort of like Steven Segall in that one movie. Although, I forget the movie. I think it has "Death" in the title or something. Wait . . . who's Steven Segall?
- **Make her bed**. Akito isn't Yurika's maid, although I imagine she would want him to dress in a French maid's uniform someday.
- **Satisfy her in bed**. I imagine Yurika would have no complaints (although Akito might), but he is not Yurika's cabin boy.

5. Everyone loves Yukito

- **Sakura**. Yukito is Sakura's schoolgirl crush. It's called a "crush" because it hurts like heck not to have it reciprocated . . .
- **Tōya**. It's only speculation that Tōya loves Yukito. But you have to admit, they are a cute pair, right?
- **Li Shaoran**. Yukito is Li Shaoran's schoolboy crush. Yup, EVERYONE loves Yukito.
- ■ **Tomoyo**. Tomoyo is too much in love with Sakura to notice Yukito at all . . .

■ **Answer to picture puzzle:** (a) Water. This is why dry clean labels are important.

1. Too touched

In the beginning episodes of *Touch*, when Minami watches Kazuya at baseball practice, there are lots of fangirls who are screaming over Kazuya. Meanwhile, Minami is being pelted with what as she attempts to continue watching him at practice?

- Pebbles
- Popcorn
- Baseballs (ouch . . .)
- Hearts from Kazuya's admirers

2. Chaste and be chased

In *Kaitō St. Tail* (Magical Thief St. Tail), Meimi-chan in the form of St. Tail steals a wedding veil that was under the guard of Asuka Jr. Why did the girl, who owned the veil, want it stolen?

- So she would not have to get married
- So her mom would not have to get re-married
- It was a gaudy-looking veil
- Just to see if St. Tail could steal it from Asuka Jr.'s guard

3. The things we do for love

In *Hana Yori Dango*, even though Dōmyōji and Tsukushi-chan are mortal enemies, what is the one thing that Dōmyōji always attempts to do to impress her?

- He tries to straighten his hair for her
- He takes his shirt off in front of her
- He hangs around celebrities and shows them off to her
- He buys entire buildings just so they can make out in them

4. Ooh, let me see!

In *Kodomo no Omocha* (Child's Toy), Sana-chan took control over Hayama and the classroom by being able to blackmail him with a picture of what?

- A picture of him getting it on with a teacher
- A picture of him stealing money from a desk
- A picture of him "fixing" his grades in the teacher's gradebook
- A picture of him with his pants down

5. Meirii Kurisumasu

It's interesting that some of the non-Christian Japanese celebrate Christmas just like Valentine's Day, where the holiday is for lovers. Which kind of makes the actual Valentine's Day all the more . . . special. Can't you just imagine the lovers in Japan saying, "Uh, didn't we just celebrate Christmas?"

In *Marmalade Boy*, what did Yū give Miki for Christmas?

- A Christmas tree
- A promise ring
- Little Yū and Miki dolls
- A one-way trip to the free clinic

© 1994 Toho, Studio Pierrot and Movic

Hiei from *Yū Yū Hakusho* (Poltergeist Report) has a glowing third eye in this scene. What is it called?

(a) Reiki (b) Yōki (c) Jagan (d) Genkai

1. Too Touched

- **Pebbles**. She that is without sin may cast the first stone. . . . I guess these girls are rather confident to say the least.

- **Popcorn**. Nah . . . Popcorn isn't aerodynamic enough or heavy enough to make an impact.

- **Baseballs (ouch . . .)**. I doubt that Kazuya was that bad a pitcher. I don't remember Minami's head being a magnet for baseballs.

- ■ **Hearts from Kazuya's admirers**. Yes, the hearts pelted Minami to her annoyance. But she shouldn't worry; she can have her pick between two twin brothers and then who would care about them?

2. Chaste and be chased

- ■ **So she would not have to get married**. Women do not need veils to get married. But the veil is symbolic of a bond that she wants to refuse! And you thought anime wasn't deep.

- **So her mom would not have to get re-married**. Nope, that's not the right answer.

- **It was a gaudy-looking veil**. Nope, it was a nice-looking veil so this can't be the right answer, either.

- **Just to see if St. Tail could steal it from Asuka Jr.'s guard**. And, it offers a chance for the young girl to be around Asuka Jr.-senpai that she likes so much!

3. The things we do for love

- ■ **He tries to straighten his hair for her**. Correct. Ever since she said that to him, he has been obsessing with straightening his hair.

- **He takes his shirt off in front of her**. If you show off the package one too many times, no one is going to want it, if you know what I mean. This answer is incorrect.

- **He hangs around celebrities and shows them off to her**. I guess he does this, but there is something more personal that he does to impress her.

- **He buys entire buildings just so they can make out in them**. No, but if Dōmyōji has hormones surging, he'd end up buying half of Japan this way!

4. Ooh, let me see!

- **A picture of him getting it on with a teacher**. Ewww . . . he's a little too young to even be doing this kind of thing!

- **A picture of him stealing money from a desk**. He may be a bully, but he's not really a thief. Wrong answer.

- **A picture of him "fixing" his grades in the teacher's gradebook**. He doesn't care about school. Why would he do this?

- ■ **A picture of him with his pants down**. Correct. There's nothing like Mr. Happy to make your blackmailer very happy.

5. Meirii Kurisumasu

- ■ **A Christmas tree**. Right! "Miki, do you wanna see my Christmas tree? It's big and full of fir!" Well, not like that. It's a glass picture of a tree, much cleaner than the statement above.

- **A promise ring**. Ah, not this time. He gives that to her later. Or was it before? Is it after the third time they broke up or after the second time they got together? Ah . . . I don't know.

- **Little Yū and Miki dolls**. Ooh! Yū's doll accidentally fell on top of Miki. Give you any idas, Miki? Um, no.

- **A one way trip to the free clinic**. How wrong could you be?

In *Marmalade Boy*, every gift seems special, regardless of what it is. "Miki, I got you a present! Dryer lint!" "Oh Yū! It's dryer lint from your favorite sweater! I love you!" "I love you Miki! When I saw this lint, I thought of you!" How romantic . . .

■ *Answer to picture puzzle:* (c) Jagan.

Science Fiction & Mecha

A long time popular genre of anime, it would be strange if I totally missed this category. So here are some questions for those who need a sci-fi fix.

1. Protective utensils

In *Tenchi Muyō*, Ayeka's guardians, Azaka and Kamadake, look amazingly like what?

- A toothpaste and a toothbrush
- A fork and spoon
- A pair of fuzzy dice
- Salt and pepper shakers

2. Dammit! I lost my connection!

In *Neon Genesis Evangelion*, how long can an Eva function after being disconnected from its power supply?

- ANSWER: _____minutes

3. We can fly, we have (Gundam) wings

In *Gundam Wing*, who could be accused of having a "Char complex?"

- Heero Yuy
- Trowa
- Zechs
- Quatre Rareba Winner

4. Chewable crises

What is the name of Priss's band in *Bubblegum Crisis*, a band which she eventually ditched to go on a solo career?

- The Revengers
- Replicants
- Rippertech
- Red Art

5. Everyone but the girl

In *Voltron* (or *Go-Lion*), when one of the fighters became injured, Princess Allura took his place. Which colored lion did she pilot?

- Blue lion
- Pink lion
- Yellow lion
- Green lion

1. Protective utensils

- **A toothpaste and a toothbrush**. Yes, these guardians are endorsed by four out of five dentists in Japan. These items are the Guardians Tooth, Justice, and the Japanese way of being! Nah, too corny.

- **A fork and spoon**. Hey look! Japanese Gothic! Nope. Sorry.

- **A pair of fuzzy dice**. They don't make great Guardians, but if you take them to a casino and prevent them from using the bathroom, you can play with a pair of loaded dice. Uh-uh.

- ■ **Salt and pepper shakers**. That's right. Azaka and Kamadake pretty much look like salt and pepper shakers for the Giant in Jack and the Beanstalk.

2. Dammit! I lost my connection!

- ■ 5 minutes

EVA's do not last long when they are not connected to their power supply. I don't know why. It's not one of the mysteries in *Evangelion*; I'm just too lazy to find out.

3. We can fly, we have (Gundam) wings

- **Heero Yuy**. Nope. Heero doesn't have a Char complex. He doesn't even have a Charmander complex either.

- **Trowa**. The only thing complex about Trowa is his past. At least, complex to us.

- ■ **Zechs**. Any guy that has to hide behind a mask has some kind of complex. It's rather symbolic of mask-ing the inner self. Either that or this guy is so narcissistic that he doesn't want to damage his pretty face.

- **Quatre Rareba Winner**. Quatre isn't very complex; he's just a sweet guy who can easily destroy things.

4. Chewable crises

- **The Revengers**. Yes, they were a band in *Bubblegum Crisis*. No, they did not belong to Priss.

- ■ **Replicants**. Yes. The names sounded good at the time: Priss Asagiri and the Replicants, Gloria Estefan and The Miami Sound Machine, Prince and the Revolution. But like all things, people go their separate ways. Apparently, Priss hogged all the bathroom space and they could not take it anymore, but those bushes they used grew real well.

- **Rippertech**. Why would you name a band after a sleazy and crooked man?

- **Red Art**. Nope. It's not this one.

5. Everyone but the girl

- ■ **Blue lion**. Yup. This Princess can handle her own and can do it all without needing cinnamon roll hair!

- **Pink lion**. There wasn't a pink lion in *Voltron*. Well, I suppose there was, but all the other pilots objected to the bright color.

- **Yellow lion**. Nope, it's not this answer.

- **Green lion**. And not this one either. There would be one little angry kid if this happened.

Amerikan Japaniizu (American Japanese)

Sailor Moon? Slam Dunk? Wedding Peach? Slayers? How come so many titles of Japanese anime are in English? In fact, not just names of anime titles, but names of products, J-pop bands, and many common expressions in Japan are also in English. Why?

In 1990, the Japanese language used approximately 20,000 English loanwords, and the number is steadily increasing. English has borrowed a couple hundred of Japanese words (note that American English gets more of its loanwords from Japanese than from any other Asian language).

After Japan opened its ports to the outside world in the mid- to late 19th century, many Western influences came into Japan, among them the German-style boys' and girls' school uniforms that one often sees in anime.

English got another infusion into Japan when during the American Occupation after World War II. The phrase "bye bye" was adopted into common Japanese use during this time. Also popular was the expression "Sankyū," for *Domo arigato*.

Two factors have increased the use of English in recent times. The Ministry of Education's requirement that junior high students take an English test in order to advance to high school has caused millions of Japanese students to begin studying English words and phrases. Also, early computers were based on English programs and came with English keyboards, making

1. A disaster of heroic proportions

By using their powers, the members of *Gatchaman* (or *G-Force* or *Eagle Riders* or whatever you call it) are affecting the environment around the world! Which of these natural disasters are most likely to be attributed to them, based on their powers?

- Earthquakes
- Floods
- Tornadoes
- Global warming

2. Shōnen toys in shōjo anime

In *Magic Knight Rayearth*, what are all the robotic-looking machines called?

- Rayearths
- Escudo
- Gekigangers
- Machines

3. How do heroes get paid anyway?

In *Shinesman*, what is Shinesman Red's day job?

- Salaryman in Sales Department
- Salaryman in Human Resources
- Salaryman in Research & Development
- Janitor for Microsoft

4. Number 2 must be really tough

In *Eat-Man,* although Bolt Crank's diet is unusual, what is he surely never going to be malnourished from a lack of?

- Fats
- Potassium
- Carbohydrates
- Iron

5. No strings attached

In *Saber Marionette J*, who makes the *otome kairō*?

- Faust
- Ieyasu
- Lorelei
- Otaru

English a necessity for many adults in science and industry. Current keyboard layout in Japan still has the "QWERTY" system printed next to the kana on the keys. Many Japanese web sites post a disclaimer if the site does not feature English.

English is indeed a universal language. But explaining why Americans cannot say the J-pop band names Hide with Spread Beaver and Ass Baboons of Venus with a straight face is a different matter.

Do you recognize these English-based terms written in romanized Japanese? (It's best to sound them out, as many Japanese do with English-based words.)

A. kamera
B. deeto
C. nyūzu
D. konpyūtaa
E. biiru
F. kurejitto kaado
G. aisu kuriimu
H. kurisumasu
I. jiinzu
J. nansensu
K. guramu
L. naisu taimingu

ANSWERS

A: camera. B: date (as in "going out on a date"). C: news (as in "news program"). D: computer. E: beer. F: credit card. G: ice cream. H: Christmas. I: jeans (as in "blue jeans"). J: nonsense. K: gram. L: "Nice timing!"

1. A disaster of heroic proportions

- **Earthquakes**. Nope. Not unless they were particularly devious and targeted their powers at a fault line.

- **Floods**. Nope. Not unless they were particularly devious and targeted their powers at a sewage tank.

- ■ **Tornadoes**. Correct. When they form their five-man pyramid, they can cause fierce tornadoes against their enemies. Also great for blowing out birthday cakes at a very far distance.

- **Global warming**. Only after they had super spicy food can they do this, except no special powers are required for this action.

2. Shōnen toys in shōjo anime

- **Rayearths**. Nope. But I should give you partial credit. One of the robots is called "Rayearth."

- **Escudo**. Nope. This is the material used to make the magical growing swords that Hikaru, Umi, and Fū hold in their hands. (Okay, think of your own dirty joke here).

- **Gekigangers**. Um … what series are you watching again?

- ■ **Machines**. Sometimes the most simple term can be most beautiful. However, with a world called "Cephiro" and one of the enemies named "Alcyone," CLAMP could have come up with a much better name, you think?

3. How do heroes get paid anyway?

- ■ **Salaryman in Sales Department**. Considering what Shinesman Red does for work, he better be paid well! At least he doesn't have to worry about dry cleaning his suit.

- **Salaryman in Human Resources**. No. Considering his busy work schedule, he'd end up giving himself constant raises! You wouldn't want to let the company go bankrupt, would you?

- **Salaryman in Research & Development**. Nah. I figure a smart cookie like him should have a plan: Research competitive salaries. Then develop a way to be paid all those salaries combined.

- **Janitor for Microsoft**. Sometimes, blackmail is the quickest way to get money …

4. Number 2 must be really tough

- **Fats**. Nope. Unless you count grease oil.

- **Potassium**. This was just a pure guess, wasn't it? I bet you haven't even seen Eat Man! (Pac-Man doesn't count here …)

- **Carbohydrates**. Uh-uh. Watch the series and you would know immediately what the answer is.

- ■ **Iron**. Correct. Well, the only thing I can say here is that I hope he stays regular …

5. No strings attached

- ■ **Faust**. Correct. This ruler of Germania equipped the *otome kairō* into each of his marionettes. I guess blow-up dolls no longer did it for him.

- **Ieyasu**. What would a shogun be doing with the *otome kairō*? He has enough problems with interns at the office!

- **Lorelei**. Nope. This female scientist probably has a lot of other things on her mind. Like the fact that she's one of the few females in the world of men! She's probably heard every pick-up line in the book, and then some …

- **Otaru**. Nope. Not him. Uh-uh. Wrong answer. Pick again.

1. Army of lovers

In *Vision of Escaflowne,* what is most notable about Dilandau's army?

- They are all pretty girls
- They are all pretty boys
- They are all battle droids
- They are all stormtroopers

2. What a long strange trip this is

In the world of *Serial Experiments Lain*, what is "The Wired?"

- A popular magazine among junior high students
- A gang of drug junkies
- A drink not unlike Red Bull
- What people would call "the world on-line"

3. The winner in LaLa Land

Who won the idol singer contest in *Martian Successor Nadesico*?

- Megumi
- Ruri
- Yurika
- Minmei

4. No sign of her in sight

In *Macross Plus*, there is a particular person named "Sharon Apple" who reigns as the idol queen of the time. Why doesn't she do autographs?

- She feels that doing them is beneath her
- Her autograph is licensed and she can only give them after getting permission
- Her jealous boyfriend does not allow her to give them out
- She's a virtual idol; she does not really exist

5. Anime cars other than the Pikachu Beetle

In Kenichi Sonoda's shows *Gunsmith Cats* and *Riding Bean*, what car is featured in both series?

- Mustang GT
- Shelby Cobra GT 500
- Pink Cadillac
- BMW 23

1. Army of Lovers

- **They are all pretty girls**. If he were Hugh Hefner, this might be a possibility.
- ■ **They are all pretty boys**. Yes, and I bet he has fun "training" them as well.
- **They are all battle droids**. The title of the question is "Army of Lovers" and you pick the most machine-like choice? Well, different strokes for different folks, right?
- **They are all stormtroopers**. Well, long ago in a galaxy far, far away . . . actually, I'm telling you how far your answer is from the correct one.

2. What a long strange trip this is

- **A popular magazine among junior high students**. You might be thinking of the magazine *Wired*, but it's the wrong answer anyway.
- **A gang of drug junkies**. Nope. But good guess.
- **A drink not unlike Red Bull**. No. And that is comfortably surprising.
- ■ **What people would call "the world on-line."** Right. "The Wired" is the Internet world and if people can actually live on-line, then we would never have to worry about growing old or being sick. Although we would have to be constantly updated and protect ourselves of from viruses. You don't know where that disk has been . . .

3. The winner in LaLa Land

- **Megumi**. Uh-uh. With a name like Megumi, it has got to be good, right? Well, not this time.
- ■ **Ruri**. Correct. Ruri won the idol singer contest. Ruri is also one of the most popular characters in *Nadesico*. All this because she calls their crewmates "idiots."
- **Yurika**. Nope, she got second place.
- **Minmei**. Uh, no . . . she's not even IN *Nadesico*! Go back to your *Macross* and don't come back until your boyfriend is someone else other than a pilot!

4. No sign of her in sight

- **She feels that doing them is beneath her**. Beneath her? Beneath her what? Circuitry?
- **Her autograph is licensed and she can only give them after getting permission**. Sounds like some comic book artists I know who'll give them out for payment. Those artist prostitutes!
- **Her jealous boyfriend does not allow her to give them out**. Everyone can become her boyfriend. Read below to see why.
- ■ **She's a virtual idol; she does not really exist**. Correct. Sharon Apple is the quintessential idol. Look but no touch. Which is why people can love her without getting rejected and obsess over her because she might be one of the few people who won't file a restraining order on a fanboy.

5. Anime cars other than the Pikachu Beetle

- **Mustang GT**. GOT Mustang? Nope.
- ■ **Shelby Cobra GT 500**. Correct. Which means that someone (no pointing of fingers) must have gotten a free car to put it in two of his anime, ne? Just kidding.
- **Pink Cadillac**. This is Kenichi Sonoda we are talking about here, not Mary Kay!
- **BMW 23**. I guess when you're a big enough company, you don't have to name your cars anymore; you just have to number them. It's not the right answer though.

Thanks to Peter Brown for this question.

1. For the love of an Ingram

Many people know that Noa Izumi's Ingram is named "Alphonse" in the anime *Patlabor*. Where did the name originally come from?

- Her grandfather was nicknamed "Alphonse"
- Her father was nicknamed "Alphonse"
- Her first crush was named "Alphonse"
- Her dog was named "Alphonse"

2. Distracting train of thought

In the game *Final Fantasy VIII*, when Rinoa's team and SeeD were planning on hijacking the President's train, they used a model train set to explain how to carry out the plan. Why does the President's car look like crap?

- Zell has been playing with it
- Selphie accidentally dropped it
- Rinoa did a bad paint job on it
- It just looked that way when they bought it at a secondhand store

3. Hey, there's no Asuka in a plugsuit in there!

In the world of *Macross*, what does "EVA" stand for?

- Enemy Valkyrie
- Evolutionary Atrophy
- Electric Variable Amplifier
- Entertainment Vor Averyone

4. Anime spinoffs

Gekiganger is a spinoff of what series?

- *Mazinger Z*
- *Astro Boy*
- *G-Force*
- *Martian Successor Nadesico*

5. Pe-ko, Pe-ko-chu!

In *Irresponsible Captain Tylor*, who was Peko-Peko?

- Ahiru no Pekkle's evil twin
- Justy Ueki Tylor
- Azalin-chan's lost pet
- The doll the twins made for the pilot

1. For the Love of an Ingram

- **Her grandfather was nicknamed "Alphonse."** Think for a moment. Why would a Japanese grandfather be named "Alphonse"?

- **Her father was nicknamed "Alphonse."** Think again for a moment. Why would a Japanese father be named "Alphonse"?

- **Her first crush was named "Alphonse."** Nope. Not correct.

- ■ **Her dog was named "Alphonse"** Bingo! There was a girl who had a dog and Alphonse was his name-o, A-L-P-H-O . . . N . . . S . . . E . . . Um, needs a bit of work.

2. Distracting train of thought

- **Zell has been playing with it.** Zell may be playful, but he did not play with the model trains.

- **Selphie accidentally dropped it.** Selphie is very **genki** ("high-spirited" is the closest translation to it), but she's no butterfingers.

- ■ **Rinoa did a bad paint job on it.** And as Rinoa brilliantly explained, her bad paint job symbolizes her hatred toward the President. To which everyone replied, "Sure," "Whatever," and some comment about how if that is what the President's car looks like, then she must REALLY hate the Preisdent.

- **It just looked that way when they bought it at a secondhand store.** Just because something comes from a secondhand store doesn't mean that it will always look like crap. Unless it's soft, brown, and attracts flies. You know, old furs.

3. Hey, there's no Asuka in a plugsuit in there!

- ■ **Enemy Valkyrie**. Correct. Do what I did; look it up in the Macross Compendium on the web and it will say **Enemy Valkyrie**.

- **Evolutionary Atrophy**. Did humans have tails? Find out in the next Geraldo! Hmmm . . . Geraldo isn't doing those type of shows anymore. Anyway, it's not the right answer.

- **Electric Variable Amplifier**. You guessed, didn't you. Good guess by the way; I would have guessed that myself.

- **Entertainment Vor Averyone**. Ja! Das ist gud, ja! Nein!

4. Anime spinoffs

- *Mazinger Z*. **Mazinger** did have spinoffs, but **Geki-ganger** wasn't one of them.

- *Astro Boy*. *Astro Boy* did not have any spinoffs, unless you count the **Astro Boy** parody on **Freakazoid!** "I will succeed!"

- *G-Force*. Well, there is a more updated *Gatchaman* in existence, but is that technically considered a spin-off? I'm not sure . . .

- ■ *Martian Successor Nadesico*. Right! Who knew that a parody of a robot show was popular enough to become something in its own right? Thanks, "Weird Al," for paving the road for us common folk!

5. Pe-ko, Pe-ko-chu!

- **Ahiru no Pekkle's evil twin**. Evil duckie. Ooh, I'm scared . . .

- **Justy Ueki Tylor**. Uh-uh. I'd knock anyone who gave me a cute nickname like that!

- ■ **Azalin-chan's lost pet**. Correct! Ah rejoice! You got this answer right! Although you actually did not find the pet and you got Azalin-chan all sad again! You're such a meanie!

- **The doll the twins made for the pilot**. Nope, this wasn't Peko-Peko. It was Chucky! The evil doll come to life in many famous horror movies and eventually became married to the Bride of Chucky. He now lives quietly as a serial killer in an unsuspecting neighborhood. At least he has stable work.

1. Things not related to Jet Li

Imagine that someone was watching *Mazinger Z* and saw the episode where the Jet Scrander was affixed to the giant robot. That person developed something similar for little kids because he knew that he could make a mint off of the merchandising. But now, what do the kids have to watch out for when using their own personal Jet Scranders?

- Cars
- Boats
- Planes
- Cowpies

2. Love triangle tangles

What happens in the movie edition of *Macross Plus* that prevents Dyson from saving Myung from the fire in the concert hall?

- He thought it was one of Kate's tricks to trick him into seeing Myung
- Guld knocked him unconscious before rescuing Myung himself
- The police barricaded the concert hall after the fire alarm went off
- He was with Lucy in bed

3. Ineligible to be Miss Macross

Which of the following character voice actor's did NOT play a *Macross* girl?

- Mika Doi
- Hiroko Kasahara
- Rica Matsumoto
- Rica Fukami

4. Shall we dance? Forever?

In *Gundam Wing*'s "Endless Waltz," what does the "Endless Waltz" refer to?

- The circle of life
- The cycle of history
- The environmental cycle
- The cycle of photosynthesis

5. Martian rock, paper, and scissors

If you were to play a match of Jan-ken-pon (rock, paper, scissors) with Yurika of *Nadesico*, what would be your most logical weapon of choice so that you would beat her, given Yurika's pose?

- Rock
- Paper
- Scissors
- Trick question! Yurika has no hands!

This character from *Sorcerer Hunters* is related to which of these other characters?

(a) Tira (b) Gateau (c) Carrot (d) Chocolate

1. Things not related to Jet Li

- **Cars**. Nope, with a Jet Scrander, you should be able to avoid cars. You can fly to school instead of walk!

- **Boats**. Unless you plan to fly like a Cessna, you have nothing to worry about here.

- ■ **Planes**. Correct. The Jet Scrander enabled the Mazinger Z to fly, and now you can fly at home, too! Just be sure to avoid the low ceilings and anything with propellers. You don't want to be responsible for jamming up a plane engine and sending passengers to their doom, now would you?

- **Cowpies**. Unless you have a Jet Scrander on a farm, you generally don't have this to worry about. Really.

2. Love triangle tangles

- **He thought it was one of Kate's tricks to trick him into seeing Myung**. Nope.

- **Guld knocked him unconscious before rescuing Myung himself**. Uh-uh.

- **The police barricaded the concert hall after the fire alarm went off**. Incorrect.

- ■ **He was with Lucy in bed**. Right, which proves one thing: there are some days you just don't wanna get out of bed . . .

3. Ineligible to be Miss Macross

- **Mika Doi**. Mika Doi played Misa Hayase of Super Dimension Fortress Macross. And for those who don't know who this person is, maybe the name "Lisa Hayes" from *Robotech* rings a bell.

- **Hiroko Kasahara**. Nope. She played Ishtar of *Macross II*. Not *Ishtar*, the movie, a much better Ishtar.

- ■ **Rica Matsumoto**. Correct. She's not a *Macross* girl. At least, not yet . . .

- **Rica Fukami**. Didn't you know? Rica Fukami is the seiyū for Myung of *Macross Plus*?

4. Shall we dance? Forever?

- **The circle of life**. What is this, *Kimba, the White Lion*? Oops, I meant *The Lion King*?

- ■ **The cycle of history**. According to the young descendant of Col. Treize, the world has a habit of building an empire that will become very powerful, only to be destroyed and then replaced with another empire, and it will continue to do that for as long as there is civilization. But if you played the game *Civilization II*, this is the one thing you try to prevent; you have to believe you can rule forever!

- **The environmental cycle**. You take up space on the earth. You pollute the earth. The earth cannot claim you back until you become worm food. That's pretty much all you need to know.

- **The cycle of photosynthesis**. Plants turn carbon dioxide into oxygen. That's your quick science lesson for today.

5. Martian rock, paper, and scissors

- ■ **Rock**. Hee hee. This is tricky! Since Yurika often poses with a Victory signal (posing with a "V" in her hand), and since "V" looks like scissors, the best way to beat her is to use "rock!" If you got this one right, you rock!

- **Paper**. Get a piece of paper and write down the letters "R," "O," "N," and "G." Now pronounce it.

- **Scissors**. You need to cut this answer out because it's not the right one.

- **Trick question! Yurika has no hands!** I could potentially make a joke about the state of being armless but because the risk of offending someone is so great (although it's never stopped me before), I won't.

■ *Answer to picture puzzle:* (c) Carrot. The pic is of Marron, and this proves that genetics only accounts for certain things in people.

Cultural

In this section are questions that require some outside knowledge, whether it is Japanese, American, or from other cultures. You'll find that anime cannot be separated from the culture where it is created, and yet it can be influenced by just about anything.

---

1. Star-crossed lovers

In Shakespeare's day, which of these characters was most likely to play Juliet in *Romeo and Juliet*?

- Akane Tendō from *Ranma 1/2*
- Nuku Nuku from *All Purpose Cultural Cat-Girl Nuku Nuku*
- Kris from *Battle Athletes*
- Subaru Sumeragi from *Tokyo Babylon*

2. Stomach CLAMP

If you are a *regular* person in *any* CLAMP manga or anime, what is the one place you need to stay away from?

- The Diet Building
- The subway
- The red-light district
- Tokyo Tower

3. If you play this backward, it sounds like Iain's theme song!

Which of these musicians have not had an anime reference in any of their videos or songs?

- Matthew Sweet
- Better Than Ezra
- Barenaked Ladies
- Michael Jackson

4. Know thy weapon

You are a ninja from the video game *Tenchū* that is sent into enemy territory to steal some weapons. You come upon an armory of weapons and you can pick and choose all you can carry. Which of these items, then, must you leave behind?

- Katana
- Kodachi
- Shinkansen
- Nagatana

5. You can never be too polite

According to *Mangajin*, the one-time magazine of Japanese popular culture, how many levels of politeness are there in Japanese?

- 3
- 4
- 5
- 7

1. Star-crossed lovers

- **Akane Tendō from *Ranma 1/2*.** A little obsessed with *Ranma 1/2*, are we? Nope. This is isn't the right answer. The clue is IN SHAKESPEARE'S DAY . . .

- **Nuku Nuku from *All Purpose Cultural Cat-Girl Nuku Nuku*.** Nuku Nuku may be cultural, but not cultured enough to play Juliet.

- **Kris from *Battle Athletes*.** In her strange little world, she probably has never even heard of this play in the first place!

- ■ **Subaru Sumeragi from *Tokyo Babylon*.** Correct! You just had to know that only men or young boys played girls' roles in Shakespeare's plays. I could make a joke here about Subaru being an effeminate boy, but I won't.

2. Stomach CLAMP

- **The Diet Building.** Nope. Although, CLAMP characters should stay away from this place. If they become any thinner, they'll disappear! Just kidding. The Diet Building is a government building in Japan.

- **The subway.** Even though the subway is a pretty dangerous place, it's not THE most dangerous place in CLAMP world.

- **The red-light district.** With some of the characters and the way they are drawn, maybe that' the first place you should visit!

- ■ **Tokyo Tower.** Correct! CLAMP has destroyed Tokyo Tower so many times that if they had to pay for permission to use the Tokyo Tower in their manga and anime, they could have built their own Tokyo Tower! Of course, it would only be good to destroy one time and then they would have to buy another one.

3. If you play this backward, it sounds like Iain's theme song!

- **Matthew Sweet.** Nope. Anime clips are spotted in his video "Girlfriend."

- ■ **Better Than Ezra.** Well, they may be better than Ezra, whoever he is, but they don't have an anime reference in their videos or music. Yet.

- **Barenaked Ladies.** Apparently, you have not been listening to their song "One Week," because the large *Sailor Moon* reference and the fact that she is an anime babe would not have missed your ears, even though they were speaking really fast.

- **Michael Jackson.** If you were watching the brother and sister duet (Janet and Michael Jackson) and the video "Scream," you would have seen anime characters screaming in the background.

4. Know thy weapon

- **Katana.** Ugh. Don't you know what a katana is? It is the most mentioned sword in anime right now! You don't have to let it hit you on the forehead to know that! Or do you?

- **Kodachi.** I know that it's the name of Kunō's sister from *Ranma 1/2*. But it also does mean "a small dagger." Which fits the character Kodachi because every time she laughs, it's like having a dagger in your ears!

- ■ **Shinkansen.** Good choice. I think stuffing a "bullet train" in your pants is rather obvious, don't you think? There's also a pick-up line there somewhere.

- **Nagatana.** Nope. This is yet another Japanese weapon that you can carry off. But if I were you, I would not stuff anything sharp and pointy into clothes that are below my waist. It's like a chef with a cleaver in a nudist colony without a metal apron. Ugh . . . chills.

5. You can never be too polite

- 3
- ■ 4
- 5
- 7

Yup. *Mangajin* listed four levels of politeness although there can actually be many more. But wisely, too many levels of politeness might scare off people from learning Japanese, and four is a pretty easy number to handle.

1. An understandable change

When *Laputa, Castle in the Sky* gets released into the U.S., it will be renamed *Castle in the Sky*. The name was never meant to offend the Spanish-speaking community; where did the name "Laputa" originally come from?

- *Gulliver's Travels*
- *Robinson Crusoe*
- *Mutiny on the Bounty*
- *Green Eggs and Ham*

2. A Japanese Pat

Which of these is NOT a gender neutral name?

- Yū
- Shinobu
- Ichirō
- Kasumi

3. Know thy enemy

According to Otaku Folklore (it's not an anime or an anime book; I'm just referring to common knowledge here), what is a fanboy's worst enemy?

- Bad dubs
- Hentai censors
- The anime industry
- Soap

4. He talks kinda funny but he can beat your @$$ with a stick

In *Rurōni Kenshin*, what is notable about Kenshin's way of speaking?

- It's very effeminate
- It's very polite
- It's very rude
- It's a nonstandard Japanese dialect

5. Second place is NEVER bad

At the time when the highest-grossing movie in all of Japan was *Titanic*, what was the second-highest-grossing movie of all time in Japan?

- ANSWER: _____

1. An understandable change

- ■ **Gulliver's Travels**. Correct. Laputa is one of the lands in *Gulliver's Travels*. I think it's south of Greece and closer to Cyprus.
- • **Robinson Crusoe**. Crusoe has Friday to keep him company. What would he need Laputa for? (Okay, bad intercultural joke. Sorry.)
- • **Mutiny on the Bounty**. Nope. Laputa is found nowhere on the *Bounty*. Because they're all men! (Sorry, could not help it. I'll be good now.)
- • **Green Eggs and Ham**. I do not like *Green Eggs and Ham*, I do not like it . . . because it's the wrong answer! Obviously!

2. A Japanese Pat

- • **Yū**. Uh-uh. Yū Matsuura (Male) and Yū Watase (female) share this name, although one exists in anime, and the other is a manga creator.
- • **Shinobu**. Sorry, the Shinobu in *Here Is Greenwood* is male and the Shinobu from *Urusei Yatsura* is female
- ■ **Ichirō**. Right on! (Um, excuse the expression, I must have been trapped in the '60s frame of mind). Generally, anything ending in *-ro* is male and anything ending in *-ko* is female. And that's your Japanese baby-naming lesson for today.
- • **Kasumi**. Yes, this surprised me, too. Most people think of Kasumi from *Ranma 1/2*, but I also know a young Japanese man by this name as well. Here's another lesson: if a name ends in *-mi*, even though the suffix means "beauty," it can be a boy's name, like "Tatsumi" (from *Bushido Blade*). Which proves that there can be beautiful boys in Japan as well.

3. Know thy enemy

- • **Bad dubs**. I bet a lot of you fell for this, didn't you? It actually isn't bad dubs. Go into a crowded dealer's room full of otaku and you'll understand why.
- • **Hentai censors**. This might be annoying, too, but when it comes to sex, we are a less restrictive about showing it on video (although more restrictive when putting it on TV).
- • **The anime industry**. Well, without the anime industry, where would we be right now? Huh?
- ■ **Soap**. I bet you had to have gone to at least ONE (probably three) anime conventions before you got this answer. People can survive bad dubs. People can survive hentai censors. And people deal with the anime industry. But come on! Is simple hygiene too much to ask?

4. He talks kinda funny but he can beat your @$$ with a stick

- • **It's very effeminate**. His voice actor may be a female, but Kenshin is very much a man! Ask Kaoru <^.^>.
- ■ **It's very polite**. Yes. Kenshin has the habit of talking politely to everyone. And there is nothing wrong that. Of course, if a person is carrying a sword around, you can't say many of the things they do are wrong unless you want to be instant shishkabobs.
- • **It's very rude**. Kenshin? Rude? You haven't mean watching this series, have you?
- • **It's a nonstandard Japanese dialect**. Nope, this isn't right either. Kenshin speaks proper Japanese. In fact, too proper.

5. Second place is NEVER bad

- ■ **Princess Mononoke**

Princess Mononoke lost only to *Titanic*; another way to think about this is that *Princess Mononoke* is the highest-grossing film ever domestically produced in Japan. See? Nothing to worry about.

Knowing Your Blood Type Can Save Your Life . . . Your Social Life!

When biographies of anime characters are made, one of the things that is always mentioned is the character's blood type. Why? Americans could care less that dedicated Street Fighter Ryu has blood type O, but the Japanese use blood types (*ketsueki-gata*) to analyze personalities. If you knew nothing about Ryu except his blood type, you would at least know he is inclined to be a determined young man with a strong sense of purpose (great qualities for a fighter, aren't they?).

This blood-type trait assessment has been scientifically researched, but it is still considered a pseudo-science at best and, like horoscopes, is used in Japan to determine a person's disposition and personality.

A: Blood Type A tends to be serious, a deep thinker, and usually introverted. A types are also responsible

1. Bald encounter

In *Slam Dunk*, why did Hanamichi Sakuragi shave his head?

- He did it on a dare
- Gum was stuck to his hair
- He wanted to impress a girl that went for bald guys
- He lost a basketball game

2. Thou shalt make life on Mars (and

In the anime *EYES of Mars*, the parents of the young psychic girl physically resemble which biblical pair?

- Sampson & Delilah
- Joseph & Mary
- Sarah & Abraham
- Sodom & Gomorrah

3. . . . Or is it Memorex?

Which of these anime do not have a live action movie?

- *Tokyo Babylon*
- *Sanctuary*
- *Mermaid's Scar*
- *Fist of the North Star*

4. Trailers not in trailer parks

When the trailer for *Princess Mononoke* came out in movie theaters in Japan, it said, "13 years since _____."

- The last war
- The end of the world
- *Nausicaä*
- We had any good anime, dammit!

5. Educational (sort of) anime

Which of these anime was not based in part on actual Chinese or Japanese literature?

- *Rurōni Kenshin*
- *Fushigi Yūgi*
- *Hakkenden*
- *Dragonball*

and obedient, and will have the coolest head of anyone in the group. A-type personalities tend to have a close circle of friends, few but committed.

B: Blood Type B is the adventurer and likes doing things his or her own way with a lot of energy and enthusiasm. Type B is creative and usually optimistic. Of all the blood types, Type B is most likely to be popular.

AB: ABs are keenly observant and like to be useful to others. They are considered good listeners, they like others to listen to them (but won't say this), and are the most diplomatic of the blood types.

O: If a person is blood type O, he or she is known to be an affectionate, caring person and even a romantic. The hard-working O Type is the is quickest to make friends of all the blood types.

Using blood typing, you can not only find out if a person is socially compatible, but if you ever need a transfusion in an emergency. . . .

Okay here's a quiz. Name the blood type of each of the following characters:

A. Sailor Moon
B. Tuxedo Mask (Tuxedo Kamen) from *Sailor Moon*
C. Ken from *Street Fighter*
D. Mitsuru from *Here Is Greenwood*
E. Yui from *Fushigi Yūgi*
F. Tamahome from *Fushigi Yūgi*
G. Lina Inverse from *Slayers*
H. Zelgadis from *Slayers*
I. Sasami from *Tenchi Muyō*
J. Sakura Kinomoto from *Card Captor Sakura*
K. Yū Matsuura from *Marmalade Boy*
L. Meimi Haneoka from *Kaitō St. Tail*

ANSWERS:

A.

A: O. B: A. C: B. D: A. E: AB. F: O. G: A. H: A. I: AB. J: A. K: B. L:

1. Bald encounter

- **He did it on a dare**. Although Sakuragi is the type that would fall for a dare, this was not a result of a dare.

- **Gum was stuck to his hair**. Hmmm . . . Sakuragi actually has great hair. It would be ashame if he shaved his head because of this. . . . Fortunately, this is not the answer either.

- **He wanted to impress a girl that went for bald guys**. Um. I would not shave my head to impress a girl. It does not mean others won't. But this is the incorrect answer.

- ■ **He lost a basketball game**. I don't know why exactly Japanese boys need to shave their heads whenever they lose face. Although I guess it's better than losing your face the same way.

2. Thou shalt make life on Mars (and not tell the zealots)

- **Sampson & Delilah**. Sampson! It's time for a haircut so you can go out in a blind rage and destroy all life on Mars so that no scientists could find it! Nope.

- ■ **Joseph & Mary**. Yes, the parents themselves look very much like Joseph and Mary, especially the mother with the veil on her forehead.

- **Sarah & Abraham**. Nah, this can't be true. Abraham has fathered more children than the MegaPlayboy in *DNA*^{2}! And in this story, the young girl is an only child of her parents, so it can't be right.

- **Sodom & Gomorrah**. Um, these are biblical cities, not people. Wouldn't work.

3. . . . Or is it Memorex?

- *Tokyo Babylon*. Yes, there is a live version of *Tokyo Babylon*. And as expected, the man who plays Subaru is cute, but he totally lacks the fashion sense that the manga character had. I guess that's what happens when Hokuto isn't around . . .

- *Sanctuary*. Yes, there is also a live version of this too.

- ■ *Mermaid's Scar*. To my knowledge, there isn't a live version of *Mermaid's Scar*. Unless you count *Splash* with Tom Hanks and Darryl Hannah.

- *Fist of the North Star*. There is also a live version of *Fist of the North Star*. One look at the main character's chest and you could tell that it came from the anime.

4. Trailers not in trailer parks

- **The last war**. What last war? You mean the war between your two brain cells to decide whether to watch *Dominion Tank Police* or *Hello Kitty*?

- **The end of the world**. Ummm . . . if that were true, you wouldn't be reading this, would you?

- ■ *Nausicaä*. Hai! *Princess Mononoke* is sort of like a sequel to *Nausicaä* except *Princess Mononoke* takes place in early Japan. Is it a prequel, perhaps, like the *Phantom Menace* without Jar Jar Binks?

- **We had any good anime, dammit!** A few people would agree, but that is not the right answer.

5. Educational (sort of) anime

- ■ *Rurōni Kenshin*. Correct. *Rurōni Kenshin* is based on some historical accounts of people who actually did exist, but that would not be considered literature.. And hey there, if you are counting the *Rurōni Kenshin* manga as Japanese literature, nope! I'm sorry! Nice try, but wrong.

- *Fushigi Yūgi*. Nope. The legend of the Four Gods is actual literature. And the names of the warriors are actual stars!

- *Hakkenden*. This anime is based on Japanese literature of the same name. And you thought this series was original!

- *Dragonball*. *Dragonball* is based on the legend of the Monkey God, hence, the prehensile long tail that follows Son Goku everywhere he went until his tail was "castrated." (Hmmm . . . I think I could have chosen a better word for this. . . .)

1. They were "another story"

Imagine that there was a person who liked the anime *They Were 11* so much that she wanted to create a story just like it. But what might be best for her is to go to the source. What kind of story was *They Were 11* based on?

- An Aesop fable
- A Shakespearean play
- A Persian folktale
- A Japanese ghost story

2. Judaism and mecha

In *Xenogears*, one of the battling empires on the continent of Ignas is called the Kislev Empire. If that empire is anything like the Jewish month of the same name, then what is the Jewish celebration that is especially prized in that empire?

- Yom Kippur
- Rosh Hashanah
- Hanukkah
- Passover

3. Finally the answer to nosebleeds

According to Gilles Poitras in his book, *The Anime Companion*, why do boys get nosebleeds when they stare at pretty women?

- Because Japanese mothers said so
- Because the shape of breasts corrodes nasal passages
- When body heat rises, nosebleeds release heat
- In being distracted, boys actually smash their noses against something and THAT causes bleeding

4. Praise Nakamori!

Again, according to Gilles Poitra's *Anime Companion*, Akio Nakamori wrote a column in 1983 that revolutionized anime/manga terminology forever. What term is he responsible for?

- Lolikon (Lolita complex)
- Mecha (mechanicals)
- Otaku (as applied to fanboys)
- *Etchi* (a derivative of *hentai*)

5. Where's Ranma?

If I walk into a house and say, "I see Ranma" and there isn't a crossdressing martial artist anywhere in the house, where am I looking at?

- The ceiling
- The fireplace
- The kitchen
- The entryway

© 1995 Hajime Kanzaka/R. Araizumi/TV Tokyo/SOFTX/Marubeni

Imagine that Zelgadis from *Slayers* ends up in the *Fushigi Yūgi* universe and has to fight one of Miaka's warriors to the death. Which warrior cannot fight him simply because Zelgadis cannot fight someone who sounded too much like him?

(a) Hotohori (b) Tamahome (c) Chichiri (d) Tasuki

1. They were "another story"

- **An Aesop fable**. Hmmm ... fables are rather too short to do anime pieces on. It wouldn't work.
- **A Shakespearean play**. Um, that *Romeo and Juliet* question never left you, did it? Are you still traumatized for getting it wrong?
- **A Persian folktale**. Protect us from the curse of this wrong answer!
- ■ **A Japanese Ghost Story**. Correct. "They Were 11" was based on a Japanese ghost story where among a group of people, people had to find out which of them was the ghost. Sort of like the board game *Clue*, but cultural.

2. Judaism and Mecha

- **Yom Kippur**. It's not "Yum, kippers!" It's Yom Kippur! But either way, it's wrong.
- **Rosh Hashanah**. Nope, this Jewish New Year is not celebrated in the month of Kislev. It's celebrated in Tishri.
- ■ **Hanukkah**. Yes, the most popular Jewish holiday (popular in the sense that non-Jewish people know about this holiday) is celebrated in the month of Kislev. Hanukkah presents for everybody!
- **Passover**. Let's passover this answer because you have the wrong one here.

If you were somehow offended by this question, I'm sorry. But I also thought that since anime often has a few Judeo-Christian references, it would be an interesting question to ask.

3. Finally the answer to nosebleeds

- ■ **Because Japanese mothers said so**. Correct. Nosebleeds of an excited nature are old wives' tales. Or more likely, it's so that you wouldn't stare at pretty women because it's rather impolite to do that.
- **Because the shape of breasts corrodes nasal passages**. Um ... no. Where did you get at idea? That's like saying bigger breasts cause men's IQ's to drop twenty points!

- **When body heat rises, nosebleeds release heat**. Nope. Nothing of the kind. Otherwise, you'd get a nosebleed every time you had a fever.
- **In being distracted, boys actually smash their noses against something and THAT causes bleeding**. Hmmm ... very much true, but not the right answer.

4. Praise Nakamori!

- **Lolikon (Lolita complex)**. Coincidentally, this answer was found in a Lolikon magazine, which means that lolikon was invented before the term that Nakamori himself invented.
- **Mecha (mechanicals)**. Nope. Not this one. A lot of people think "mecha" means giant robot, but not necessarily. "Mecha" is used for an item when a sufficient amount of detail has been paid to its mechanical design. Don't quote me on that, though.
- ■ **Otaku (as applied to fanboys)**. Correct. Wanna know more about how this word came to be applied to "fanboys?" Pick up a copy of *The Anime Companion* by Gilles Poitras and find out!
- *Etchi* (a derivative of *hentai*). Etchi is just the katakanized spelling of the letter "H," which is an abbreviation for *hentai* or "perversion."

5. Where's Ranma?

- ■ **The ceiling**. Yes, according to the *Anime Companion*, a *ranma* is an open grating near the ceiling that allows light and air to come into a room. And it does not close when you throw cold water at it.
- **The fireplace**. I never figured Ranma to be a "flamer," but I guess there is a first time for everything.
- **The kitchen**. Only if Kasumi is around to cook him something, or if he is in a cooking challenge with Akane
- **The entryway**. Nope. Not here at all.

■ ***Answer to picture puzzle:*** (b) Tamahome. They are played by the same voice actor: Hikaru Midorikawa.

1. That name rings a bell

The name of a character in *Marmalade Boy* is also the name of the bell that is placed in front of the picture of the deceased. What is the name of the bell?

- Kei
- Yū
- Ginta
- Arimi

2. 20/20 = 1

The news show *20/20* used a clip from the anime, *Robot Carnival* to show:

- How Japanese anime is violent
- How cartoons are influencing vehicle designs
- How robots are taking jobs away from humans
- How subliminal advertising works

3. Ooh, what big eyes you have!

This sentence could apply to any anime, but this sentence refers specifically to a little anime called *Akazukin Cha-Cha* (Red Riding Hood Cha-Cha)

Akazukin Cha-Cha is not based on the original tale of "Little Red Riding Hood" at all. If it was, which of these things would happen?

- Dorothy-chan would get her lost
- Shiine-chan would strip her naked
- Riiya-kun would eat her
- Seravi-sensei would chop her up into pieces

4. So, which guests are coming to Lolicon?"

The infamous word "Lolikon," which means lusting after young girls, comes from the term "Lolita Complex." The male equivalent is called "Shotakon." So where does the "Shota" in "Shotakon" come from?

- From a common boys' name in Japan: Shotaro
- From a novel where a young boy was the equivalent of Lolita
- From a young boy who testified against his teacher in court
- From a lollipop company that made a bunch of suckers that looked like little boys

5. In a perfect world

The shōnenai ("boy's love") anime *Ai no Kusabi* (Love's Wedge) portrays what would be an ideal society for which writer?

- Plato
- Machiavelli
- Locke
- Marx

1. That name rings a bell

■ **Kei**. Correct. Kei is the name of the bell in front of the deceased. Although with Kei's musical talent, I'm surprised it's not a chiming bell that plays a popular piano piece. That would not be very respectful toward the deceased, however . . .

• **Yū**. Nope. Yū has enough confusion with his name in English. Let's not depress him anymore.

• **Ginta**. Nice try, but choosing a bell sound effect name does not score you any bonus points here.

• **Arimi**. Neither does this choice. Good guess.

2. 20/20 = 1

• **How Japanese anime is violent**. I imagine that somewhere else in America, someone has made a report on cartoons (not just anime) being violent, but if Yosemite Sam did not have a gun, he would be out of business!

• **How cartoons are influencing vehicle designs**. I imagine that anime must have influenced vehicle designs. I mean, the Pikachu Volkswagon Beetle does exist, you know . . .

• **How robots are taking jobs away from humans**. As long as there are labor unions, I doubt that this would happen.

■ **How subliminal advertising works**. Yes, believe it or not. They used a clip from the anime *Robot Carnival* to demonstrate this. A girl quickly passed by on screen holding a can of what was unmistakably the red can of Coca-Cola. And I don't even want to get into how they managed to sneak in a beer logo into a cartoon!

3. Ooh, what big eyes you have!

• **Dorothy-chan would get her lost**. Although Dorothy-chan might like to get Chacha lost, she really isn't THAT mean.

• **Shiine-chan would strip her naked**. Um, Shiine-chan might enjoy this, but they are kids for God's sake! In the original tale of "Little Red Riding Hood," Red's grandma makes her take off her clothes before getting into bed with her, something very much edited out of the story today.

■ **Riiya-kun would eat her**. Correct. Riiya-kun transforms into a wolf, and if this were the real story, he would eat Cha-Cha. Eating the one you love may not be such a good or pleasant idea.

• **Seravi-sensei would chop her up into pieces**. Seravi-sensei is too nice to chop up anything. Besides, he's a magician, not a woodcutter. He'd probably use a magical axe, just like Mickey and his magical broomsticks in *Fantasia*, to do all his work for him.

4. So, which guests are coming to "Lolicon?"

■ **From a common boys' name in Japan, Shotaro**. Yup. That is how "Shotakon" got its name. If "Baro" was a common name, then it might have been named "Bakon." If "Daichi" was the common name it would have been "Daikon." You can probably go on and on with these, but I won't.

• **From a novel where a young boy was the equivalent of "Lolita."** Nope. Even though there are such stories in ancient Japanese literature, the term "Shotakon" did not come from there.

• **From a young boy who testified against his teacher in court**. Uh-uh. I think it would have been more tasteful if the press kept the young boy's name a secret.

• **From a lollipop company where they made a bunch of suckers that looked like little boys**. Ewwww . . . that's almost too scary a thought to make that kind of connection.

5. In a perfect world

■ **Plato**. Correct. I imagine this was not an easy one at all. In *The Republic,* Plato endorsed the idea of genetic superiority to maintain order in society, and this occurs in *Ai no Kusabi*, based on hair color.

• **Machiavelli**. Nope. If the writer of *The Prince* took hold of the place, there would be a lot less people in it, since the book takes an unabashed look at how power works.

• **Locke**. Locke is the proponent of democracy. *Ai no Kusabi* is in no way democratic.

• **Marx**. Nor is *Ai no Kusabi* a communist anime either.

Anime Math

And who said math was useless? You've heard of anime physics, now it's time for anime math, with word problems that will do your algebra teacher proud!

1. No need for geometry!

Actually, geometry is rather useful. Without it, I would never be able to cut square sandwiches into triangles for dinner parties.

In *Tenchi Muyō in Love*, what shape did the Jurai power make around Tokyo Tower when it was activated at the Fudō temples?

- Triangle
- Square
- Pentagon
- Hexagon

2. *Final Fantasy* math

Doesn't having so many sequels defeat the purpose of calling this game "*Final*" Fantasy?

Multiply the American *Final Fantasy* (released for Super Nintendo) with Cyan and the American *Final Fantasy* with Squall, then subtract the number by the Japanese *Final Fantasy* with Tifa and what kind of number do you have?

- A prime number
- A number divisible by 2
- A number divisible by 3
- A number divisible by 5

3. Key fractions

Were Key the Metal Idol and Casper the Friendly Ghost separated at birth? They both aren't exactly human. They both are quite pale. They both want to make friends. And most importantly, their second names match.

Feeling sorry for Key, Sakura convinces Key that she only had to make one-sixth the number of friends that Key was told she needed in order to be human. How many friends would that be?

- ANSWER: _____

4. Does size matter?

Of course it does! If a man is with a woman and as much as she tries, she yells "It won't fit!" he should tell her to buy a more comfortable pair of shoes and she'll feel a whole lot better.

If your Gundam model of Nataku was 1/144 scale and the model stood 8 inches high, then using those numbers, how big would the actual Nataku Gundam be?

- ANSWER: _____

5. They look good in tight pants but will that affect their singing?

The Backstreet Boys ate way too much chocolate, plumped up, got a terrible case of acne and can't go out on stage. Which of these group of boys can replace them on stage because the group has the same number of people as the band?

- The Gundam Wing Boys
- The Fushigi Yūgi Boys
- The Here Is Greenwood Boys
- The Hardy Boys

1. No need for geometry!

- **Triangle**. You must be distracted by that sandwich anecdote, aren't you?

- **Square**. You have to be such a "square" to use this answer.

- ■ **Pentagon**. Yes! When Jurai power was released from each of the temples, they formed a pentagon around Tokyo Tower.

- **Hexagon**. Nice try, but remember to lay off the scotch when you're counting the temples and tracing the pattern.

And once the Jurai power formed a Pentagon, it declared war on a small country and tried to take it over. Those shapes just never behave, do they?

2. *Final Fantasy* math

- ■ **A prime number**. Good going, math major! Cyan (3) x Squall (8) = 24 - Tifa (7) = 17, which is a prime number.

- **A number divisible by 2**. Baka baka!

- **A number divisible by 3**. Baka baka baka!

- **A number divisible by 5**. Baka baka baka baka . . . aw forget it, by this time it's not funny anymore. (Was it even funny in the first place?)

Final Fantasy Axiom: As long as fans demand *Final Fantasy*, there will never be a "final" *Final Fantasy*. Isn't capitalism wonderful?

3. Key fractions

- ■ **5,000**. In the story, Key needs to make 30,000 to become human, so a sixth of that is 5,000.

The answer to Key's problem seemed rather obvious; become an idol and you will be adored by many. But . . . isn't standing still on top of a mantelpiece rather tiring after a while?

4. Does size matter?

- ■ **96 feet high**. This is just simple mathematics here but be careful on the measurements because they are tricky. I gave you the inches, but I wanted the answer in feet. So for your mathematical pleasure, I'll work this out for you: $x/144 = 8$. Multiply both sides by 144 to leave x alone. Here, $x = 1152$ inches. To convert into feet, you have to remember that 12 inches makes a foot so: 1152 inches divided by 12 = ? feet. The answer is 96 feet. And you thought you could just leave your algebra behind–didn't you? Of course, since when is a 1/144-scale model 8 inches?

5. They look good in tight pants but will that affect their singing?

- ■ **The Gundam Wing Boys**. Correct! Hey with the five Gundam Wing boys matched up with the five Backstreet boys, you can pass off Quatre as Nick and then match up the rest!

- **The Fushigi Yūgi Boys**. Nope. There are seven of them so you know that they'll all be fighting over the spotlight and Tasuki will accidentally burn the stage to a crisp.

- **The Here Is Greenwood Boys**. Well, depending on how you interpret this, you could just be talking about the four main characters of the entire dorm of boys; either way is wrong by the way.

- **The Hardy Boys**. What the heck? They're not even anime characters! Besides, there's only two of them!

Of all the guys in anime those Gundam boys scream "boy band." As long as Wu-Fei does not sing about making love with his Shen-long in full operation, I think they can get a good contract deal.

1. Maison math

Admit it. If you have ever fallen in love, you and your lover have played little games with your names to see how compatible you two are. Just remember, though, the anagram of "mother-in-law" is "woman Hitler." Sorry to spoil the party.

Godai's room number - Ichinose's room number = ?

- Yotsuya's room number
- Roppongi's room number
- Otonashi's room number
- Mitaka's room number

2. Date and time

Whenever you go on a date, it is important to be punctual. And if you are a guy asking a young lady on a date with a father around, treat her like a library book. You can fondle though the pages but if you bring her back late, you'll have to pay.

Kazuya Hasukawa has a date. (Okay, go ahead and die from shock if you want to.) The date says that she'll meet him 20 minutes after the number posted on his dorm room. What time is she meeting him?

- 1:40
- 2:30
- 2:50
- 3:40

3. A product of love

Love is a many-splendored thing. And things like the Overfiend need to keep those splendors to itself. *Gundam Wing* names follow a number system. That's why Heero and Duo yaoi fics (stories of love between men written for women) are abbreviated as 1 x 2. If Trowa x Quatre are in a yaoi fic, which of these pairs would be a product equivalent?

- Heero x Wufei
- Heero x Treize
- Zechs x Duo
- Trowa x Noin

4. Evil deeds never go unpunished. Stupid deeds just get laughed at.

An evil version of Astro Boy roamed around the universe determined to stop Astro Boy from his good deeds. The problem was, he was not very bright. Evil Astro Boy rounded up 90,000 horses from Japan and put them into a large tank to use their energy in order to crush Astro Boy. However, Astro Boy just extended his arms and the horses collapsed. At least how many more horses should Evil Astro Boy have used to run over Astro Boy?

- ANSWER: _____

5. Oh my goodness, they're multiplying like . . .

Ryo-Ohki and Ken-Ohki from *Tenchi Muyō* have survived nuclear winter and are the only creatures left on Earth. They produced 2 children, and each of those 2 children produced 2 more children and so on and so forth. By the time all the great-great grandchildren were born, how many cabbits have populated the earth in the span of a mere 2 hours?

- ANSWER: _____

© GAINAX/Project Eva • TV Tokyo

"When I, Shinji Ikari, go for a swim, I wear Evangelion™ swim-trunks, for the young man without . . . hey? Where's my trunks?" In this scene, who was closest enough to Shinji to actually snatch his swimwear?

(a) Rei (b) Asuka (c) Misato (d) Pen-Pen

1. Maison math

■ **Yotsuya's room number**. Hai, hai! Godai (5) - Ichinose (1) = Yotsuya (4). And if you knew Japanese, this was way too easy since "Go" in Godai means "five," "Ichi" in Ichinose is "one," and "Yo" in Yotsuya is "four."

• **Roppongi's room number**. Nope. Besides, what are you doing in Roppongi's room anyway? Looking at that see-thru nightie, weren't you?

• **Otonashi's room number**. Kyōko Otonashi has no number on her room since she is the manager of the apartment. Looks like someone hasn't been watching his/her *Maison Ikkoku*!

• **Mitaka's room number**. Are you serious? Why would a rich guy like him live in *Maison Ikkoku*? So he can catch Kyōko as she is bathing herself? Hmmm . . . Mitaka may not think it's such a bad idea after all . . .

Someone started a false rumor that the reason why Room 2 was vacant in the anime series is because it is symbolic of Kyōko and Godai not getting together as a couple. So why is Room 3 vacant?

2. Date and time

• **1:40**. Nope. Incorrect. Sorry, domo sumimasen.

■ **2:30**. All right! The number on Kazuya's room is 210 so if you converted that into a time, it would be 2:10 and add 20 minutes and you got 2:30. Hee hee, you're one smart cookie. And hopefully as tasty.

• **2:50**. Sorry, wrong answer. And now that Kazuya has arrived late, um . . . wait a minute, she never exactly told you where to meet, did she?

• **3:40**. Dang, you don't know your *Greenwood*, do you? You need to pay more attention to useless things like room numbers on people's doors so you can answer trivia questions like these!

And like a library book, make sure that she comes home with a jacket to cover all those hickeys.

3. A product of love

• **Heero x Wufei**. No. Heero (1) x Wufei (5) = 5. Which leaves Wufei by himself. All alone again. Naturally.

• **Heero x Treize**. Uh-uh. Heero (1) x Treize (13) = 13. Heero always disappears out of these equations, doesn't he?

■ **Zechs x Duo**. Correct. Trowa (3) x Quatre (4) = 12 and Zechs (6) x Duo (2) also equals 12.

• **Trowa x Noin**. Nope. Trowa (3) x Noin (9) = 27. Of course, this is also Trowa x Trowa x Trowa for people who have triplet fantasies.

You can get fairly creative with this math. Heero x Duo x Trowa is as much fun as Zechs by himself. Go figure.

4. Evil deeds never go unpunished. Stupid deeds just get laughed at.

■ **10,001 horses**. Astro Boy has the power of 100,000 horses (at least that's what it said on his tag line), so Evil Astro Boy needs at least 100,001 horsepower to beat him. Thus 90,000 + 10,001 = 100,001.

Okay. I'll admit there is very little logic to having a tank filled with 90,000 horses, but isn't it also unwise that a little robotic boy powered by a nuclear core can potentially eat Mexican food?

5. Oh my goodness, they're multiplying like . . .

■ **62 cabbits**. 5 generations of cabbits: 2+4+8+16+32=62. I hate to think about this but if there is a nuclear winter and there are no other animals around and all the plants are contaminated, they better adapt to the taste of cabbit stew fairly quickly.<*.*>

1. Do you have the dragonballs to do it?

You decide to get smart and fool the dragon. Instead of finding the actual dragonballs, you have the audacity to create papier-mâché balls and stick red stars (the kind elementary teachers give you for good quiz scores) onto the gold spray-painted balls. Well, apparently, the good scores from the teacher weren't in math because the dragon bluntly says you added three more stars on the set of dragonballs. In a short moment before he fries you, how many stars did you put on your dragonballs?

- ANSWER: _____

2. <^.*>

Greater than and less than problems have got to be the easiest in math. Always remember, that Pac-Man likes to eat the bigger piece. Or is it that the bully likes to point at the smaller kid? Whatever mnemonic you use, just be sure it works! Tell me if the following math problems equal less than a thousand or one thousand and more ...

- The year the world ends in X minus the number of the *Galaxy Express* train
- *Fushigi Yūgi* episodes times *Here Is Greenwood* episodes
- All the *Sailor Moon* episodes
- *Tokyo Babylon* episodes times *Rurōni Kenshin* episodes
- Number of Sailor Senshi in *Super S* series cubed
- Gross box office receipts of *Princess Mononoke* in yen divided by the collection cels used to make the movie
- Number of times Misato kisses Shinji on the lips in the *Evangelion* TV series times the amount of food in pounds eaten by Lina Inverse, Usagi, Ranma, and Miaka after being lost in the desert for days without food.

3. Suddenly, I'm not half the man I used to be.

Do you think that if the water were neither hot nor cold, if someone splashed Ranma with it, he could be a hermaphrodite?

In Japan, *Ranma 1/2* is called *Ranma Nibun-no-ichi*. If it was called *Ranma Yonbun-no-san*, what would that look like in ciphers?

- Ranma 3/4
- Ranma 2/3
- Ranma 4/3
- Ranma 3.14 ...

4. Solving for the "X" variable

I've always wondered why math teachers usually wanted students to solve for "x" as opposed to any other letter of the alphabet. It's not like they're going to find buried treasure when they solve it!

Number of members of the Dragons of Earth + number of members of the Dragons of Heaven - Number of all those members who were in *Tokyo Babylon* = ?

- ANSWER: _____

5. Lessons with Lina

Lina Inverse from *Slayers* saved your life and for some reason, you decided to treat her to dinner. Worried about having to mortgage your house when you feed her, you were relieved to find that the bill for the food came out to only $1,200.00. With the standard tip to be added to the bill, how much did this lesson of remembering that Lina has a bottomless stomach cost you?

- ANSWER: _____

1. Do you have the dragonballs to do it?

■ 31 stars.

The original seven dragonballs have 1+2+3+4+5+6+7=28. And then the three extra stars that you mistakenly put on the papier-maché balls come out to 31. Moral: No matter how clever you may be, a dragon will always know if you are holding his balls …

2. <^.*>

■ **The year the world ends in X minus the number of the *Galaxy Express* train**: 1000 or more (1999 - 999 = 1000).

■ ***Fushigi Yûgi* TV episodes times *Here Is Greenwood* OAV episodes**: less than 1000 (about 50 x 6 = 300).

■ **All the *Sailor Moon* episodes**: less than 1000 (more than 200, but not even close to 1000).

■ ***Tokyo Babylon* OAV episodes times *Rurôni Kenshin* episodes**: less than 1000 (*Tokyo Babylon* only had 2 OAV's, RK would need 500 episodes and it hasn't reached that point).

■ **Number of Sailor Senshi in *Super S* series cubed**: 1000 or more (10 x 10 x 10 = 1000).

■ **Gross box office receipts of *Princess Mononoke* in yen divided by the collection cels used to make the movie**: 1000 or more. (*Princess Mononoke* was the highest-grossing film in Japan after *Titanic* when it was released; the end result would definitely be 1000 or more.)

■ **Number of times Misato kisses Shinji on the lips in the *Evangelion* TV series times the amount of food in pounds eaten by Lina Inverse, Usagi, Ranma, and Miaka after being lost in the desert for days without food**: less than 1000. (Misato never kissed Shinji in the TV series. And anything times zero is zero!)

If you did not do well in this section, don't worry. Neither do most dogs, cats, or well-trained monkeys.

3. Suddenly, I'm not half the man I used to be

■ **Ranma 3/4**. Right. "Yonbunnosan" is "3 of 4 parts" in Japanese. Although with Ranma, I don't want to guess which body parts this number is referring to.

· **Ranma 2/3**. Nope. I guess it make sense if he took a dip in the spring of drowned piglet and transformed into a pig woman, I guess.

· **Ranma 4/3**. That doesn't make much sense! That's like Ranma with an extra appendage. Well, I guess if he really wants to prove if he's a guy …

· **Ranma 3.14**. Ranma pie. Changes flavors depending on the type of water you used in the pie mix. Yum.

I bet you someone, someone out there is going to try to find out at what temperature point does Ranma change sexes and how much water is required to make the change. Scientists have enough trouble with cold fusion and this guy exists out there? What gives?

4. Solving for the "X" variable

■ **12**. There are 7 dragons of Heaven and 7 dragons of Earth - 2 from *Tokyo Babylon* (Subaru and Seishirô) = 12

5. Lessons with Lina

■ **$1,380**. $1200 plus the standard tip of 15% ($180) equals $1380. You may be civilized enough to know the proper etiquette for a tip, but treating Lina Inverse to dinner? Tsk, tsk tsk.

Lina never seems to get fat from all the food that she eats. She's on the animation plan diet: as long as she is a popular character, her animators will never draw her fat.

Manga, Anime's Onēchan ("Older Sister")

Manga is generally used to means "comics" and is translated as such. (Although "comics" is the closest translation, it is not entirely accurate. "Comics" has a kiddie connotation (as does "cartoons"), but manga are not just for children and not always comedic in nature. Manga come in all forms, from comedy to adventure to drama to historical pieces and yes, even cooking. Some 50% of all Japanese read manga (both adults and children), a number high enough to make manga a major mass-market industry.

What we know as manga started in the 12th century with a monk's drawings of animals acting as humans, although the term "manga" came into use in the 19th century. In the early 20th century, manga took on a more Westernized look, with strip-style panels and speech balloons. In 1931 Henry (Yoshitaka) Kiyama produced America's first manga, *Yonin Shosei* (The Four Students Comic), about Japanese immigrant life in the

1. Pokemath

Don't worry, I'm not going to ask you something like give me the square root of the number of electric Pokemon that currently exist. That's just plain mean. However, this question is no less than heinous. You'll see what I mean.

In the Pokemon League Test, what is James's badge number divided by Ash's badge number?

- 73
- 78
- 86
- 92

2. There's plenty of me to go around

The F4 are so popular and so rich, they think cloning themselves would multiply their coolness. They all clone two others of themselves, except Hanazawa, who thinks this is a bad idea. Dōmyōji liked the way the clones turned out, so he clones three more to go on four times as many dates. So now, how many clones are running around the campus, giving Tsukushi-chan a nervous breakdown?

- ANSWER: _____

3. Anime title arithmetic

No fuss here or snappy intro while I check my funny bones for dry rot. Just add the numbers in the following titles and give an answer.

_____ T.T.S. Airbats + They Were _____ =

- ANSWER: _____

4. It's all relative

People often treat relatives differently from how they treat their friends. The fact that you share your gene pool with your relatives makes it more important that you weed them out for sanity than anything else.

Who would qualify as Ranma's "fiancée's" brother's classmate's sister's fiancé's father?

- Soun
- Genma
- Principal Kunō
- Your mother

5. 17 pound gospel

Kyōsuke Hatanaka is known for his weight problem in *One-Pound Gospel*, although he does not seem to get fat; he just gains muscle (I wish I could do that <*.*>). If Kyōsuke was 17 pounds over his weight limit, and if 1 pound = $1.50, how much is that in American money?

- ANSWER: _____

United States. It is also the first bilingual manga, written in a mixture of Japanese and English.

After World War II, Osamu Tezuka, considered the "god of manga," began using manga as a storytelling medium like cinema (Tezuka was heavily influenced by animation, especially Disney animation). Tezuka, who created *Astro Boy* (*Tetsuwan Atom*), *Kimba the White Lion*, and *Adolf*, often used a few lines to convey a lot of expression (if you want to know why many manga and anime characters have large eyes, a minimal nose, and a small line for a mouth, Tezuka is the one who started that style). Tezuka's narrative and artistic style influenced many other artists and helped fuel the popularity of manga today not only among children but adults as well.

Manga is so important to anime because most anime in Japan started out as manga. Shows such as *Ranma 1/2*, *Here Is Greenwood*, *Fushigi Yūgi*, and many others had popular followings as manga and then developed as an anime series.

1. Pokemath

- **73**. No, I don't think so.

■ **78**. Wow! I'm impressed! James's badge number (546) divided by Ash's badge number (7) yields 78.

- **86**. Hey, Pokemasters have to know these things! Or people who have too much time on their hands . . . like me.

- **92**. Nope, you're way off. I guess you're not a die-hard *Pokemon* fan. Awww . . . did I make you cry?

If you got this question right, congratulations! You would do well on the Pokemon League Test. Just remember your Voltorbs from your Pokeballs. You don't want to blow up your Pikachu into bits when you want to catch one.

2. There's plenty of me to go around

■ **9**. Rui had no clones, Akira had 2 clones, Sōjirō also had 2, and Tsukasa had 5. Which makes Rui more collectable than all the others in the set.

F4, collect them all! Costs as much as the Mona Lisa x The Eiffel Tower x The Statue of Liberty, but collectors are known to shell out the bucks for things they want anyway.

3. Anime title arithmetic

■ **812**. *801 T.T.S. Airbats + They Were 11* = They Were 812 T.T.S. Airbats.

I was kind this time. If I had asked a different kind of question, the answer could have been "They Were 11 La Blue Girls."

4. It's all relative

- **Soun**. Soun has enough problems as it is. A dojo with barely any students and two freeloading houseguests. Don't bother him with a logic problem right now . . .

■ **Genma**. Good job! Ranma's "fiancée's" (Kodachi) brother's (Tatewaki) classmate's (Nabiki) sister's (Akane) fiance's (Ranma) father (Genma). It's important to pay attention to the quotes in fiancée and the second fiancé doesn't have an extra "e," and that indicates a man engaged to be married.

- **Principal Kunō**. With Principal Kunō as an in-law, who needs to search in your own gene pool for sanity? In fact, the whole Kunō family should be committed!

- **Your mother**. Correct! You mom is a man, apparently, and endorses beard-dyeing products at the circus sideshow . . .

I believe in the six degrees of separation theory. If you move away from your relatives, the area where your relatives live will be six degrees better than wherever you are now . . .

5. 17 pound gospel

■ **$25.50**. 17 pounds x 1.5 (conversion rate) = $25.50. Which is just enough to buy to three kernels of popcorn from Jenny Craig.

Losing weight is supposed to be easy: Exercise and eat right. However, just eating chocolate is much, much easier.

1. Maison math (part 2)

Kyōko needs more money badly because the city inspectors found out that the sewage systems have overloaded and are going to blow any minute. The Gundam Wing Boys are looking for apartments to rent in the same area. Based on the numbering system of both the *Maison Ikkoku* anime and *Gundam Wing* anime, which pilot can rent a room if they are limited to renting under similar numbers? (Note: Kyōko *cannot* rent to a pilot whose equivalent-numbered room is occupied.)

- Heero
- Duo
- Quatre
- Wufei

2. Spiked in the heart with love

There is no sport like volleyball that shows sheer grace and power. Unless you count ballerinas slamming balls with baseball bats.

Natsu, the volleyball player in *Rival Schools*, has a lot of fans. One day a guy came up to her and gave her the number of flowers that is the same as her volleyball uniform number. If the flowers cost $30.00 a dozen, then how much did it cost for the boy to gave Natsu those flowers?

- ANSWER: _____

3. Macross math

Lynn Minmei is such a good singer, she can stop wars by singing that her boyfriend is a pilot. If I sang that, I would end up causing wars. People would fight to decide who would beat me up first.

According to the *Macross Chronicles*, how many have passed between Lynn Minmei's farewell concert and Sharon Apple's debut concert?

- 14 years
- 27 years
- 53 years
- 77 years

4. Basketball math

Math is important and is everywhere in basketball. It's in everything from the number of points needed to win a game to the amount of money needed to win a paternity suit.

Rukawa's shirt number + Sakuragi's shirt number + Mitsui's shirt number / Kogure's shirt number = ?

- Miyagi's shirt number
- Akagi's shirt number
- Kogure's shirt number
- Haruko's bra size

5. Final math question

In *Final Fantasy III* (in America, it is *Final Fantasy VI* in Japan), if Cyan has a fast sword that has a successful hit rate of 70%, and if he hits he averages 63 points of damage against a strong enemy, then what is the average points of damage during the other 30% of the hit rate?

- ANSWER: _____

Mitsuru and Shinobu from *Here Is Greenwood* look quite evil here. And why not? They can control anything. Which of these people is an officer at the dorm?

(a) Shinobu (b) Mitsuru (c) Both of them
(d) Neither of them

1. Maison math (part 2)

- **Heero**. Nope. If Heero threatened Mrs. Ichinose (their names are both represented with the number 1) and said he would kill her to get her apartment, she would just smack him and tell him to shut up.

- ■ **Duo**. Correct! Duo's name in the Gundam system is 2 and room 2 of Maison Ikkoku is free to rent. That is if he can stand to stay there after a night of the tenant's sake party.

- **Quatre**. No. Quatre would blush many times for walking in on Yotsuya (both their names are represented by a 4). He would have keeled over if he had walked in on Akemi's room!

- **Wufei**. Uh-uh. Wufei, whose name is represented by a 5, would walk in on Godai who lives in Room 5, who is already stressed out enough as it is because of finals. After going mad, Godai would attack Wufei and well . . . let's just say that Godai does not have to worry about finals . . .

Duo, being the nice guy that he is, would probably squeeze all the Gundam boys into the room, leaving yaoi fanfic writers plenty of material.

2. Spiked in the heart with love

- ■ **$25.00**. Natsu's uniform number is "10" so you would have to take 10/12 of $30.00 to get the amount.

Math is important. It costs money to be romantic.

3. Macross math

- **14 years**. 14 years isn't long enough between the two singers. Tabloids will still print sightings of big, bloated Minmei by then.

- ■ **27 years**. All right! According to the *Macross* chronicles, Lynn Minmei's farewell concert was in year 2012 and Sharon Apple's debut concert is in year 2039.

- **53 years**. By this time, Lynn Minmei's songs would be the music that your grandmother listens to if Sharon Apple drew a crowd this late.

- **77 years**. "Lynn who?"

I understand no one has bought tickets for Lynn Minmei's concert just yet . . . The BASS ticket outlet does not reserve that far ahead of time (but it doesn't mean people haven't tried!).

4. Basketball math

- ■ **Miyagi's shirt number**. Either you're lucky or you've really worked at this, haven't you? Rukawa (11) + Sakuragi (10) + Mitsui (14) / Kogure (5) = Miyagi (7).

- **Akagi's shirt number**. So close and yet . . . heck, you were probably guessing! Get outta here!

- **Kogure's shirt number**. Nope. Actually try paying attention to insignificant details for once!

- **Haruko's bra size**. <*.*> That is just plain wrong!!!

If you got this answer right, I'm duly impressed. You are a true *Slam Dunk* fan. Which in the course of world events does not mean anything, but I'm still proud of you nonetheless!

5. Final math question

- ■ **0**. Sorry for the trick question. But namely, if you fail the hit rate, you can't damage your opponent.

And if you think you can damage just using the residual wind of your swinging effect, you gotta remember that this isn't Guile's sonic boom from *Street Fighter* that we're talking about here!

■ **Answer to picture puzzle:** (b) Mitsuru. Mitsuru is President of the Dorms. Shinobu is President of the Student Council, but just happens to be roommates with Mitsuru.

Merchandise

It's not enough for an anime to be well-watched for it to be considered successful. You also have to be able to sell products related to the anime; anything from dolls, to plushes, and even toothbrushes. How much anime stuff do you know about?

1. All that training has done him good

In the card game *Ani-Mayhem*, Boy-type Ranma looks particularly buff. From which OAV episode did the image come from?

- The "Christmas" episode
- The "Cursed Jewel" episode
- The "Cooking" episode
- The "Cursed Doll" episode

2. Weak points

In the *Pokemon* card game, Staryu is weak against what?

- Lightning Pokemon
- Psychic Pokemon
- Fire Pokemon
- Triple Chocolate Fudge Cake

3. Mega who?

If you are looking for Megaman merchandise in Japan, you won't find anything remotely close to a man in blue armor. What name do you have to look under?

- Rockman
- Alphaman
- Ironman
- Spiegelman

4. Non-existent alma maters

Sometimes in anime conventions, there are people who wear "Furinkan High School" T-shirts. Before people ask about what kind of tapes they have at the Furinkan High School anime club, to which anime series does this particular high school refer to?

- *El Hazard*
- *Sailor Moon*
- *Ranma 1/2*
- *Haunted Junction*

5. Versatile, but not THAT versatile

Nabiki has this way of being able to get her way most of the time by blackmailing and profiting off of other people. My friend said that she was the most American anime character that she had ever met.

In the *Ani-Mayhem* card game, which is NOT one of Nabiki Tendō's abilities?

- Survival
- Bureaucracy
- Streetwise
- Savoir-faire

1. All that training has done him good

- **The "Christmas" episode**. Uh-uh. This was basically an "omake" episode full of characters and singing and a particularly nice shot of Kasumi in her nightgown....

- **The "Cursed Jewel" episode**. Nope. This is the episode where Ranma wears a tuxedo, remember?

- ■ **The "Cooking" episode**. Yup. Don't you remember the part when Ranma is training outside just before his mom comes to visit the Tendō dojo? That's where the image comes from. Wow. Ranma, finally has muscles. And Akane has silicone.

- **The "Cursed Doll" episode**. Ranma may be wearing a tanktop to show off his arms, but that's not where the image comes from.

2. Weak points

- ■ **Lightning Pokemon**. This is pretty simple. Just read the bottom of the card (Japanese or English) and the weakness is printed right there.

- **Psychic Pokemon**. Nope. Psychic Pokmon is unusual because they can be weak against other psychic Pokemon.

- **Fire Pokemon**. Uh-uh. What puts out fire? Water does. And therefore Fire Pokemon are weak against water attacks!

- **Triple Chocolate Fudge Cake**. This might be a weakness for Pokemon trainers, but I'd hardly consider slapping a cake on Staryu any form of an effective attack.

3. Mega who?

- ■ **Rockman**. Correct. I could not begin to tell you why he is named Rockman, but this information is pretty handy if you want to look for Megaman toys. And believe me, they are out there!

- **Alphaman**. Tried to be logical, eh? If you thought the opposite of Megaman is Alphaman, you're close. It is actually Omegaman. But one needs to be modest, you think?

- **Ironman**. Who do you think this is, Tony Stark? Sorry.

- **Spiegelman**. Wrong answer. Batsu, batsu!

4. Non-existent alma maters

- *El Hazard*. Sorry. Makoto, his classmates, and Fujisawa-sensei go to Shinenome High School (is that how you spell it?) where Makoto spends his time beating Jinnai at everything.

- *Sailor Moon*. Why bother to learn the name of this school? Serena (Usagi) spends half of her time sleeping through it anyway.

- ■ *Ranma 1/2*. "Furinkan High" is the high school that Ranma goes to. Very early in the series, even we hear that Kunō is the "Blue Thunder of Furinkan High." Hmmm ... I didn't even know that thunder had colors.

- *Haunted Junction*. Furinkan High isn't spirited enough to be the school of choice for the holy student council. Although it does have its own cast of weirdos.

5. Versatile, but not THAT versatile

- ■ **Survival**. This answer makes sense. If you ask in the middle of the woods, what good is paper money other than never needing to use oak leaves for those personal moments?

- **Bureaucracy**. Hey, this girl knows enough red tape to use it as a martial arts weapon! I think there is even a fanfic that mentions this.

- **Streetwise**. Well, according to *Ani-Mayhem*, this is one of her abilities. But knowing Nabiki as money-hungry as she is, I hate to think of what she'll do on the streets for money.

- **Savoir-faire**. You have to admit, Nabiki is rather sophisticated among that entire cast of *Ranma 1/2*. Then again, if you did not have to worry about changing your sex or into an animal every time it rained, you'd be sophisticated too. Although, in Ranma's case, it would not necessarily apply.

1. Pocket sailor

There are cute little 2-inch Super Deformed *Sailor Moon* figures that come in a cast of characters by Irwin. So which cast member gets ready with lawyers because there is no figure made for that character?

- Molly
- Luna
- Queen Beryl
- Artemis

2. Pokemon . . . original recipe or extra crispy?

When Kentucky Fried Chicken had *Pokemon* collectibles for sale, which of these characters weren't sold (and probably was served extra crispy?)

- Vulpix
- Zubat
- Charmeleon
- Dratini

3. Playing favorites

Let's say that you were in Japan (or more likely, Japantown) and you went to a Japanese bookstore like Kinokuniya and dozens of anime-related magazines to choose from. Which magazine has a character ranking list of the most popular anime characters?

- *AX*
- *Animage*
- *Newtype*
- *Hyper Hobby*

4. Playing favorites (part 2)

In the magazine where this character ranking list is, there is one character that has stayed on the ranking list for years and years. Name her:

- ANSWER: _____

5. Before going to Grandma's house

When *Vampire Savior* dolls were made, Bulleta (Baby Bonnie Hood) and Jon Talbain came as a package that let people re-enact sick little fantasies of Little Red Riding Hood. And Bulleta has lots of treats, but which of these items is not one of her goodies that comes with the figure?

- A picnic basket
- A puppy
- An apple pie
- A semi-automatic gun

© 1992 Clamp/Shinshokan/MOVIC/Sony Music Entertainment (Japan) Inc.

This is yet another Subaru and Seishirō from *Tokyo Babylon* by CLAMP. In what other CLAMP series does this couple appear?

(a) *CLAMP School* (b) *Clover* (c) *Magic Knight Rayearth*
(d) *X*

1. Pocket sailor

- **Molly**. Nope. The Brooklyn-accented young class-mate of Serena is a little doll herself. A doll in this packaging, that is.
- **Luna**. Nope. Luna comes in a package with Artemis so that Luna wouldn't be lonely.
- ■ **Queen Beryl**. Queen Beryl should thank her lucky stars that a super-deformed character was not made of her. She would have looked like a mini drag queen. Wrong kind of queen.
- **Artemis**. Uh-uh. Artemis comes in a package with Luna so that Luna was one cat to turn to when she's in heat.

2. Pokemon . . . original recipe or extra crispy?

- **Vulpix**. This cute foxlike Pokemon was one of the more popular characters. Of course, he'd be one of them!
- **Zubat**. Zubat has no eyes so if you kept this Pokemon in the shower, you'd never have to be embarrassed. But its hearing is superb, so it could probably hear you break wind from a mile away.
- ■ **Charmeleon**. Charmeleon is the only one in the group that was not a beanie for Kentucky Fried Chicken. But I imagine that he'd be one of the few Pokemon with experience to work there.
- **Dratini**. "Uttini!" (Translation: "Wrong!")

3. Playing favorites

- *AX*. AX this answer because it's wrong!
- ■ *Animage*. Yup. A*nimage* has a top character ranking list. It's sort of like a popularity contest except less

■ *Answer to picture puzzle:* (d) *X*. And in the animated movie, they last less than two minutes. . . .

painful since no one is laughing at you if you didn't make it.

- *Newtype*. *Newtype*? Try a new choice, pal!
- *Hyper Hobby*. Uh-uh. Sorry, that is incorrect.

4. Playing favorites (part 2)

- ■ **Nausicaä**

Nausicaä is one of Japan's most beloved characters. Sort of like Superman, but without a weakness from an element that is supposed to be found from a destroyed planet and yet villains happen to have it handy every time cape boy is around.

5. Before going to Grandma's house

- **A picnic basket**. No little girl going through the woods would be complete without a picnic basket full of grenades and mace. A girl has got to protect herself, you know?
- **A puppy**. Oh yes! Puppies are an essential part of being cute. And they look even cute when eating the remnants of those skinned wolves that Bulleta seems to be fond of.
- ■ **An apple pie**. Unless this pie is laced with knock-out juice, Bulleta would have no need for it
- **A semi-automatic gun**. I guess there is money to be made in wolf fur.

1. One item per kart

It would be nice for the figures in *Mario Kart* to have their choice of weapons, but they can only be packaged with one. What item from the video game *Mario Kart 64* does Yoshi come with?

- A spiked turtle shell
- A question box
- A mini boo (ghost)
- A row of bananas

2. I'm #01!

Which figure among the Bandai Dragonball Z Action Figure Series is number 01 of the series?

- Son Gokou
- Son Gohan
- Vegeta
- Piccolo

3. I'm #01! (part 2)

Which figure among Tomy's 2-inch PVC figures of *Pokemon* characters is number 01 of the series?

- Pikachu
- Bulbasaur
- Charizard
- Donald Duck

4. Hmmm . . . what's the Japanese for "Pikachu?"

I overheard this question asked in all seriousness. Yes, I know it's hard to believe. Try to contain your laughter. I couldn't.

In the Japanese Team Rocket booster cards for the *Pokemon* collectible game, what is different about their *Pokemon* cards from regular *Pokemon* cards?

- Members of Team Rocket are treated as Pokemon
- All their Pokemon are colorless
- There are no trainer cards in those boosters
- There are evil Pokemon in these cards

5. God is my pilot . . . literally

Not to be sacreligious or anything, but suppose that the Pope needed to make a robot that symbolized holy power to vanquish coming demons. Because this Gundam from the *Endless Waltz* series has angelic-looking wings, which Gundam does the Pope choose to pilot?

- Tallgeese III
- W-Gundam Zero Custom
- Gundam H-Arms Custom
- Gundam Sandrock Custom

In Japan, 16 is a marriageable age. Which is why anime such as *Marriage* and *Wedding Peach* feature characters that seem to us too young to even consider marriage. In *Sailor Moon Stars,* when Usagi enters high school, she dreams about turning 16 so she can marry Mamoru.

In Japan, school is compulsory until the end of junior high (9th grade), while in America, school from K to 12 is compulsory. In order to get into high school in Japan, a student must take an entrance exam for each high school he or she wants to go to.

In Japan, the depiction of breasts, butts, and penises (on little boys) is considered no big deal. In Japan, with its public bathhouses where naked bodies are in full view of others, animated body parts do not seem so alarming. When anime is brought to America, these body parts are treated with "digital underwear" or careful editing; this is most notably seen in *Dragonball Z* when Gohan loses his clothes and a piece of clothing masks over the appropriate place.

Needless to say, in Japan there's a lot more stuff like this!

1. One item per kart

- **A spiked turtle shell**. We're the rebel shell! We cry, "More! More! More! Pick a more likely answer!"

- **A question box**. What would Yoshi be doing with a question box anyway? Making a castle that only required one block?

- **A mini boo (ghost)**. What is the ghost of Yogi's pal, Boo-Boo, doing with Yoshi? Let's hope it does not have to involve Yoshi's tongue!

- ■ **A row of bananas**. Correct. Who knew that a universal slipping agent could be used as a strategic device against drivers who are directly behind you? Are you taking notes, Jeff Gordon?

2. I'm #01!

- ■ **Son Gokou**. Hee hee. Rather the obvious answer, isn't it? Who else would you put as #1 other than the main character?

- **Son Gohan**. It would make sense to make Gohan #1, but Goku looks more impressive, don't you think?

- **Vegeta**. He may be #1 on some people's lists, but he is not #1 in this series of toys.

- **Piccolo**. Piccolo may have his fame in being one of the most popular toys, but that still does not make him #1 of the series.

3. I'm #01! (part 2)

- **Pikachu**. Too obvious! Pikachu isn't even #1 on the Pokedex!

- **Bulbasaur**. Bulbasaur may be number #1 on the Pokedex, but he is not number one in the series. Hmmm . . . how can we tell if Bulbasaur is a guy without having to turn him upside-down?

- ■ **Charizard**. Correct. You definitely know your Pokemon! Can't give you a badge or anything except for a heartfelt "Good Job!" I imagine that you'd rather have the badges anyway.

- **Donald Duck**. Wow, you've been locked up in Disneyland for the past thirty years, haven't you?

4. Hmmm . . . what's the Japanese for "Pikachu?"

- **Members of Team Rocket are treated as Pokemon**. And I guess one of James's attacks would be bashing an enemy with a ladies' pump? I don't think so.

- **All their Pokemon are colorless**. Ooh, they can get away with being the ultimate baddies if that were true, but that is just an ugly rumor.

- **There are no trainer cards in those boosters**. Actually, there are VERY useful training cards in the Team Rocket Booster Pack. If Jesse and James knew how to use half of those effectively, Ash would be nothing but a pile of . . . ash.

- ■ **There are evil Pokemon in these cards**. Ooh! Evil Pokemon! I thought that Ekans said that only if the masters are evil, then the Pokemon are evil, too. Lies! Lies! All lies!

5. God is my pilot . . . literally

- **Tallgeese III**. That answer is almost as annoying as this name. Isn't a name supposed to inspire or strike fear, not remind you of farm animals?

- ■ **W-Gundam Zero Custom**. Sure, angelic feathers may not be aerodynamic on a Gundam, but who cares? It looks cool! *Gundam* is not about reality; it's about getting someone to drop their jaw when they see a piece of well-designed metal, drop to their knees, and say, "We're not worthy! We're not worthy!"

- **Gundam H-Arms Custom**. H-Arms? What dirty things do arms have to do in order to be called those?

- **Gundam Sandrock Custom**. Uh-uh. This ain't the answer.

1. Never stand behind a "Yak Bak"

The items known as "Yak Baks" in America originally came from the show *Kodomo no Omocha* (Child's Toy). What were these called in the commercials in Japan?

- Burucha
- Squeakmaker
- Voice Change
- Helium Machine

2. The world is coming to an end. Now, smile!

On the *X* red poster or wall scroll where the Dragons of Heaven are all wearing red outfits and standing in front of a destroyed Tokyo Tower, who is standing at the very bottom among the group?

- Kamui
- Subaru
- Karen
- Sorata

3. Who's "Daman?"

If you gotta "B-Daman" in Japanese, who do you got to be in America?

- Megaman
- Bomberman
- Anpan-Man
- Doraeman

4. Barubi daru

The Japanese have a doll that is the Japanese equivalent to Barbie, except she has a more "anime" looking appearance. What's her name?

- Naoko
- Hanako
- Natsumi
- Jenny

5. So mad that I couldn't find it

In the preview edition of the card game *Anime Madness*, what is used as a source of power (the equivalent of energy cards in the *Pokemon* collectible card game)?

- Animators
- Anime fans
- Business people
- Swamps and forests

Ah, another romantic pic of Kaede and Mamoru from *Blue Seed*! And another question: Kaede has a sister named Momiji. "Kaede" and "Momiji" are also names of what?

(a) Maples (b) Drums (c) Flowers (d) Meat buns

1. Never stand behind a "Yak Bak"

- **Burucha**. Nope. Burucha is a vibrating machine. Often found in men's pockets nowadays.

- **Squeakmaker**. Nah. If you step on a mouse, you would get this effect. Inhumane, but fun for some.

- ■ **Voice Change**. Correct. Sana-chan's famous voice changing machine was simply called "Voice Change" and it was often advertised during the commercials in the *Kodomo no Omocha* show. However, the biggest seller is that hyper little Sana-chan is using the "Voice Change" machine in the anime itself.

- **Helium Machine**. Uh-uh. Helium to shrink a voice is a novelty that should only be limited to kids' birthday parties. To hear it all the time would be annoying.

2. The world is coming to an end. Now, smile!

- ■ **Kamui**. Correct. The young man that is going to decide the fate of the world stands at the bottom center of the picture.

- **Subaru**. Nope. He stands to the right side of the picture.

- **Karen**. Uh-uh. She is standing to the lower left of the picture in a corset that looks like a remnant prop of Madonna's Blonde Ambition tour.

- **Sorata**. No. Sorata is standing on the upper left of the picture, looking studly in a pilot's uniform.

3. Who's "Daman?"

- **Megaman**. Maybe you weren't paying attention, baka! I already told you earlier that "Rockman" is the Japanese name for "MegaMan."

- ■ **Bomberman**. Correct. This guy, who has a lot of cool toys made to his name is also called "Bomberman" in the U.S. He is also called "Bomberman" in some parts of Asia as well because hey, he plays with more bombs with the cast of Looney Tunes. It makes sense.

- **Anpan-Man**. Hmmm . . . a guy made of bread filled with sweet stuff inside his head. I guess he can be better than Mr. Bill, ever since teachers told me not to eat Play-Doh or paste.

- **Doraeman**. Nope. Besides, it's not "Doraeman," it's "Doraemon," a well-loved blue robotic cat who almost reaches the merchandisable status of Hello Kitty in Asia.

4. Barubi daru

- **Naoko**. Uh-uh.

- **Hanako**. Nope.

- **Natsumi**. Not this one either.

- ■ **Jenny**. Correct. Not only does this doll have "anime-like proportions," but she has long blonde hair and is given an English name! Omoshiroi, ne? (Interesting, isn't it?) We could talk about the invasion of American culture into foreign societies, but let's not cause a ruckus here!

5. So mad that I couldn't find it

- ■ **Animators**. Correct. In this game, you receive your power pool from your animators (there are even cards called "Overworked Animator," "Underpaid Animator," and "American Hack Animator") and I guess you draw up characters with it. But I wouldn't know since I lost the directions for it. But no one plays it so it's just as well.

- **Anime fans**. Um, what would they be doing with their powers? Crowding into convention rooms? Getting fansubs of everything? Paying $100 for an autographed balloon that is eventually going to pop later? Puh-leeze!

- **Business people**. Um, if this ever happened, expect a revolt from anime otakudom.

- **Swamps and forests**. Nope. You're obviously thinking of the template game that started it all: *Pokemon: the Gathering*. Oops! I mean, *Magic: the Gathering*.

■ *Answer to picture puzzle:* (a) Maples. Hee hee <^.^>, if you read the *Anime Companion*, you would have known that <^.^>.

1. It's MY Cutie Palace! You can't HAVE it!

In Rei's Cutie Palace, what accessory does she have that the other Sailor Senshi Cutie Palaces do not have?

- Medical Equipment
- Beauty Salon
- Small Shrine
- Karaoke Machine

2. Things too dense to be Block Headds

On the *Five Star Stories* Mortar Headd LED Mirage, what design is on its shield?

- A cross
- A chevron
- A penatacle
- A sign that says "Don't Hit Me!"

3. Sympathetic cards, for the simp and the pathetic in you

In the *Neon Genesis Evangelion* card game, how are the cards set up at the beginning of the game?

- In a triangle around Shinji
- In a square around Shinji
- In a pentagon around Shinji
- Everyone is piled on top of Shinji, demonstrating his burden of angst and suffering

4. She's got the whole universe in her hands

In the *Fushigi Yūgi* UFO Catcher dolls series, what is Miaka holding in her tiny little hands?

- A book
- An unfolded scroll
- A bouquet of flowers
- A very tiny Tamahome doll

5. I figured that Rukawa's package would be that big

There is an 11-inch Kaede Rukawa doll from the Star Member Series of *Slam Dunk* who comes with everything in the package but . . .

- A basketball uniform
- A school uniform
- A basketball
- Underwear

Here in *My Dear Marie*, "Hiro" has managed to take an incredible amount of steroids to impress the ladies. However, the man named Hiro who is considered the "Natural Playboy of town" comes from where?

(a) *Bust-A-Groove* (b) *Gundam Wing* (c) *Tenchi Muyō* (d) *Goldenboy*

1. It's MY Cutie Palace! You can't HAVE it!

- **Medical Equipment**. Do not trust any Sailor Scout with syringes handy.

- **Beauty Salon**. Hey, the Sailor Senshi never had a bad hair day or pimples! They don't need this.

- **Small Shrine**. A small shrine to herself? You mean with a large picture of Rei and Rei dolls everywhere? I imagine there must be some fanboy that's done this already.

- ■ **Karaoke Machine**. Correct! Rei has her own karaoke machine so she can sing to her heart's content! And to everyone's annoyance!

2. Things too dense to be Block Headds

- ■ **A cross**. I guess this design never goes out of style. It's pretty popular for any shield, whether they are Christian or not.

- **A chevron**. Nope. Now *Five Star Stories* does not want to get into a tangle with a certain gas company, would it?

- **A pentacle**. Nope. The pentacle is not on this particular shield.

- **A sign that says "Don't Hit Me!"** Hey, sometimes it works! Give peace a chance. Word to your mother.

3. Sympathetic cards, for the simp and the pathetic in you

- **In a triangle around Shinji**. Uh-uh. The triangle may have mystic properties but is not mystical enough for the *Evangelion* card game.

- **In a square around Shinji**. What is Shinji expected to do? Do-si-do and swing his partner? (Or swing WITH his partner?)

- ■ **In a pentagon around Shinji**. Correct. Shinji is surrounded by the other characters in *Evangelion* around him. This way, there's no escape.

- **Everyone is piled on top of Shinji, demonstrating his burden of angst and suffering**. Um . . .no.

4. She's got the whole universe in her hands

- **A book**. Miaka? Studying? Nah . . .

- ■ **An unfolded scroll**. Correct. Along with the Miaka UFO Catcher doll is a red unfolded scroll that is supposed to represent the scroll with the Universe of the Four Gods. But it looks more like a red hanky that's been stiffened by continuous nose blowing.

- **A bouquet of flowers**. Ah, how lovely. How wrong, but lovely.

- **A very tiny Tamahome doll**. I've heard of fetishes for short people, but this is a little out of hand.

5. I figured that Rukawa's package would be that big

- **A basketball uniform**. Rukawa without a basketball uniform? What planet are YOU from? Oh yeah, the REAL world. You probably have a life, don't you?

- **A school uniform**. Hey, Rukawa needs a school uniform. What else is he going to sleep in?

- **A basketball**. Rukawa needs a basketball. What can Rukawa do without balls?

- ■ **Underwear**. Correct. If you strip him down, he has no underwear except for the flesh-colored speedos permanently crafted to his body.

■ ***Answer to picture puzzle:*** (a) *Bust-A-Groove*. Because every playboy has gotta dig those 70s threads.

Gender Confusion

Anime has its fair share of guys that look like girls and girls that look like guys and love regardless of whoever that person is. So here are the questions on alternative lifestyles as presented by anime:

1. "Hand me those pumps!"

(Above is an actual quote from James in *Pokemon*). In *Pokemon*, which of these outfits did James NOT cross-dress into in the first season?

- A nurse's uniform
- A schoolgirl uniform
- A hula outfit
- A Marie Antoinette–style dress

2. A rather flat-chested girl

A lot of people already know that, to make him "acceptable," Zoicite from *Sailor Moon* was originally a man who, due to his feminine appearance and relationship with another man, was rewritten as a female character when he was brought over to the United States. However, that was not the only change. What was Malachite's original name in Japan?

- ANSWER: _____

3. Closet fighters

After the first few episodes of *Street Fighter II V*, Ryu and Ken yaoi (male-male love) stories suddenly popped up on the Internet. What is one evidence in the anime that hints at this kind of relationship?

- They looked like they were picking up guys at a bar, although it was for a fight
- They admired Guile's muscles more than they should have on the military base
- They swam together butt naked, frolicking in a penthouse pool
- Ryu calls Ken "Pretty Boy" and Ken calls Ryu "Stallion"

4. The crying game

In *Here Is Greenwood*, how did Kazuya find out that his girlish guy-impersonating roommate, Shun, was actually a real guy?

- He saw him using a urinal
- Kazuya walked in as Shun was taking a bath
- Kazuya saw a "stiffie" in Shun's pants
- Kazuya, in a moment of passion, threw himself on Shun and something did not seem right between Shun's legs

5. James isn't the only one with the fetish

There was a time when Ash brought out his feminine side by wearing a long, blonde wig and an orange dress. Why did he do it?

- So he can go to a woman's restroom without causing a riot
- To sneak into Erika's gym
- To stop Duplika from copying him
- To distract Brock, although it worked a little too well

1. "Hand me those pumps!"

■ **A nurse's uniform**. Don't worry. James will wear this outfit soon enough. Just not in the first season.

• **A schoolgirl uniform**. James dressed as Jesse's schoolgirl companion when they were trying to give tickets away.

• **A hula outfit**. James and Jesse dressed in hula outfits to greet Ash and his friends at Saffron City.

• **A Marie Antoinette–style dress**. James donned this when she was battling at the infamous Salon Roquet.

It's rather disturbing that I remember all this, isn't it?

2. A rather flat-chested girl

■ **Kunzite**

I'm not sure exactly why they made the change. Maybe Malachite sounds more manly and impressive? Perhaps . . .

3. Closet fighters

• **They looked like they were picking up guys at a bar, although it was for a fight.** They actually were picking up guys. And once they lifted them over their heads, Ken and Ryu gave them back-breakers they'll never forget. But that's wrong.

• **They admired Guile's muscles more than they should have on the military base.** I would not worry about that. Body worship is normal. Just don't let it distract you from fighting.

■ **They swam together butt naked, frolicking in a penthouse pool.** And until I saw that scene, I did not know that a butt can actually have muscles. . . .

• **Ryu calls Ken "Pretty Boy" and Ken calls Ryu "Stallion."** Well they do. Just not in public.

Ryu and Ken, the ambiguously gay duo of anime!

4. The crying game

■ **He saw him using a urinal**. Well that proves that Shun is a boy or a very talented girl.

• **Kazuya walked in as Shun was taking a bath**. That would prove he was definitely a guy, but it did not happen that way.

• **Kazuya saw a "stiffie" in Shun's pants**. Hmmm . . . it did not happen this way, although it would be a pretty bad way to find out.

• **Kazuya, in a moment of passion, threw himself on Shun and something did not seem right between Shun's legs**. All I can say is that that's no way to treat a lady. Then again, he isn't a lady so you're forgiven.

5. James isn't the only one with the fetish

• **So he can go to a woman's restroom without causing a riot**. Hee hee. Ash would be a naughty little boy if he did that! Why wait in line when a bush will perfectly suit his needs?

■ **To sneak into Erika's gym**. Correct. He could not get into the gym otherwise. Hey, you have to admire Ash for wanting those badges so much.

• **To stop Duplika from copying him**. Nope. Even if he tried it, it wouldn't work. Duplika is just too good.

• **To distract Brock, although it worked a little too well**. If Brock calls Ash's name in his sleep, Ash is in big trouble.

1. When did you get THOSE?

When Sailor Uranus appears in the *Sailor Moon* anime, who initially has a huge crush on her because she thought she was a cute-looking boy?

- Sailor Mercury
- Sailor Venus
- Sailor Mars
- Sailor Jupiter

2. A rather flat-chested girl (part 2)

At what moment in *Fushigi Yūgi* did Miaka find out that Nuriko was a guy?

- She found that Nuriko did not need to squat to relieve himself
- The top of his blouse came open and he had no breasts
- He never had "that time of the month"
- Tamahome told her after he found out the "hard" way

3. Oh my goodness, you're . . . normal

Utena usually wears a boys' school uniform and is often admired by other girls wherever she goes. So what event happened that made her decide to wear a girls' uniform?

- Girls kept bugging her for a date
- Her boy's uniform was ruined and she had nothing else to wear
- She lost a rose duel and felt humiliated
- Fanservice (I don't know to whom, but fanservice nonetheless)

4. Cos-play king (or queen?)

In *Ranma 1/2*, Tsubasa Kurenai is a ball of gender confusion and the bane of Ukyo's existence. But he is a costume king. Which of these things has he NOT disguised himself in the first episode where he appears?

- A mailbox
- A one-eyed mushroom
- A tree
- A vending machine

5. First kisses . . . how disgusting!

Where did Ranma receive his first kiss, with actual lip contact, from a guy?

- In the dojo
- On stage
- On a skating rink
- At a bathhouse

1. When did you get THOSE?

- **Sailor Mercury**. Mercury just never has time to date, so it can't be her.

- ■ **Sailor Venus**. Correct. Boy crazy Venus thought he snatched herself a cute guy, but this handsome girl has already been snatched by Neptune.

- **Sailor Mars**. Sailor Mars was also trying to look for the cute guy, but all she found was a girl who had two things in her blouse that would be rather unbecoming on a guy....

- **Sailor Jupiter**. Sailor Jupiter can easily pick up guys. Over her head!

2. A rather flat-chested girl (part 2)

- **She found that Nuriko did not need to squat to relieve himself**. And if Miaka followed Nuriko around just to catch him squat, Miaka has a rather serious problem, doesn't she?

- ■ **The top of his blouse came open and he had no breasts**. Correct. It just came open. That would be a rather good excuse if he tried this with Hotohori.

- **He never had "that time of the month."** Of course Nuriko doesn't have that time of the month. Since when does Nuriko have to pay bills anyway?

- **Tamahome told her after he found out the "hard" way**. And how would Tamahome explain why he was looking there?

3. Oh my goodness, you're . . . normal

- **Girls kept bugging her for a date**. That never stopped Utena before.

- **Her boys' uniform was ruined and she had nothing else to wear**. Do you think the tomboyish Utena would make a fussy complaint like that?

- ■ **She lost a rose duel and felt humiliated**. Right. She no longer felt that she wanted to be a prince. There are already enough obscure symbols in anime that are difficult to pronounce!

- **Fanservice (I don't know to whom, but fanservice nonetheless)**. Aside from this, this isn't the correct answer.

4. Cos-play king (or queen?)

- **A mailbox**. Talk about romance going postal!

- **A one-eyed mushroom**. How could you forget the one-eyed mushroom? And no, that is NOT a metaphor for anything! He really was a one-eyed mushroom!

- **A tree**. Well, Tsubasa was this as well. You can tell by the presents left behind by robins that tried to nest in his hair.

- ■ **A vending machine**. Correct. I don't want to think of where you are going to have to stick those 100-yen coins!

5. First kisses . . . how disgusting!

- **In the dojo**. Nope. The only thing Ranma's lips touched on that dojo was the floor whenever Akane smacked Ranma's head down to the ground.

- **On stage**. Fooled you! It's technically not a kiss when there's tape involved. Otherwise, Ranma gave Kunō one smack of a kiss!

- ■ **On a skating rink**. Correct. Mikado had his way with girl-type Ranma when she was helpless on the ice. I guess Mikado knows how to take advantage of a situation. But how can you be proud of kissing 1,000 girls? Whatever happened to the fear of "mono"?

- **At a bathhouse**. Ranma is naked and in a bathhouse. And the only thing she wants to do is kiss?

Need to Overthrow a Government? Try Anime!

In the 1970s, the most popular anime in the Philippines was *Voltes V*. There were many young fans of the series who watched it every time it came on until, suddenly, it was pulled off the air. Ferdinand Marcos, the dictator-president of the Philippines, had signed a directive that banned all robotic anime from Japan from being broadcast in the country.

According to Marcos, anime such as *Voltes V* were responsible for making children violent, and thus would eventually produce a violent society. Children, he claimed, would begin to glorify robots and value machinery over humanity..

These is more to this than what Marcos claims, how-

1. Love that dares not speak its name, but has one

Stories about two guys in love are called "yaoi" (male sex) or "shōnenai" (boy's love) stories. Stories about two girls having sex or in love are called what?

- Duet stories
- Yuri stories
- Margaret stories
- Male fanservice

2. A kiss doesn't mean anything, right?

In *Fushigi Yūgi*, which of these pairs of men did NOT kiss in the anime?

- Nakago/Tamahome
- Tamahome/Nuriko
- Hotohori/Nuriko
- Amiboshi/Suboshi

3. The denizens of Lesbos are everywhere

Which of these anime does NOT feature a lesbian relationship?

- *Sailor Moon*
- *Fushigi Yūgi*
- *El Hazard*
- *Revolutionary Girl Utena*

4. Lessons in seduction

In *Kizuna*, how does Ranmaru's professor attempt to seduce him?

- Blackmail with grades
- He drugged his drink
- Blackmail with a scandalous photo of him
- He was whipped vigorously until he met with no resistance

5. Faking it

In *Fake*, why did the captain let Dee have the same time off as Ryo?

- Dee got time off for good service
- Dee got time off because he was too stressed
- Dee got time off because he had to use his vacation time before it expired
- Dee pleaded and begged and pleaded and begged until he got time off

ever In *Voltes V*, a central theme in the plot was about the oppressed masses intending to rebel and overthrow an elitist government headed by a despotic family. Obviously the subject was a bit too close to home for Marcos, who took a typically despotic action. To make things worse, *Voltes V* was pulled off the air before the audience could find out what happens at the end of the series.

It wasn't until recently that *Voltes V* was put back on the air in the Philippines and shown in its entirety. Some Filipinos claim it is the #1 most loved anime in the country. And why not? Sometimes you don't know how much you love something until it's gone....

1. Love that dares not speak its name, but has one

- **Duet stories.** Nope. Even when two woman make beautiful music together, it is not called by this name.

- ■ **Yuri stories.** Correct. Is it from fantasies of Kei and Yuri going at it? Probably not. But it's fun to speculate!

- **Margaret stories.** Nope. And my friend Margaret would kill me if I even suggested such a thing! Actually, this idea came from Margaret Comics, which originally produced a yuri story that did not do well.

- **Male fanservice.** Wow, what isn't fanservice to guys nowadays?

2. A kiss doesn't mean anything, right?

- **Nakago/Tamahome.** You're in the middle of battle and your opponent is standing in front of you, face to face. So what do you do? You kiss, of course! Then you drop your weapons and skip down the yellow brick road....

- **Tamahome/Nuriko.** It's one of the earliest kisses in the series. Of course, Tamahome thought Nuriko was a girl at the time.

- ■ **Hotohori/Nuriko.** Awwwww . . . Unrequited love. How sad. Although I would not know how to explain why Hotohori's . . . oops! Let's stop here before we spoil anything, shall we? ::wink::

- **Amiboshi/Suboshi.** Nope. This kiss is here to satisfy the twin brother fetish in you....

3. The denizens of Lesbos are everywhere

- *Sailor Moon*. Nope. Sailor Uranus and Sailor Neptune would be a pair that would protest your ignorance.

- ■ *Fushigi Yūgi*. Yes, Yui may care about Miaka very strongly, but they just remain best friends. Although it's interesting that the guys in the anime are always willing to experiment.

- *El Hazard*. Hmmm . . . did you forget the servant and ruler relationship, Alielle and Fatora?

- *Revolutionary Girl Utena*. <*.*> You obviously have not watched Utena at all . . . You learn about this relationship, not just in episode one, but in the opening credits!

4. Lessons in seduction

- **Blackmail with grades.** It would work if Ranmaru is a bad student, but he's a straight A student. Let me rephrase that: he's a student with good grades.

- ■ **He drugged his drink.** Yes, drugs. The universal seducing agent. They are never around when you need them and even if you were a fanboy, people couldn't be that drugged up enough to go with you.

- **Blackmail with a scandalous photo of him.** Oh my goodness! Ranmaru was eating paste! How scandalous can Ranmaru be?

- **He was whipped vigorously until he met with no resistance.** Than after being baked, he will manage to serve four, or more if your friends aren't greedy.

5. Faking it

- **Dee got time off for good service.** Nope. More like good riddance!

- **Dee got time off because he was too stressed.** Stressed over the fact that if he did not get the time off as Ryo, he was going to quit. The boss didn't mind.

- **Dee got time off because he had to use his vacation time before it expired.** Hey, cops are fighting crime all the time! When do they have time for vacations?

- ■ **Dee pleaded and begged and pleaded and begged until he got time off.** And if you plead and beg and whine enough, you can actually get your way. And the fact that Dee is handy with a gun never hurt him.

1. Is everyone visiting the drowned springs?

Which of these characters is NOT gender-changing?

- Ranma from *Ranma 1/2*
- Dilandau from *Escaflowne*
- Maze from *Maze*
- Nuriko from *Fushigi Yūgi*

2. The unbishōnen bishōnen

Despite what everyone calls Nakago *from Fushigi Yūgi*, he is NOT a bishōnen. Why not?

- He's not a homosexual
- He's not a boy
- He's not Japanese
- He "pitches," but he doesn't "catch"

3. The unbishōnen bishōnen (part 2)

Despite what everyone calls Ryōga *from Ranma 1/2*, he is NOT a bishōnen because he is not drawn as a pretty man to titillate women. What is a better word that fits him describing someone who is handsome and manly?

- Otokorashii
- Otokonoko
- Otokomae
- Otokodōsei

4. Yaoi as good as . . .

What is the sequel to the yaoi story *Zetsuai*?

- *Golden*
- *Silver Tongue*
- *Bronze*
- *Platinum Visa*

5. That woman was so ugly . . .

That woman was so ugly, the doctor slapped her mother at birth. That woman was so ugly, her mother shaved her butt and made her walk backwards. That woman was so ugly, she has to sneak up to a mirror just to look at herself. Which woman? How about this one?

Mitsukake cross-dressed in the omake scene of the *Fushigi Yūgi* OAV series was so ugly, that . . .

- The writers wrote it out of the script
- The animators censored his face
- He was the only man allowed to be dressed as a guy
- They made him a woman with a hormone problem

© 1997 B-Papas/Chino Saito/TV Tokyo/Shonen Inkai

In this scene in *Utena*, Miki appears to be looking at something. What is he looking at?

(a) A musicbox (b) A dead rat (c) A piano (d) A box of silk clothes

1. Is everyone visiting the drowned springs?

- **Ranma from *Ranma 1/2*.** DUH!!!! NO!!!! BAKA!!!

- **Dilandau from *Escaflowne*.** You can't lead an army of pretty boys and not have some suspicion thrown in your face, now can you?

- **Maze from *Maze*.** If you don't know what *Maze* is, think of *Ranma 1/2*, except when Maze is a guy, he is hornier than a junior high kid with an issue of *Victoria's Secret*.

- ■ **Nuriko from *Fushigi Yūgi*.** Quite easy, wasn't it? Not Nuriko, the question!

2. The unbishōnen bishōnen

- **He's not a homosexual.** Whether he is or is not does not affect the status of that term.

- ■ **He's not a boy.** Correct. "Bishōnen" means "beautiful boy" or even "pretty boy," but he is not a boy. The proper term for a beautiful man is "biseinen," or as other girls call him, "Mine."

- **He's not Japanese.** Nope. "Bishōnen" is not a Japanese-only term.

- **He "pitches," but he doesn't "catch."** This isn't baseball, you know. But while we're on the subject, he's more likely to be the one who bats with a big stick.

3. The unbishōnen bishōnen (part 2)

- **Otokorashii.** Nope. This word is used to describe men who don't ask for directions. The word means "typical of a male."

- **Otokonoko.** Nope. This word means "young boy."

- ■ **Otokomae.** Correct. This term applies to characters like Ryōga from *Ranma 1/2* and Tasuki from *Fushigi Yūgi*. And men can use it on other men too without having to compromise their sexuality.

- **Otokodōsei.** Nope. This is the word for "male homosexual," and this would be the perfect place to introduce that meaning.

4. Yaoi as good as . . .

- **Golden.** Sorry. That's not the sequel for this story.

- **Silver Tongue.** Ah! Kōji! You have swallowed mercury to prove your love to me! And then the young soccer star, Izumi, drops dead and can never find love again. Nope.

- ■ **Bronze.** Correct. Here, Kōji and Izumi continue their love from the story in *Zetsuai*. *Zetsuai* is often translated as "No love" or "Zero love," so hopefully, they made progress from that point or they stopped playing tennis.

- **Platinum Visa.** It would be everywhere you want to be, but not here. Sorry.

5. That woman was so ugly . . .

- **The writers wrote it out of the script.** Think about this. If the writers wrote it out of the script, then why are we even talking about this?

- ■ **The animators censored his face.** Correct. Even for the moment when you actually did see his face and the bad makeup job. So much a man that the women forced him to "breed" with women as per the custom of their land! How difficult . . .

- **He was the only man allowed to be dressed as a guy.** Nope. It would not be as much fun!

- **They made him into a woman with a hormone problem.** And I'm sure people would love that . . .

■ *Answer to picture puzzle:* (c) A piano.

1. Top or bottom?

Like any genre, yaoi has its own terms and vocabulary. In yaoi, "seme" is the equivalent of "top" and "uke" is the equivalent of "bottom." However, while "uke" literally means "receive," what does "seme" literally mean?

- To give
- To seed
- To spend
- To attack

2. Why do all the girly men get the girls?

In *Five Star Stories*, how does the effeminately beautiful man, Ladios Sopp, know the Clothos, Atropos, and Lachesis?

- He helped raise them
- They are his maidservants
- He knows them in the biblical sense
- By reading Greek mythology, silly!

3. You must really want your job . . .

In *Boku no Sexual Harassment*, since Mochizuki-kun is so cute, what does his boss do?

- Makes him wear a dress to work
- Makes him pose nude for an ad campaign
- Rents him out to other executives as a "toy"
- Tries to marry him even though they are both men

4. Fast times at Seiran High

In the game *Graduation* by GAS (one of the few computer yaoi dating games translated into English), if you reach the goal area on your date on Sunday, where have you and your date ended?

- The swimming club
- A park at nighttime
- The front of the school
- A love hotel

5. Aoki Rōtachi no Densetsu (Legend of the Blue Wolves)

In the above-named yaoi anime, if Leonardo DiCaprio played the character that shared his first name, then what is to be his destiny at the end of the anime?

- He would die of disease from space
- He would die at the knife of his lover in space
- He would die from an exploding ship in space
- He would die while Celine Dion sings that her heart will go on

1. Top or bottom?

- **To give**. If someone asked you to give to the poor, would they enjoy it if you meant "give" this way?

- **To seed**. What? Do you expect roses to come out of Nuriko's . . .

- **To spend**. I heard of people getting orgasms while shopping but this is ridiculous!

- ■ **To attack**. Take this! And this! And this! Hey, I'm beating you up! Why are you enjoying this?

2. Why do all the girly men get the girls?

- ■ **He helped raise them**. Correct. They have a fond memory of him and one of them longed to be his Fatima.

- **They are his maidservants**. Nope. Not correct.

- **He knows them in the biblical sense**. Hey, knowledge is power! But he never knew them that way.

- **By reading Greek mythology, silly!** Uh-uh. And yet the names of the three primary Fatimas share the names of the Fates. Oh well, anything is possible in anime!

3. You must really want your job . . .

- **Makes him wear a dress to work**. Only if it's not plaid. Plaid is out this season. Nope, not this one.

- **Makes him pose nude for an ad campaign**. Nope, Mochizuki-kun is not that type of guy. (It does not exclude him from being another type, though . . .)

- ■ **Rents him out to other executives as a "toy."** Correct. Why sleep your way to the top when you can have someone else do it for you?

- **Tries to marry him even though they are both men**. Well, this anime does not take place in Hawaii so we can effectively rule that out.

4. Fast times at Seiran High

- ■ **The swimming club**. Correct. And those shorts are rather short. Thank God! Um . . . ahem . . .

- **A park at nighttime**. Yes, your date will end in a mugging in the middle of a dark park. How romantic.

- **The front of the school**. Where everyone can see you? No way!

- **A love hotel**. Hee hee. You wish!

5. Aoki Routachi no Densetsu (Legend of the Blue Wolves)

- **He would die of disease from space**. They aren't dead moon people, you know!

- ■ **He would die at the knife of his lover in space**. Correct. And if you only knew what that same knife was used for earlier in the anime. . . . Let's just say Bobbitt would have said. "Been there, done that."

- **He would die from an exploding ship in space**. Nope. How boring! Try something original!

- **He would die while Celine Dion sings that her heart will go on**. Near, far . . . Actually quite far from the actual answer I'm looking for.

Translations

Japanese isn't exactly the language most easily translatable into English. But we certainly have to appreciate the efforts of translators to get anime understood on this side of the Pacific. How attentive are you to translations? Try these questions for size.

1. What kind of man is he?

When anime comes to America, in order not to have to explain what a "nikuman" is, what do English-dubbed characters often call them instead?

- Donuts
- Pizza
- Cheesecake
- Marshmallow bunnies

2. Water-fighting techniques

In the later episodes of *Sailor Moon* (when the Sailor Scouts encounter members of the Dark Moon Kingdom like Diamond, Sapphire, and Emerald), Sailor Mercury has an attack called "Shine Aqua Illusion." What did they rename this attack in North America?

- Water Hyperblast
- Mercury Ice Storm
- Mercury Crash Wave
- Shine Aqua Illusion

3. How to be an instant millionaire

In the North American *Sailor Moon*, the penniless Yachirō gets turned into what when he appears at Raye's temple?

- Police cadet
- Male model
- Corporate executive
- Rock star

4. Protection by paperwork

In *Pokemon*, both Ash's team and Team Rocket buy wards to guard themselves from a beautiful ghost's curse. What were these wards called in English?

- Ghost wards
- Spirit protectors
- Soulburners
- Anti-ghost stickers

5. Tiramisu? Is that like a disease or something?

In *Here Is Greenwood*, Agent D is sent out to get some "Tiramisu" in the English dubbed translation. What did Agent D think Tiramisu was in the first place?

- A type of dress
- A video game
- A slang term for "sex"
- A lost woman looking for "Carrot"

Yūsuke from *Yū Yū Hakusho* (Poltergeist Report) stands here posed without his weapon. What does he normally use to fight enemies?

(a) A sword (b) A whip (c) His fists (d) His words

1. What kind of man is he?

- ■ **Donuts**. Yup. Although they never explained why these donuts don't have holes....

- • **Pizza**. You might be thinking "okonomiyaki." And I bet the only reason you know that word if you are an anime fan is because of Ukyo in *Ranma 1/2*! Am I psychic or what?

- • **Cheesecake**. This should be a pretty "cheesecake" question to an anime fan.

- • **Marshmallow bunnies**. Nope. Wrong on that one.

2. Water-fighting techniques

- • **Water Hyperblast**. Nope. Sailor Mercury doesn't have this attack in her arsenal.

- • **Mercury Ice Storm**. There was an attack that was called this, but it did not appear in the later episodes of *Sailor Moon*.

- • **Mercury Crash Wave**. Nope. Sailor Mercury doesn't have this move in her arsenal either.

- ■ **Shine Aqua Illusion**. Correct. In the "lost episodes" (lost where, in Canada?) the words did not change at all.

3. How to be an instant millionaire

- • **Police cadet**. No police cadet would be as bumbling as he is.

- • **Male model**. Nope. That was Darien's job.

- • **Corporate executive**. What? With that haircut? Pretty unlikely.

- ■ **Rock star**. I guess it sounds more impressive than "bum" anyday. But the title was a giveaway, wasn't it? <^.^>

4. Protection by paperwork

- • **Ghost wards**. Nah, too obvious.

- • **Spirit protectors**. Nah, too complicated.

- • **Soulburners**. Nah, too scary.

- ■ **Anti-ghost stickers**. Yes! And if some companies have their say, they can be selling these alongside talking Pikachu keychains!

5. Tiramisu? Is that like a disease or something?

- • **A type of dress**. Nope, it's not a type of dress.

- ■ **A video game**. Correct. Well, he could have found out the hard way and left a mess on the console.

- • **A slang term for "sex."** You can have Tiramisu and eat it, too! But most escorts will charge extra for that.

- • **A lost woman looking for "Carrot."** And is "carrot" a slang term for something rather obvious?

■ ***Answer to picture puzzle:*** (c) His fists. Selection (d) would only be correct if he was going to throw a dictionary at his enemies.

1. Firetrippy

What is the most interesting thing about the English dub of *Firetripper*? Um . . . let me rephrase that. What is the most "notable" thing about the English dub of *Firetripper*?

- They speak English in a French accent
- They speak English in a British accent
- They speak English in a Japanese accent
- The timing between the voices and the mouths in the dub is worse than those old *Godzilla* movies

2. Japanese checkers

You adopt a sweet-looking dog that has white fur on one side and black fur on the other side. You could go for the American version of Ryōga's dog's name which is "Checkers" (which is given in the *Ranma 1/2* translated manga) but a U.S. president already used it for his dog so you decide on the original Japanese name of the dog ,which is:

- Shirokuro
- Chocovan
- Blackwhite
- Monochrome

3. Showgirl by night

The English voice for the main character in *Armitage* did which TV show?

- *Degrassi Jr. High*
- *90210*
- *Saved by the Bell*
- *Sweet Valley High*

4. Expressions that don't translate well from English

In the dubbed version of *Ranma 1/2*, boy-type Ranma once used a phrase that did not have a Japanese equivalent. Which one?

- "Raise the roof!"
- "C'mon ride the train!"
- "Who's the man?"
- A Nine Inch Nails lyric dealing with animals and feeling inside something

5. Expressions that don't translate well from Japanese

The commercially translated English title of *Urusei Yatsura* is "Those Obnoxious Aliens." If literally translated, what does "Urusei Yatsura" mean?

- Noisy Aliens
- Those People from Planet Uru
- Obnoxious Foreigners
- Princess in Tiger-Striped Bikinis

1. Firetrippy

- **They speak English in a French accent**. Nope. This is not Nadia and the Secret of Blue Wah-tère!

- ■ **They speak English in a British accent**. Correct. The accent was so strong, for a moment, I thought the anime was set in Great Britain!

- **They speak English in a Japanese accent**. And manage to offend both English speakers and the Japanese at the same time? They're not stupid, you know.

- **The timing between the voices and the mouths in the dub is worse than those old *Godzilla* movies**. Hee hee. That actually might be fun to watch.

2. Japanese checkers

- ■ **Shirokuro**. Correct. "Shirokuro" means "white-black," although the name "Checkers" in the translation makes sense because it is an actual dog's name. Of course, there's nothing wrong with leaving it "Shirokuro" as well.

- **Chocovan**. Nope, they may be a "Chocolate" and "Vanilla" mix, but that is not what the dog is called.

- **Blackwhite**. This would make sense in English, but it might be awkward in Japanese.

- **Monochrome**. It may but be a good idea to give your dog a name where the nickname could sound like a potentially contagious infection.

3. Showgirl by night

- *Degrassi Jr. High*. What's that? It's a Canadian high school drama. Oh, I see. No wonder I didn't get it.

- *90210*. Nope. They're all pretty busy spending money and having sex to do this type of work.

- ■ *Saved by the Bell*. Correct. The young lady in red is played by Elizabeth Berkeley, and if you paid attention to the title of this question, you would have gotten this right away.

- *Sweet Valley High*. Would be perfect if Armitage featured a pair of girls who are twins, but it didn't happen. Sorry.

4. Expressions that don't translate well from English

- **"Raise the roof!"** Ranma can probably do that by knocking it down.

- **"C'mon ride the train!"** All I can say is that he has enough fiancées to do his special kind of train.

- ■ **"Who's the man?"** If you knew one ounce of Ranma, you would have known this was the answer. You have got to admit that this is something that Ranma would say, isn't it?

- **A Nine Inch Nails lyric dealing with animals and feeling inside something**. No!!! Not it!!! Not it at all!!!

5. Expressions that don't translate well from Japanese

- **Noisy Aliens**. What other kinds of aliens are there?

- ■ **Those People from Planet Uru**. Correct. "Urusei" or "Planet Uru" sounds remarkably like "urusai" or "noisy." If you don't know Japanese, it's rather hard to get.

- **Obnoxious Foreigners**. Where do you think we are? France?

- **Princess in Tiger-Striped Bikinis**. Hmmm . . . I'm not sure what the Japanese is for "tiger-striped . . . ." but I'm sure that it was wrong.

1. Things that come before your bladder

Why is "Gall Force" called "Gall Force?"

- "Gall" is the name of the ship
- "Gall" is the name of the corporation that made the ship
- "Gall" is the name of the owner of the corporation that made the ship
- "Gall" and "Girl" are the same word in Japanese

2. Baby Food

"Tamagotchi" means "little egg" in Japanese. If creatures were born from cherries, what would we carry in our pockets to annoy us once every fifteen minutes?

- Ichigotchi
- Budotchi
- Okonomiyakitchi
- Sakuranbotchi

3. Americans can't handle that . . .

Which of these changes did editors NOT make when they brought the video game *Revelations: Persona* from the Japanese to the American version?

- They put digital underwear on the nude main boss
- They turned one character into an African-American
- They took out Budweiser advertisements from the convenience stores
- There were fewer playable characters than in the Japanese version of the game

4. Something ripped other than Ryu's muscles

If in the middle of a fight, you tore Ryu's *hachimaki* into shreds, what would you be able to get a better look at?

- His chest
- His forehead
- The knuckles on his hands
- Nothing. But Ryu would suddenly feel a draft.

5. How do you know what he's saying?

When Pikachu says "Pi-ka-pi" in the anime, what does he usually mean?

- He is saying his owner's name, "Satoshi"
- He is saying danger, "Abunai"
- He is calling someone an idiot, "Bakaro"
- Pikachu needs to go to the bathroom

1. Things that come before your bladder

- **"Gall" is the name of the ship**. No.
- **"Gall" is the name of the corporation that made the ship**. Nope.
- **"Gall" is the name of the owner of the corporation that made the ship**. Uh-uh.
- ■ **"Gall" and "Girl" are the same word in Japanese**. Correct. And this is yet another reason why Japanese is difficult to translate into English and why you have to love the translators you got.

2. Baby Food

- **Ichigotchi**. Nope. That would be a creature born from a strawberry.
- **Budotchi**. Uh-uh. That's a creature born from a grape.
- **Okonomiyakitchi**. Okay, what kind of creature would be born from okonomiyaki? Would you really want to know?
- ■ **Sakuranbotchi**. Correct. Sakuranbo is Japanese for "cherry." So I guess when a creature is born, it has to break it's own cherry, doesn't it?

3. Americans can't handle that . . .

- ■ **They put digital underwear on the nude main boss**. Nope. The main character is nude. Of course, this is only relevant if you are turned on by women whose body is split in half and somehow spliced with another creature. . . .
- **They turned one character into an African-American**. True. Although some people question this decision, I thought that it was nice of them to make this consideration.
- **They took out Budweiser advertisements from the convenience stores**. Yup. Those advertisements may

be on your local neighborhood convenience store but they don't belong on an American video game.

- **There were fewer playable characters than in the Japanese version of the game**. Correct. Yuki is a character that you get in the beginning, but because an entire quest is missing, that is all the playtime she gets in America.

4. Something ripped other than Ryu's muscles

- **His chest**. After you stop staring at Ryu's pectorals, you realize that his *hachimaki* is still on.
- ■ **His forehead**. Right! A *hachimaki* is your basic bandana that you sport over your forehead.
- **The knuckles on his hands**. Nope. *Hachimaki* isn't the name of those knuckle guards that Ryu wears. However, I don't know what they are called either, so you'll need to ask someone else.
- **Nothing. But Ryu would suddenly feel a draft**. How you got your hands there in a fight is beyond me and I don't want to go there right now . . .

5. How do you know what he's saying?

- ■ **He is saying his owner's name, "Satoshi."** Right! It's probably the only thing that anyone can understand from Pikachu. Why can't he take a cue from Genma and start holding signs to communicate? I guess it takes the fun out of guessing.
- **He is saying danger, "Abunai."** Nope. Good guess though. You definitely get an "A" for effort with that answer.
- **He is calling someone an idiot, "Bakaro."** Pikachu is rather too nice to do that, although he was raised to kick some tail.
- **Pikachu needs to go to the bathroom**. This is information that we just simply do not need to know.

Redefining Anime

How can someone tell if something is "anime" or not? The question is pretty simple on the surface, but to some anime fans there is a need to separate "anime" from "non-anime." Why? I'm not exactly sure why. But the term "anime" itself in America is not simple. The word is considered to identify both "something from a different culture" and an "art style" at the same time.

If something looks like anime, is it anime, even if it is not produced in Japan? Some say "yes" while others say "no." People have tried to separate "Japanese anime" (produced in Japan) and "American anime" (produced in America and looks like anime), until you point out that the term "American anime" really means "American Japanese animation." Which it is, but that's messy. A term like "fusion anime" might be better since it suggests an American take on Japanese animation. If

1. Why would you put monsters there?

In Japan, *Pokemon* is called *Poketto Monsutaa* (Pocket Monster). Why the name change?

- Because saying "monster" to little children will scare them
- There was already a cartoon in the U.S. with a similar name
- Nintendo will not allow the same name to be used in the U.S.
- People just decided that *Pokemon* sounds better

2. Mr. A (alias Mr. B)

In America, the Street Fighter character known as "Balrog" is "Bison" in Japan. In America, the character known as "Bison" is "Vega" in Japan. The character we know as "Vega" is "Balrog" in Japan. So why the heck did they do this in the first place?

- The characters were misnamed when translated and it was just never corrected
- "Vega" sounded more Spanish and that was given to the character from Spain
- "Bison" sounded too much like an American boxer with a similar name
- To discourage the Japanese from playing the American version of *Street Fighter*

3. Foo-she-gee Yoo-gee?

I guess one of the great things about being an anime fan is listening to how new fans attempt to pronounce the name of the anime with Miaka and

Tamahome in it. Of course it is just as precious as when people pronounce the word "anime" itself.

Fushigi Yūgi can be translated into several phrases. Which one of these phrases would be an incorrect translation?

- Mysterious Play
- Mysterious Game
- Miraculous Play
- Miraculous Puzzle

4. A genderless name for a "genderless" sailor

The good thing about a "genderless name" is that if a baby is a boy or girl, it is appropriate. The bad thing is that if it looks anything like "Pat" from *Saturday Night Live* . . . According to Irwin Toys, what is Sailor Uranus's English name?

- Corrin
- Dana
- Toni
- Bobby Ann

5. Are you sure that's not Chinese food?

The first line of Ranma's first season opening song is: "Yappapa, yappapa, II-SHAN-TEN." What game is the expression "II-SHAN-TEN" used for?

- Shogi
- Mah-jongg
- Go
- Go Fish

chefs in Japan can have "fusion cuisine," why can't Americans have "fusion anime?"

The other issue that anime fans have to deal with is the anime art style. Many people have an idea what an "anime art style" is, but if you consider *Doraemon*, *Crayon-Shin-chan*, and, to some extent, *Crying Freeman*, you find works that do not fit into the current American notion of how anime is supposed to look. These works don't have the huge eyes, the little knob for a nose, the small mouth. The idea that anime looks like "that" comes mainly from Osamu Tezuka, who influenced many artists with his economical yet expressive style. What many people think of as the "anime" art style is actually "Tezukan anime" (for lack of a better term).

Someday, someone might be able to answer this question. But then who would care? I would.

1. Why would you put monsters there?

- **Because saying "monster" to little children will scare them**. Although a kindergarten teacher told me how true this was, it's not THE major consideration for the change.

- ■ **There was already a cartoon in the U.S. with a similar name**. Right. The name of the original cartoon was called *Monsters in my Pocket*. But with copyrights as they are, they just changed the name to *Pokemon*, which is faithful to the Japanese because they also use that term as well.

- **Nintendo will not allow the same name to be used in the U.S**. Nope. In fact, it would have been cheaper to use the same name.

- **People just decided that *Pokemon* sounds better**. And now that I'm used to it, it already does sound better.

2. Mr. A (alias Mr. B)

- **The characters were misnamed when translated and it was just never corrected**. I doubt Capcom is that sloppy . . .

- **"Vega" sounded more Spanish and that was given to the character from Spain**. Although "Vega" is a Spanish name, that is not the main consideration.

- ■ **"Bison" sounded too much like an American boxer with a similar name**. Correct. A certain boxer with a penchant for ears comes close to Bison's name. In order to avoid the hassle, the switch was made and people who play the Japanese *Street Fighter* games have to keep this in mind.

- **It was done to discourage the Japanese from playing the American version of *Street Fighter***. Who needs discouragement when you have the original game in Japanese at home?

3. Foo-she-gee Yoo-gee?

- **Mysterious Play**. Well, no. This is the official English title of the anime.

- **Mysterious Game**. This was a translation from a Japanese web site before *Fushigi Yūgi* was commerically available in the U.S.

- **Miraculous Play**. This was another translation from a Japanese web site.

- ■ **Miraculous Puzzle**. Well, *fushigi* can mean "mysterious," "miraculous," or "wondrous," while *yūgi* means "play" or "game." "Puzzle" is just beyond the scope of *yūgi*'s meaning.

Like many things in Japanese, things don't translate easily into English.

4. A genderless name for a genderless sailor

- ■ **Corrin**. Correct. And the only way to know this is either through Irwin or the *Sailor Moon* role-playing game book.

- **Dana**. Nope.

- **Toni**. Uh-uh.

- **Bobby Ann**. Wrong.

Sailor Uranus could possibly use any of these names. The rest of these can be saved for the gender bending Sailor Stars.

5. Are you sure that's not Chinese food?

- **Shogi**. Shogi, or Japanese chess, does not have this term in its vocabulary.

- ■ **Mah-jongg**. Correct. The expression is used to denote being two tiles away from a winning hand. Which, in my experience in playing Mah-jongg, doesn't mean diddly.

- **Go**. Nope. No such term exists here.

- **Go Fish**. And what is so complicated about Go Fish that you would need to have a term like that?

1. No wonder he's gone for days at a time . . .

In the parody fandub "Ranma 1/3: Notes from the Closet," what is Ryōga's spare time occupation?

- Gigolo
- Pimp
- Bacon fryer
- Colombian drug lord

2. Ooh, where can I get those princess dolls?

Sidenote to this question: Whoever did the translation for the "Princess Doll" episode of *Pokemon* did an excellent job. Translating an entire culture without serious compromises and making it accessible to an American audience without the use of cultural notes is VERY difficult. I applaud you all.

In the American version of *Pokemon,* Misty competed in the "Princess Festival" for a grand set of "Princess Dolls." In Japanese, what is this festival called?

- The Princess Festival
- The Doll Festival
- The Queen Fesitval
- The Empress Festival

3. Sign of the Cross

When the fansub group White Cross subtitled the first episode of *Weiss Kreuz,* what was the biggest mistake they made?

- The timing of dialogue to speech was off by five seconds
- The subtitles were white, making it difficult to read
- They translated *weiss* as *bice*
- Many of the subtitles were in romanized Japanese and the audience was automatically expected to know those words

4. Whodunit?

Who fansubbed *Kaitō St. Tail*?

- Project Genki
- Project Ogenki
- Project Ogenki Clinic
- Project Ogenki Clinic Fanboys

5. Censored *Pokemon* episodes that don't have seizures

In the first season of *Poketto Monsutaa,* there was an episode that featured Satoshi (Ash) and his group at the beach. Why did they not bring that episode to America?

- There was Pokemon "mating"
- Kasumi (Misty) steals Satoshi's swimsuit and Satoshi is totally nude
- Satoshi steals Kasumi's top and she is bare from the waist up
- Kojirō (James) enters the ladies swimsuit contest in a bikini and inflatable breasts

© 1991 Yuike Nasu/Hakusensha/Victor Entertainment, Inc./Pierrot Project

Mitsuru and Shinobu from *Here Is Greenwood* share an intimate moment here. So where are they sharing this moment with the audience?

(a) In their dorm room (b) In the bathtub (c) In the dorm hall (d) In class

1. No wonder he's gone for days at a time . . .

- **Gigolo**. You wish! But you better go to him rather than have him come to you.

- **Pimp**. Ryōga a pimp? Wouldn't that be Nabiki's job?

- **Bacon fryer**. <*.*> Must I explain why this isn't correct?

- ■ **Colombian drug lord**. I always wondered about those nosebleeds that Ryōga always seemed to get . . .

2. Ooh, where can I get those princess dolls?

- **The Princess Festival**. No. I wouldn't be asking this if the question were that straightforward.

- ■ **The Doll Festival**. Correct! Every March 3, there is a Doll Festival, and all households with daughters participate.

- **The Queen Festival**. If James were to enter this kind of contest, he'd win for sure! That French outfit is simply fabulous!

- **The Empress Festival**. Although it is wise of you to remember that Japan is ruled by an emperor or empress, the answer is still not correct. Sorry.

3. Sign of the Cross

- **The timing of dialogue to speech was off by five seconds**. Nope. This wasn't the Kizuna subtitling we're dealing with here.

- **The subtitles were white, making it difficult to read**. Nope. This isn't a Japanese subtitling project.

- ■ **They translated "weiss" as "bice."** Correct. Wow. Sugoi, ne? That's pretty bad. . . .

- **Many of the subtitles were in romanized Japanese and the audience was automatically expected to know those words**. I hate when people assume this. Please, show a little courtesy to a new anime fan, okay?

4. Whodunit?

- ■ **Project Genki**. Correct.

- **Project Ogenki**. No.

- **Project Ogenki Clinic**. No!

- **Project Ogenki Clinic Fanboys**. No!!!!!!!

Come on! They fansubbed *St. Tail*, not *Mistress Cat O' Nine Tails*!

5. Censored *Pokemon* episodes that don't have seizures

- **There were Pokemon "mating."** Do I make you horny, baby? Uh. no.

- **Kasumi (Misty) steals Satoshi's swimsuit and Satoshi is totally nude**. Yeah, but isn't that rather easy to cover up with digital underwear? Unless Satoshi proves to be a bigger man than everyone thinks he is?

- **Satoshi steals Kasumi's top and she is bare from the waist up**. Well, that would be pretty easy to cover up with a digital bra, so there should be no problem there.

- ■ **Kojirō (James) enters the ladies swimsuit contest in a bikini and inflatable breasts**. Correct. And because of that one scene, the entire episode stayed in Japan. But what disturbed me more was that Kojirō said the word "Service" as he inflated his realistic breasts. . . .

■ *Answer to picture puzzle:* (c) In the dorm hall. In front of others just to see them bug out..

Seiyū & Music

Seiyū (voice actors) and music are a category in itself. If you are a beginning anime fan outside of Japan, you may not necessarily care for voice actors just yet. But seiyū are celebrities in their own right, even releasing CDs next to J-Pop stars (although in a few cases, whether they can actually sing well is another matter . . .)

1. Megumi!

Megumi Hayashibara may be the most famous seiyū. She is listed in the credits for *Pokemon*, but she is not credited for playing Musashi (Jesse) in the American version. Which Pokemon's voice is she credited for in the American version?

- Pikachu
- Arbok
- Pidgeotto
- Charmander

2. Voice recognition test

If you listen to someone long enough, you can imitate the way they speak and predict what they would be likely to say. But then again, so can parrots and mynah birds. Therefore, we have the intelligence of mynah birds. Don't you love syllogistic thinking? In *Sakura Taisen* who says "Watakushi no teban desu wa, ne?"

- Iris
- Sakura
- Sumire
- Ōgami

3. Idol Chatter

Karaoke scoring machines are rigged! I know they are! Why is it that when I sing that I can never get higher than 80 and my friend manages to get a 99? Sure, she's a classically trained opera singer, but since when has the "Yappapa, Yappapa" song from *Ranma 1/2* ever been sung that way?

In *Ranma 1/2*, the voice actors playing female Ranma, Akane, Nabiki, Kasumi, and Shampoo formed a singing group that released a number of albums. What were they called?

- Loco
- Doco
- Tako
- Yugo

4. Hey! Hey! Hey!

Hey! Since when did Fat Albert start popping up in anime huh? Is he trying to get a job as Snorlax in *Pokemon*?

You are an anime fan and a musician. You want to compose an anime song that will be very famous. According to "Hey! Hey! Hey! Music Champ," every song featured in a particular anime hit the top of the J-Pop charts. Which anime do you beg to write for?

- *Shōjo Kakumei Utena*
- *Sailor Moon*
- *Rurōni Kenshin*
- *Macross Plus*

5. Yū can sing most anything

"When you know the notes to sing, Yū can sing most anything!" And Yū, from *Marmalade Boy*, can too. He has a really good voice. Speaking of Yū:

If you were Yū, and I was me, and I saw Yū at concert, which Madonna song would you be singing because it had the same title as a song that Yū sang in the *Marmalade Boy* series?

- "Frozen"
- "Rain"
- "Like a Virgin"
- "For You"

1. Megumi!

- **Pikachu.** Let's give credit where credit is due! Pikachu is voiced by Ikue Ōtani. Which makes me wonder why people claim that the Japanese version of *Pokemon* has a Pikachu that "sounds more Japanese."

- **Arbok.** Megumi hissing? Well, she can certainly hiss, but not for this Pokemon.

- ■ **Pidgeotto.** Yes, Megumi does the voice of Pidgeotto in the American version of *Pokemon*. You have to admit that even if she is relegated to doing a character voice, Pidgeotto's voice DOES take some talent to reproduce!

- **Charmander.** Charmander might be cute (let's face it, he's extremely cute!), but he is called "Hitokage" in Japan and thus would not even be able to say the word "Charmander."

2. Voice recognition test

- **Iris.** Nah. Iris would sound cuter than that. And in French!

- **Sakura.** Nope. Although it's her rival that says it (hint, hint)

- ■ **Sumire.** Yes, that haughty and very self-important voice belongs to none other than Sumire. And even if you did not know that statement from the *Sakura Taisen* video game, "Watakushi" is the giveaway because it seems very self-important.

- **Ōgami.** Um, what self-respecting man in Japanese would use the feminine "wa, ne?" (Uh, don't answer that.)

As much as you might love to speak Japanese, please do not say "Watakushi wa otaku desu, ne." You will see people slowly start to move away from you like moths to bug spray.

3. Idol Chatter

- **Loco.** You have to be loco in the head to have come up with this answer.

- ■ **Doco.** Correct. This is an easy one for *Ranma 1/2* fans. Consider it a birthday present.

- **Tako.** Why would this girl group be named after an "octopus"? Or for some of you, why did you assume that this group would be named after something made in Taco Bell?

- **Yugo.** Named after a car? There have been stranger names for bands, but this one is not correct.

4. Hey! Hey! Hey!

- *Shōjo Kakumei Utena*. Nope.

- *Sailor Moon*. Whoa, you either really are a *Sailor Moon* fan or you have heard nothing outside of *Sailor Moon* music ...

- ■ *Rurōni Kenshin*. Yes! You know your anime and J-Pop well, don't you?

- *Macross Plus*. Even though the songs on *Macross Plus* are composed by the music goddess herself, Yoko Kanno, this is not correct.

Ever since that idea of anime songs doing well on J-pop existed, a lot more famous bands are doing anime songs. And you have Rurōni Kenshin to thank for that.

5. Yū can sing most anything

- **"Frozen."** Um, you would be frozen on stage if you found out that this wasn't the correct answer.

- ■ **"Rain."** Yes, Yū did a very sweet song called "Rain" with a really cool voice.

- **"Like a Virgin."** <*.*> No.

- **"For You."** Uh-uh. This is the name of the piano piece that Kei played for Miki.

It technically would not be correct for Yū to sing "Like a Virgin" if he actually is one. Unless there is something about Yū that we don't know ...

1. Farewell to arms

Parting words (not just parting) are such sweet sorrow. Because most of those lines are cornier than a pan full of Jiffy-Pop!

In *DNA2*, what are Karin's last words to Momonari-kun before she shoots him?

- "Sayonara"
- "Nothing personal"
- "Eat this!"
- "Bye bye, Mega Playboy!"

2. Sing for me

Which of these J-Pop musicians have NOT sung for Rurōni Kenshin?

- Judy and Mary
- Namie Amuro
- TM Revolution
- Yellow Monkey

3. Singing soprano

You are a guy and someone just kicked you in the groin. You can now hit the high notes from that one opera song in *Memories*. From which opera did it originally come from?

- *The Magic Flute*
- *La Boheme*
- *Madame Butterfly*
- *The Rocky Horror Picture Show*

4. Midorikawa-love

The only reason why this title is here is that my friend, the *karaoke-joō* (karaoke queen), Eileen, is a big fan of Hikaru Midorikawa, and when she writes his name she writes "Midorikawa-love" in the middle. And next week, she is going to Japan to stalk him.

Which of these roles has Hikaru Midorikawa not voiced?

- One of Miaka's Senshi
- A shapechanging mascot
- A Gundam pilot
- An American exchange student

5. Mr. Clean, Mr. Clean!

One great thing about anime parodies of anime like *Project A-ko, Nadesico*, and *Shinesman* is, obviously, that they don't take themselves too seriously AND that, if you do get the insider jokes, it is one more indicator you are an anime fan. And it is a warning not to see *Otaku no Video*.

In the anime sentai parody *Shinesman*, what is notable about the voice actors in the series?

- They are the same cast from *Fushigi Yūgi*
- The voice actor's names all ended in "da"
- All the voice actors were female
- All the voice actors' last names were the same for the character they played.

Ah, here is yet another pic of Subaru and Seishirō from *Tokyo Babylon*, but Seishirō is 17 in this pic and Subaru is about 5. If Subaru were a legal consenting adult in the U.S., how old would Seishirō be before he tried to make the moves on him?

(a) 25 (b) 28 (c) 30 (d) 34

1. Farewell to Arms

- **Sayonara**. Well, because we are an English-speaking audience, it sounds impressive, but it's pretty ordinary for a Japanese audience.

- **Nothing personal**. Nope. This is what Misato in the *Evangelion* movie says as she wastes the man that was going to kill Shinji.

- **Eat this!** Well, they are at a café when she says it, but Karin isn't exactly talking about quiche!

- ■ **Bye bye, Mega Playboy!** Correct. This memorable phrase was uttered by Karin just as she shot him. A fitting ending. And a fitting beginning as well.

2. Sing for me

- **Judy and Mary**. Well, they did a little song called "Sobakasu" (Freckles) at the beginning of the first season of *Rurōni Kenshin* so this would be incorrect.

- ■ **Namie Amuro**. Can you celebrate? You got this one right!

- **TM Revolution**. Well, TM did the song "Heart of the Sword," so this answer would be wrong, too.

- **Yellow Monkey**. Yellow Monkey did the ending song "Tactics." I guess when the lyrics "I need your love" are in the song, I'm assuming the tactic is begging.

3. Singing soprano

- *The Magic Flute*. Well, if someone kicked you hard enough to sing the song that has the highest notes in all of opera, you would be dead.

- *La Boheme*. Umm . . . probably not. Although an opera about slackers might be a popular one in this generation.

- ■ *Madame Butterfly*. Well, Yurika from *Nadesico* came in at second place. But second place still makes you a loser!

- *The Rocky Horror Picture Show*. I said you were kicked in the groin, not made-to-wear fishnet stockings!

4. Midorikawa-love

- **One of Miaka's Senshi**. Hikaru Midorikawa played a small role, maybe you've heard of it, called "Tamahome."

- ■ **A shapechanging mascot**. Correct. Who can imagine a cute little mouse or pig with Heero's voice saying "Omae o korosu" (I will kill you)?

- **A Gundam pilot**. He played the hero of the story, Heero!

- **An American exchange student**. Midorikawa not only demonstrates his ability to play a red-haired blue-eyed boy, but he speaks English as well!

5. Mr. Clean, Mr. Clean!

- **They are the same cast from *Fushigi Yūgi***. Nope, sorry.

- **The voice actor's names all ended in "da."** No "da!" No "da!" No "da!" (This is Chichiri from *Fushigi Yūgi* telling you that you were wrong.)

- **All the voice actors were female**. Hey! This isn't the *Utena* musical! (Where all of the parts WERE played by women).

- ■ **All the voice actors' last names were the same for the character they played**. Correct. Which is why, although the dubbed version was okay, if you are a seiyū fan you definitely want the subbed version to get those jokes.

■ ***Answer to picture puzzle:*** (c) 30. Subaru has to be 18 to be a consenting adult, right? If Seishirō has to wait 13 years for him to turn 18, then Seishirō would have to be 30. But age has never stopped Seishirō before…

1. Tin roof rusted!

You thought the lyrics in B-52's "Love Shack" were hard to discern, what about this one? What is the "Third Word" in the *Macross* song "Voices?" And I don't mean the third word sung in the song, but what is called the "Third Word?"

- Kaze (wind)
- Yume (dream)
- Kami (god)
- Hmmm (a hum)

2. The boy who cried like a wolf

Better than a boy who's "Hungry Like the Wolf" . . . (Duran Duran songs are now stuck in my head; forgive me), *Akazukin Cha-Cha* (Red Riding Hood Cha-Cha) features a voice actor who plays Riiya-kun, a boy who changes into a wolf. The voice actor himself actually comes from which Japanese boy band?

- SMAP
- Saruganseki
- Pool Bit Boys
- X-Japan

3. Thou shalt not worship idols

If you're relgious, demons and devils are not cool, but Japanese pop singers should be okay. . . . In *Perfect Blue*, what is the name of Mima's idol singing group?

- Double Bind
- Love Wave
- Cham
- Sasshi

4. Songs with a bit of class

Who says that anime music must be poppy? There are some serious classical pieces used in anime, thus giving anime the dignity it deserves. Like this one:

What is the classical music piece that serves as the base for the *Dragonhalf* ending song?

- Brahm's "Lullaby"
- Mozart's *Requiem*
- Beethoven's Symphonies 1–9
- Wagner's "Ride of the Valkyries"

5. More than just a great movie

I love *Princess Mononoke*. Go see it! Go see it! Go see it! And one more thing: GO SEE IT!!!!

The *Princess Mononoke* theme song won which award at the Japanese Record Awards?

- Best Composition
- Best Lyrics
- Song of the Year
- Best Promotion

© GAINAX/Project Eva • TV Tokyo

"Shinji here from *Neon Genesis Evangelion* and when I play music, I use nothing but the best. Evangelion™ cello strings, the ONLY strings your own father never pulls. . . ." In the *End of Evangelion*™ movie, what is the name of the classical piece that Shinji, Asuka, Rei, and Kaworu play as a quartet?

(a) "Requiem" (b) "Kanon" (c) "Air" (d) "Prelude to Carmen"

1. Tin roof rusted

- **Kaze (wind)**. Nope, this is the "First Word." Or is it the "Second?"
- **Yume (dream)**. Nope. This is the "Second Word." Or is it the "First?"
- **Kami (god)** Uh-uh.
- ■ **Hmmm (a hum)** I guess the lyricist ran out of words. But she could not come up with more than just *kaze* and *yume*? But it's quite nice, isn't it?

2. The boy who cried like a wolf

- ■ **SMAP**. Correct. The young man known as Shingo from SMAP played Riiya-kun in *Akazukin Cha-Cha*. I forget what SMAP means. I know that S and M means Sports and Music but isn't AP sort of like those super hard classes you take for college credit?
- **Saruganseki**. Nope, neither of the Saruganseki boys played any roles in that anime.
- **Pool Bit Boys**. These boys did not even have bit parts in anime!
- **X-Japan**. Oh yes, of course. Can you imagine these highly stylized J-Rockers playing the voices of cute boys? I think not.

Of course, the S and M in SMAP could mean other things as well, but since none of them have any scars or liked to be spanked, I'm pretty sure it's not the other thing.

3. Thou shalt not worship idols

- **Double Bind**. Nope, this is the name of Mima's drama.
- **Love Wave**. Sounds like a J-Poppy enough name but it's not the name of Mima's idol singing group
- ■ **Cham**. Yup. I have no idea where the name Cham comes from. But I guess as long as the members are cute and the songs are catchy, you can call a J-Pop group "Poopies" and no one in Japan will think twice.
- **Sasshi**. Totally made up name. And you fell for it! Damn, I'm good <^.^>

4. Songs with a bit of class

- **Brahms's "Lullaby."** Good night! ::bops you on the head with an interdimensional hammer::
- **Mozart's *Requiem***. I guess a requiem will have to be played for you getting the wrong answer here!
- ■ **Beethoven's Symphonies 1–9**. Correct. You are a refined and sophisitcated person. But why do you have that copy of *Urotsukidōji* back there?
- **Wagner's "Ride of the Valkyries."** Kill the fanboy! Kill the fanboy! Kill the fanboy! La-la-la!

Now, you never have to worry about that the classical music collection from those places that offer 12 CDs for a penny! Just get this song and play it extra slow and you got them all!

5. More than just a great movie

- ■ **Best Composition**. Correct. The theme song of *Princess Mononoke* is such a beautiful song, that only a guy can hit those high notes. That's right, this song is sung by a countertenor (read: a guy with a range equivalent to a soprano).
- **Best Lyrics**. Well, if half of the song goes "la, la, la, la, la, la, la, la," I'm sure they won't get this category.
- **Song of the Year**. Nope. That went to Namie Amuro's "Can You Celebrate?" Apparently, she could not because she always cries in the middle of performing this song.
- **Best Promotion**. Only in Japan would a song win just from its advertising. Of course, *End of Evangelion* was nominated this way.

■ ***Answer to picture puzzle:*** (b) "Kanon." "Air" is also in the movie, but not played by the quartet.

1. The Merry Fish

Kikuko Inoue is the voice of so many sweet characters, and she believed that she was a fish in her past life. Not to say that these two things are related, but they are just two interesting facts about this popular seiyū.

Which of these anime features does not have Kikuko (say that name five times fast) Inoue in it?

- *Ranma 1/2*
- *Ogenki Clinic*
- *Fish in the Trap*
- *Boku no Sexual Harassment*

2. The scarce emus in Japan

Emus are a scarce animal and should be protected under the Endangered Species Act. I mean, other than E.M.U. and Weiss Kreuz, what other all male seiyū bands are there? What does E.M.U. stand for?

- Entertainment Magic Unit
- Excellent Music Understanding
- Emergency Medical Unit
- Enter My Universe

3. Strange things other than Sarah

Girls do boy voices all the time. Why can't boys do girl voices? Or at least girls with hormonal problems? Which of the following boys was NOT voiced by Megumi Ogata, the voice of Sailor Uranus?

- Shinji from *Evangelion*
- Young Mamoru from *Sailor Moon*
- Akito Hayama from the *Child's Toy* TV series
- Young Keiichi from *Ah! My Goddess*

4. The human memory jukebox

It is not unusual for a person to know the track numbers of the songs on a CD, but to imitate everything on the *Ranma Kurata* CD is to call a person's sanity into question....

Who sings track number 3 on the *Ranma Kurata* CD?

- Ryōga
- Ranma-chan (Female Ranma)
- Nabiki
- Akane

5. Dun-da-da-da

Here's a simple question: When did Megumi Hayashibara get married?

- April 1, 1998
- March 30, 1998
- November 14, 1998
- She's not married! She's not! She can't be! Noooooooo!

1. The Merry Fish

- *Ranma 1/2*. Well, she did kind of play a role named "Kasumi" in *Ranma 1/2* . . .
- *Ogenki Clinic*. Hee hee. That sweet little person played the very busty nurse in *Ogenki Clinc*. I think the character holds the world's record for staying the longest underwater without needing to come up for air! I guess being a fish in a past life helps a lot.
- ■ *Fish in the Trap*. I bet you didn't know what this anime was, but you had to play a hunch and go for the most obvious answer. Yoku dekimashita!
- *Boku no Sexual Harassment*. No! She played an office lady who gets rejected by the men in her office. Why? Because all the men are dating each other!

2. The scarce emus in Japan

- ■ **Entertainment Magic Unit**. Yup. Who knew?
- **Excellent Musical Understanding**. If they had a little more understanding, their songs would hit the charts!
- **Emergency Medical Unit**. Get your head fixed! No!
- **Enter My Universe**. You tried to enter their universe, only to find it was locked because it is the wrong answer!

3. Strange things other than Sarah

- **Shinji from *Evangelion***. Hmmm . . . you must not know Megumi Ogata at all because this is her most well-known role. You have her to thank for Shinji's bouts of depression and freaking out.
- **Young Mamoru from *Sailor Moon***. Sorry. Megumi has a penchant for young boys and this one is no exception (uh, let me rephrase that . . .).
- ■ **Akito Hayama from the *Child's Toy* TV series**. Correct! Actually, Megumi Ogata DID play this voice . . .

for the OAV series when Sana-chan happened to be blonde. For all of Sana-chan's money, I guess she ran out of peroxide.

- **Young Keiichi from *Ah! My Goddess***. Cute little Keiichi? Yup, Megumi voiced this character too.

It must suck to be known as "the other Megumi."

4. The human memory jukebox

- ■ **Ryōga**. Correct! He sang "Uketotte My Song" and I remember someone playing it over and over again just so she could hear Ryōga sing the words "I love you" to her. Man, this girl needs help.
- **Ranma-chan (Female Ranma)**. Nope. Ranma-chan had nothing to do with track 3, except maybe pretending to be an ardent admirer of Ryōga in order to get him to blush like heck.
- **Nabiki**. Sorry. Nabiki, for what it's worth, sang some really cute tracks on this CD. They're my favorite. Aside from Ryōga's, of course.
- **Akane**. Nope. Not Akane. She was busy knocking the stuffing out of Ranma's head for calling her, yet again, an unsexy tomboy. Well, not in the way of Red Asphalt when I say knock the stuffing out of his head, but you get my meaning.

5. Dun-da-da-da

- ■ **April 1, 1998**. April fools! She DID get married on this day to the regret of fanboys everywhere. Although there are no legal things about just marrying a voice, since that is what a lot of people know her for. Forget her! Just marry the voice!
- **March 30, 1998**. Hmmm. . . . I wonder why no one's here at the wedding yet? It's the right place, right? But it's the wrong date!
- **November 14, 1998**. What? Still in denial?
- **She's not married! She's not! She can't be! Noooooooo!** Oh yes she is. Get over it!

Hey Where's the Rest of Sailor Moon?

With the exception of Sailor Pluto, America has not had the official privilege of meeting any of the other Sailor Scouts outside of the core team of Sailor Moon, Mercury, Mars, Jupiter, and Venus because only the first two seasons of the five seasons of *Sailor Moon* have been dubbed into English.

There is a reason for this.

In the third season of *Sailor Moon*, Sailor Uranus and Sailor Neptune are introduced. These two women are lovers. Sailor Uranus acts and dresses masculine, so much so that Minako and Usagi fawned over her because she made such a handsome boy. In Japan this can be depicted in young children's anime without causing much hassle. Not so in America.

1. I'm not half the man I used to be

If Nuriko from *Fushigi Yūgi* was your favorite character of all time and you wanted to get a CD of the same voice, which of these would be your most logical choice?

- *Boogie Queen*
- *Osakana Penguin*
- *Caramel Pop*
- *Mega Babe*

2. March madness

Let's see if you are truly a *seiyū guru* (or a person way too obsessed with the lives of Japanese voice actors to have a life). Which of the following seiyū was not born in March?

- Megumi Hayashibara
- Chieko Honda
- Shiina Hekiru
- Megumi Ogata

3. Sounds like chicken

In the song "Yasashii Ii Ko ni Narenai" (I Don't Wanna Be a Nice Girl), how many times does Akane say *baka*, not counting the 0.5 in some people's calculations?

- 64
- 96
- 128
- 156

4. A drug or a virus?

THTC is a band name made up of the male seiyū from what series?

- *Gundam Wing*
- *Here Is Greenwood*
- *Saint Seiya*
- *Fushigi Yūgi*

5. Final seiyū/music question

Last question!

Rica Fukami is a seiyū who has a CD called *La _____*. It has one English song on it (and the one-word name of the song is in the title). What is so significant about that song?

- ANSWER: _____

The last episode of the third season of *Sailor Moon* in America was not Rini reuniting with Queen Serenity but a teaser episode that included Sailor Uranus and Neptune shrouded in mystery. Although the story had a perfect ending up to this point, this episode let *Sailor Moon* fans know was that more *Sailor Moon* lay ahead.

Will these later episodes ever become available? *Sailor Moon* fans already organized once, as SOS (Save Our Sailors), to bring back the show to American TV after it was cancelled part way through its second season. The *Sailor Moon* movies that include Sailor Uranus and Neptune are now available in the U.S.. There is definitely a market for it, as large numbers of fans must still be wondering, "What happened to all the Sailor Scouts after Sailor Jupiter and before Sailor Pluto?"

1. I'm not half the man I used to be

- ■ **Boogie Queen**. *Boogie Queen* is an album by Chika Sakamoto, who plays the voice of Nuriko. I guess "Boogie Queen" is kinda appropriate for Nuriko, ne?

- **Osakana Penguin**. No. This was done by Junko Iwao, who played Key in *Key the Metal Idol* and Kikuko Inoue, who played Kasumi in *Ranma*.

- **Caramel Pop**. This is done by Yuri Shiratori, who plays the Japanese voice of Alice in *Please Save My Earth*, or more popularly as Mokona on *Magic Knight Rayearth*.

- **Mega Babe**. Mega Babe belongs to Noriko Hidaka who plays Akane, Ranma's fiancée, which according to Ranma is NOT a babe . . .

2. March madness

- **Megumi Hayashibara**. For shame! You did not know that the big M herself was born on March 30? What kind of a Seiyū fan are you anyway?

- **Chieko Honda**. Nope, this young lady who did the voice for Miya Igarashi in *Here Is Greenwood* was born on March 28.

- **Shiina Hekiru**. Uh-uh. This lady who played Hikaru in *Magic Knight Rayearth* was born March 12.

- ■ **Megumi Ogata**. Correct! This young man . . . I mean, er, lady, was born on June 6. Which means that you have time to get her a present. A role as a female character, I suppose?

3. Sounds like chicken

- • **64**. Much higher.

- • **96**. Higher.

- ■ **128**. Sugoi! I don't know whether to be proud or scared that you know this. . . . But thanks to Young Yoo and Soung Lee for actually counting and giving me this question.

- • **156**. Lower.

4. A drug or a virus?

- • **Gundam Wing**. Tell me why . . . this group of boys aren't actually performing somewhere when boy bands are really hot right now?

- • **Here Is Greenwood**. They actually sing well together, but this Greenwood group is not THTC.

- • **Saint Seiya**. Action figures by day, nightclub singers at night! No.

- ■ **Fushigi Yūgi**. If you thought about it carefully, you would know that THTC stands for Tamahome, Hotohori, Tasuki, and Chichiri; four of the characters from *Fushigi Yūgi*. Although if this were a sickness, I don't think some girls would mind catching the fever!

5. Final seiyū/music question

- ■ **Venus**. And the significance? Rica Fukami is the voice actress behind Sailor Venus in the *Sailor Moon* series. Eat your heart out, Bananarama!

Watch Carefully

Are you pretty observant? Can you look for details? Do you know when something is mispelled or can you spot bad English a mile away? Did you know "mispelled" was just misspelled? Try your powers of observation on these questions.

1. Life can be heck on earth

On the American versions of *Dragonball Z*, the word "HELL" on the demons' tanktops has been edited out. What "word" now graces the front of their tanktops and probably will if Miller's Outpost gets a hold of them?

- HFIL
- IELI
- BBII
- HEII

2. The power of suggestion

In the second *Fatal Fury* movie, when Mai Shiranui watches Joe Higashi's kickboxing match, what word is printed across her chest?

- Milk
- Bazookas
- Melons
- Tomatoes

3. Butt out

Deciding to show your butt is a big deal in movies, but in anime, it's an ordinary thing. Then again, how excited can people be about anime characters showing their behinds on the screen? You'd be surprised. Sad, isn't it? In *Ranma 1/2*, only one male character's butt was fully exposed on screen (no side views or simple cracks; the whole thing) by the time the second season rolled around. Whose?

- Ranma
- Ryōga
- Mousse
- Kunō

4. Near, far, wherever you are . . .

The ladies of *Mahō Tsukai Tai* are aboard the *Titanic*. The *Titanic* hits an iceberg and sinks. The ladies are panicking because there are three life jackets and four ladies. Based on chest size, which of these ladies has her own set of "floatation devices?"

- Sae
- Akane
- Nanaka
- Miyama

5. Open wide!

One thing that is great about anime is the opening sequences. There are some shows that I watch only for the opening sequences because they are done so well. But if the animation in the opening is supposed to compensate for the crappy animation of the actual show, I won't be so forgiving . . .

In the first opening animation sequence in the American version of *Pokemon*, which Pokemon is NOT featured?

- Raichu
- Lapras
- Oddish
- Cubone

1. Life can be heck on earth

■ **HFIL.** It's correct. Although I don't know what HFIL is supposed to mean. Is it supposed to be like a FILA brand or something?

• **IELI.** What's an IELI? For that matter, what's a HFIL? Sorry.

• **BBII.** Awww . . . My little BBII! I don't think a hulking weightlifting demon is going to be wearing something like that.

• **HEII.** Heii! L'eggo my eggo! Nope.

Only in America would we create a combination of letters that could not even form a word or have some sense of meaning and wear it on our bodies. I would say the Japanese, but they are better at this than we are.

2. The power of suggestion

■ **Milk**. Correct. I noticed that this little detail hasn't escaped your attention!

• **Bazookas.** Wow! Talk about merely stating the obvious!

• **Melons.** Sounds like some word Mai would wear, but just not to the kickboxing event.

• **Tomatoes.** Umm . . . I guess melons would be more appropriate . . .

Milk does a body good. . . .

3. Butt Out

• **Ranma**. We are more likely to see Ranma's groin than his behind, but he's much more of a tease when he turns into a girl

■ **Ryōga**. Poor Ryōga has the terrible habit of losing his clothes. Well, for the ladies, not too terrible . . .

• **Mousse**. Mousee has a pretty well developed upper body that he'll show off, but the nether region is off-limits except to Shampoo.

• **Kunō.** Kunō? Show off his proud, regal buttocks? He can probably be suckered into it if you stroke his ego enough, but he hasn't flashed it out yet.

Well, I bet all that walking and getting lost has probably done Ryōga wonders for that area . . .

4. Near, far wherever you are . . .

• **Sae.** Um . . . Sae doesn't even wear much of a training bra . . .

• **Akane.** She certainly likes to show off her body, but she doesn't have the biggest chest in the group.

• **Nanaka.** No, that's incorrect too. Get her a life jacket!

■ **Miyama.** Correct! The head of the manga club bounces everywhere she goes, causing nosebleeds among all the young men everywhere. And of course, since she doesn't need a life jacket, she'll be the first to jump ship!

I heard Miyama has been accepted to a private American college. Miyama is now known as the "Hunchfront of Notre Dame."

5. Open wide!

• **Raichu.** Nope. Raichu is there lunging at Pikachu. Raichu isn't that cute. No wonder Ash doesn't want to evolve him!

• **Lapras.** Lapras, the ferry boat monster of the *Pokemon* world is definitely in the opening sequence.

■ **Oddish.** This cute little plant with legs is not anywhere in the opening sequence of *Pokemon*. I guess it would not stay in one place long enough to have it filmed.

• **Cubone.** This little shy Pokemon who hides behind a skull is also in the opening sequence. Although he's still camera shy.

1. Call your psychic friend!

I always wanted to run a psychic hotline but I could foresee that it wouldn't work . . .

After Yūsuke was resurrected in *Yū Yū Hakusho* (Poltergeist Report), he encountered a fortune teller in an alley who saw big things in his future. What did the fortune teller wear on the top of her head?

- A pentacle
- A Star of David
- A cross
- Golden arches from a fast-food restaurant

2. Wild jaguars

You are an eccentric millionaire (you wish!). You own five Jaguars and decide to paint them in different colors. You decide to paint them in the Shinesman team colors because they are sophisticated and subdued, although not very heroic. Although your car is not built like *Speed Racer*'s Mach 5 so you don't particularly care to be heroic. Anyway, the colors are so subdued you almost forget which colors are Shinesman colors. Which of these is not a Shinesman Team color?

- Moss green
- Sepia
- Salmon pink
- Turquoise

3. They're not scars . . . they're really long beauty marks

Scars can ruin a modeling career. But the following guys have never had problems attracting a flock of women like seagulls to a piece of bread. Okay, so maybe they aren't exactly ripping their clothes off, but scars make them a part of what they are.

Which of these characters do not have a scar on their face?

- Chichiri from *Fushigi Yūgi*
- Mitsuru from *Here Is Greenwood*
- Kenshin from *Rurōni Kenshin*
- Captain Harlock from *Starblazers*

4. Da plane! Da plane!

Sae from *Mahō Tsukai Tai* is a very energetic girl. But as she gets older, she gets more practical. She watches the anime *Tattoo Master* and decides getting a tattoo of the shape that unlocks her power would be handy somewhere on her body because she doesn't always have a pen and paper ready on hand. What tattoo would unlock Sae's full power and freak out her mom?

- A spiral
- A triangle
- A heart
- A teddy bear

5. Itsy bitsy teenie weenie

There is something unnerving about any piece of clothing that has less material than a handkerchief. It is even more unnerving if women in anime actually use it as formal wear. . . .

In the second *Fatal Fury* movie, when the Fatal Fury team goes to explore a beach cave, who is wearing the skimpiest outfit?

- Terry Bogard
- Andy Bogard
- Joe Higashi
- Mai Shiranui

1. Call your psychic friend!

- **A pentacle.** Nope. You're evil, dude.

- **A Star of David.** Nope. Not this either.

- ■ **A cross.** Good job! Fortune tellers usually do not have crosses attached to the top of their robes like that, but then again, why are skaters wearing the yin-yang sign?

- **Golden arches from a fast food restaurant.** No! She's telling fortunes, not tossing fries!

I can see another thing in your future . . . ummm . . . you are going to watch anime sometime within the next month. Am I psychic or what?

2. Wild jaguars

- **Moss green**. Sorry! This subdued forest green color is also a Shinesman color

- **Sepia.** Nope. This color used to take pictures of your great-grandparents is indeed a Shinesman color.

- **Salmon pink.** Uh-uh. Salmon pink is a Shinesman color, with none of the smell!

- ■ **Turquoise.** Correct. This color is not a Shinesman color. But it is most of the jewelry that you'll find at an Indian trading outpost.

Picking Shinesman colors for your Jaguars does not make you eccentric. It's taking the time to find jaguars who would be willing to be painted without trying to kill you that does.

3. They're not scars . . .they're really long beautymarks

- **Chichiri from _Fushigi Yūgi_**. On his smiling mask, he has no scars, but under it, he hides a handsome mug as well as a scar over his eye.

- ■ **Mitsuru from _Here Is Greenwood_**. Correct! Not only is his face ever so pretty but all scars heal in less than a minute on his face.

- **Kenshin from _Rurōni Kenshin_**. Wow, you must have no idea who Kenshin is, do you? Kenshin would be high on this list of men who have scars, especially since he has two of them crossed on his cheek!

- **Captain Harlock from _Starblazers_.** My guess is that you're not old enough to remember _Starblazers_ and that's why you guessed this one, right?

Everyone wants to either be Mitsuru or date him. This guy is popular, pretty, has a face that heals all scars and has to eat a lot just to keep that process up. Dang, if that was true for everyone, some fanboys would be some of the most beautiful men on earth!

4. Da plane! Da plane!

- ■ **A spiral.** Yes, the magic spiral is the key to unlocking Sae's power. Which also makes fishcakes in your udon magical as well.

- **A triangle.** No, this is Takeo-kun's shape that unlocks his power. And I bet Aburatsubo-senpai does not mind trying to unlock him while he's at it.

- **A heart.** Sentimental and probably cute on Sae, but it's wrong.

- **A teddy bear.** Let me be your teddy bear! I'll be cute and adorable and remind you of Sae's friend, Jeff-kun, and I'll keep you warm in bed!

But where is Sae going to put the tattoo where she'll have easy access to it, where her mom can't see it, and where boys will stop asking her to show it off so they'll get a free peep show?

5. Itsy bitsy teeny weenie

- **Terry Bogard.** He wears the same thing wherever he goes! Even weddings! I doubt it.

- **Andy Bogard.** Sorry. Incorrect. Wrong. No.

- ■ **Joe Higashi.** Correct! All he is wearing is . . . bikini briefs. He does not have to moon anyone by taking his shorts down. All he has to do is turn around and . . .

- **Mai Shiranui.** You wish, fanboy! Just because she bounces does not mean that she's going to wear a headband over her . . . body.

If Joe Higashi needs to wear anything skimpier than bikini briefs, might I suggest a black dot, large enough to cover his itsy bitsy teeny weenie . . .

1. Oh my God!

In *Haunted Junction*, Haruto Hōjō tries to submit his resignation from the Holy Student Council as he always does. However, another evil school spirit has come and Haruto has to take care of the situation. But when he attempts to resign, he puts six of the school badges on his uniform into the resignation letter to show how serious he is. He is stuck with the badge that was originally the center badge of the seven badge formation. Which character can Haruto only summon now?

- The girl in the mirror
- Toilet Hanako
- The large foot
- The principal

2. Why do men have nipples?

In which of the following anime do the men have no nipples?

- *Dragonball Z*
- *Video Girl Ai*
- *Ranma 1/2*
- *Kizuna*

3. Rephrase: Why do cartoon men have no nipples?

I never understood what is wrong with drawing them. I mean, they occur naturally and everyone has them. Except on Robin's armor in the *Batman and Robin* movie, now that was plain weird . . .

In one of the *Fushigi Yūgi* CDs, the characters are drawn in white silk pajamas and holding flowers. Which male character is shirtless?

- Tamahome
- Chichiri
- Tasuki
- Nuriko

4. Refusing to let go

Well, no jokes here. When you're dealing with an anime that features the aftermath of World War II in Japan, it's a little difficult to find something amusing. In *Grave of the Fireflies*, what does the main character, Seita, hold on to at the end of his life?

- A picture of his sister
- A crumpled letter
- A tin full of ashes
- A dirty, ragged bunny slipper

5. Natural talent

You decide to join the basketball team. For good luck, instead of deciding to wear Michael Jordan's number on your uniform, you wear Sakuragi Hanamichi's number to indicate that you are a natural athlete. So what number are you wearing when you go from that slam dunk (and find that you fouled because you forgot to dribble the ball)?

- 10
- 15
- 18
- 23

1. Oh my God!

- **The girl in the mirror.** Take a good look in the mirror and what do you see? A loser! Wrong!

- **Toilet Hanako.** Great for fanservice and although she would be nice to summon right now, she's not the one that's coming to irriatate Haruto right now.

- **The large foot.** Ack! Bigfoot's alive! And he's eating a peanut butter and banana sandwich! No.

- ■ **The principal.** Yup. As annoying as he is, the principal is the only one Haruto's got. But at least if the Principal doesn't get summoned, Haruto can finally resign without any objections.

2. Why do men have nipples?

- *Dragonball Z.* Nope. If a *DBZ* character takes off his shirt and they aren't there, then he has to be an impostor!

- *Video Girl Ai.* In one of the omake (gift) scenes, Yōta and Takeshi are posing nude together and they're right there! (I'd rather not explain how they got into that position right now).

- ■ *Ranma 1/2.* Yup. All those buff bodies and nary a "nyūrin." But they are suddenly there if the character is female. Hmmm ...

- *Kizuna.* As a standard rule, in any anime where two men are making out, you need something to "tittilate" the audience.

3. Rephrase: Why do cartoon men have no nipples?

- **Tamahome.** He's wearing an open shirt, but he still has a shirt on. Sorry.

- **Chichiri.** Well, he has never taken his shirt off during the OAV series, but as one FY fan said, wait until you see him in the OAV! Then she fainted. Go figure.

- ■ **Tasuki.** Yes, Tasuki is Mister Manly in the *Fushigi Yūgi* series. So manly that he can wear earrings and still smell of masculinity. Especially after he's had cabbage.

- **Nuriko.** Nuriko, the drag queen? I don't think so.

4. Refusing to let go

- **A picture of his sister.** Nope. It wasn't this, although it was a good guess.

- **A crumpled letter.** Uh-uh.

- ■ **A tin full of ashes.** Yes. Interestingly enough, you see the end of Seita's life at the beginning of the movie. Although it would be too much to tell you what those ashes were made of.

- **A dirty ragged, bunny slipper.** Ha ha, vain attempt at humor. Nope.

Like I said, it's fairly difficult to joke on this question. I remember after watching this on screen, no one was in the mood to stick around for *Kimagure Orange Road* and watch Kyōsuke get torn between two lovers.

5. Natural talent

- ■ **10.** Alright, you got it! You can celebrate! Until you realize that he's been rejected 50 times by women and you have to wonder why you chose the number in the first place.

- **15.** Sorry. Actually, I'm not sorry ... you were just taking a stab here, weren't you?

- **18.** Nope. Not this one.

- **23.** Read the question carefully! I said like Sakuragi, not Jordan!

All you have to do is count the fingers on your hands to remind you of this number. Just be happy if you're a forgetful guy that your number isn't 21! (You have to think below the waistband for this one ...)

"Sub"marines vs. "Dub"marines: The Classic Anime Fan Battle

One of the oldest battles in anime fandom revolves around one question: "Which is better? Subtitled anime or anime dubbed in English?" The argument seems trivial but it has become complicated (and tiresome).

Sorry to bring it up again ...

SUBTITLED ANIME

Advantages: If you are a student of Japanese, subtitled anime helps you get a feel for how the language is naturally spoken (although people learning Japanese should be wary of actually using "anime" language before native speakers). Japanese cinema is subtitled; why not anime?

Disadvantages: You are at the mercy of subtitlers. You are relying on their interpretations, and if they are

1. What's under there?

In *Akazukin Cha-Cha* (Red Riding Hood Cha-Cha), what does Shiine-chan wear under his robe?

- Boxers
- Briefs
- Lace panties
- Nothing, except then the wind picks up, a censored bar in the appropriate area

2. Idol hands

You are a press member covering Mima's last idol singing performance in *Perfect Blue*. Based on the outfit she was wearing when she announced that she was leaving the music scene, which of these captions would be the most fitting beneath her picture?

- Pretty in Pink
- Love Is Blue
- Purple Rain
- Yellow Submarine

3. Oh, I watch these for the plot . . .

No big joke here, except the one about you if you actually get this right! In the infamous anime *Urotsukidōji*, which character did the Demon attack first when he awakens in the first episode?

- A schoolgirl
- A nurse
- A schoolteacher
- An office lady

4. Idol hands (part 2)

Thank goodness idols have choreographers. The last thing I want to see is a woman clutching her microphone so tightly that in her nervousness, it slips out of her hand, falls into the stage, causes her distress, forces her into early retirement, and is suddenly featured in VH1's "Where Are They Now?" In *Idol Project*, what was Mimu's entry number?

- 48
- 36
- 44
- 32

5. And yet another man without . . .

In *Nadesico*, Akiko Tenkawa takes off his shirt and embarrasses which character to the point that she is unable to interact with him?

- Erina
- Yurika
- Ines
- Jun

wrong. . . . Timing subtitles is critical because it must appear as the dialogue is said, stay long enough for a person to read it without rushing, and allow the audience to see the action. Correct spelling and grammar are especially important here.

DUBBED ANIME

Advantages: If anime is English-dubbed, it can get airplay on television. Dubbed anime is better for younger audiences, and there is no struggle to understand the dialogue. Because Japanese is a punny language, you aren't going to miss the puns (unless you know Japanese).

Disadvantages: Even though the puns are in English, creating English equivalents is difficult. Japanese dialogue must be translated *and* the English dialogue must fit the mouth movements of characters, so the execution can be awkward. English voice actors for the characters must be chosen carefully; otherwise the voice will seem off or even grating.

One sub supporter said he wanted to see no dubs because subbed and dubbed tell different stories, even if the episode is the same. But as another person said, the stories told by the English sub and the original nontranslated Japanese are just as different. This classic battle of subs vs. dubs has nothing to do with the story or content but is really all about how the story is told and, most important, how people want to have it presented to them.

1. What's under there?

■ **Boxers.** Yup, Shiine-chan wears a pair of clean white boxers. At least they're clean when he's not nervous.

· **Briefs.** Nope. Like his choice in clothes, briefs would be a little too "inhibiting."

· **Lace panties.** I imagine there is a fetish for little boys wearing lace panties, but that fetish is definitely not entertained in this show!

· **Nothing, except when the wind picks up, a censored bar in the appropriate areas.** Uh . . . no.

I always wondered why is it called a "pair of underwear" when there's actually one item? Why try to make it sound like a two-for-one bargain when everyone has to wear them anyway?

2. Idol hands

■ **Pretty in Pink.** Yup. Mima's pink costume is the epitome of adorable idol outfits with enough sugar to rot your teeth.

· **Love Is Blue.** The fans may be blue that Mima is leaving, but Mima's costume isn't.

· **Purple Rain.** There may have been a rain of tears when Mima "chose" to leave the singing scene, but none of it stained her dress purple.

· **Yellow Submarine.** Well, wearing yellow is like eating a stick of butter, it does tend to make people look fat. . . .

And what caption will you use for her nude photos???

3. Oh, I watch these for the plot . . .

· **A schoolgirl.** Um, I doubt that this would make it to America at all . . .

■ **A nurse.** Well, this demon definitely wanted to play doctor . . . by exploring her insides!

· **A schoolteacher.** Yes, I bet the demon could teach her a few things . . . like staying away!

· **An office lady.** It would be business as usual for the demon, but the OL was not the demon's first target.

And what better way to explore her insides than having her explode in your face?

4. Idol hands (part 2)

· **48.** Nope.

■ **36.** Yup.

· **44.** Uh-uh

· **32.** No.

What can I say? This was a pretty straightforward question . . .

5. And yet another man without . . .

■ **Erina.** Yes. Apparently, Erina finds him so studly that she blushes a lot and has to leave the room. Before her nose bleeds, of course.

· **Yurika.** Actually, I think she might be rather thrilled at the prospect!

· **Ines.** No. Ines would not be embarrassed by anything.

· **Jun.** Hey, wait a minute, Jun is a guy! Although, he is rather pretty and if you were drunk enough . . .

1. Aw, nuts!

In *Neon Genesis Evangelion*, Shinji is naked when he confronts Misato about Pen-Pen in the bath. What item covers his groin area frm our point of view after Misato takes away the beer can?

- A cup of noodles
- A plate of salami
- A box of toothpicks
- A bowl of sausages

2. Soon we'll be making another run

If you've ever been on a cruise ship or watched *Love Boat*, then you know that there are always certain people that you meet over and over again, which isn't always ideal even if you are on a singles cruise. Sure you can say there are plenty of fish in the sea, but if you mess with too many people, that's where you'll end up!

In the *Minky Momo* OAV, which character does Minky Momo NOT repeatedly meet on the bridge?

- A jogger
- A flower girl
- An older lady with a poodle
- A peanut salesman

3. It's a bird, it's a plane, it's . . . no, I think it's a bird . . .

Why do superheroes need capes to fly? And for that matter, why do superheroes wear their underwear outside their uniforms?

In the anime *Tonde Būrin*, what is Būrin?

- A tiger
- A bat
- A squirrel
- A pig

4. The popular vote

I never liked popularity contests in school because it made 1% of students feel better about themselves while everyone else feels like they suffer in

anonymity. Of course, if anything happens to them, we are allowed to laugh long and hard at their expense.

In *Touch*, how many votes did Tatsuya get in the male student popularity contest?

- He won the popularity contest by one vote
- He tied with his twin brother in the popularity contest
- He lost being the most popular guy by one vote
- He received one vote. Period.

5. For your eyes only

Only otaku who are real otaku would actually slow down a tape frame by frame on a *Tenchi Muyō* tape just to see of there is a hidden frame where Mihoshi's clothes "accidentally" disappear. But while looking for that, I found something else interesting:

In *Tenchi Muyō in Love*, which of these products is subliminally advertised?

- Reese's Pieces
- Three Musketeers
- M&Ms
- Butterfinger

© SA-RO-MW/BA-TX-SE

Who is the Japanese voice actress behind this character from *Sorcerer Hunters*?

(a) Megumi Hayashibara (b) Aya Hisakawa (c) Noriko Hidaka (d) Atsuko Tanaka

1. Aw, nuts!

- **A cup of noodles.** Noodle to cover his wet noodle? Try again.
- **A plate of salami.** Well, THIS is subtle, isn't it? But this too is wrong.
- ■ **A box of toothpicks.** Correct! And degrading . . .
- **A bowl of sausages.** If Shinji jad a "sausage" in this bowl of sausages, I don't hink anything could hide it.

2. Soon we'll be making another run

- **A jogger.** Nope. He's constantly training on the bridge. And finally stops when he crosses the finish line tape. Goodness, his legs must be tired!
- **A flower girl.** Uh-uh. The flower girl is always there, regardless of what season it is.
- **An older lady with a poodle.** Nope, she is definitely dedicated to walking that poodle, who is good enough not to do her dirty business on the bridge. And I'm referring to both of them.
- ■ **A peanut salesman.** Right! There is no peanut sales-man on that bridge. He would end up colliding with the jogger, competing against the flower girl, and bit-ten by the poodle on this busy bridge.

3. It's a bird, it's a plane, it's . . . no, I think it's a bird . . .

- **A tiger.** A flying tiger. Yeah, uh-huh, whatever.
- **A bat.** Ummm . . . not exactly original, is it? No.
- **A squirrel.** What do you think this is, *Rocky and Bull-winkle*? Uh-uh.
- ■ **A pig.** *Tonde Būrin* is about a young teenage girl who transforms into a flying pig to rescue people. I'm sur-prised Osamu Tezuka had not thought of this sooner!

4. The popular vote

- **He won the popularity contest by one vote.** Not even close.
- **He tied with his twin brother in the popularity contest.** Still not close.
- **He lost being the most popular guy by one vote.** Try even less votes.
- ■ **He received one vote. Period.** Sad but true. But at least he was not completely shut out. Then again, wouldn't this serve as a constant reminder of how unpopular he is?

5. For your eyes only

- **Reese's Pieces.** I don't about know, but Kiyone does not look like E.T.. But Tenchi does. Sorry.
- **Three Musketeers.** Kinda reminds me of Tenchi, actually. Soft on the inside and no nuts. But not the right answer.
- ■ **M&Ms.** Correct! When the spaceship Yagami was supposed to get a signal from Galaxy Police HQ, Mihoshi falls backward and food flies up in the air, including a few frames of M&Ms.
- **Butterfinger.** No one better lay a finger on my But-terfinger. Although every woman in the show wants to lay hers on Tenchi's. Nope.

You guys are REAL otaku! I'm so proud!

■ *Answer to picture puzzle:* (a) Megumi Hayashibara. When in doubt about a female voice, assume it's Megumi. Some fans do.

Random A

These are questions that I could not fit anywhere else. How convenient!

1. How do you say Montezuma's Revenge in Japanese?

In an *Animaniacs* comic book, Dot goes to Japan while a character from Japan comes to the Warner Brothers. The character that comes from Japan is a parody of:

- Hello Kitty
- Pikachu
- Astro Boy
- Totoro

2. Canon ball

Do you remember English class? (I have to know this because I'm an English major; although not a grammar major.) There were certain books that you had to read because they were part of the English Canon of Literature. For the longest time, I thought that meant that those books were insidious enough to become either torture devices or sleeping aids. But a canon actually seems to be a list of readings intended to be representative of all literature in general. In other words, it's the basic stuff one needs to know.

Now that I've bored you enough, answer this question: Which of the following anime is least likely to fall under the North American anime canon?

- *Ranma 1/2*
- *Sailor Moon*
- *CLAMP School*
- *Tenchi Muyō*

3. Spoon!

In *Pokemon,* why does Kadabra fight with a spoon in his hand?

- He tries to scoop out the eyes of his opponents
- He likes to eat while fighting
- He uses it to show he is psychic
- He can fling sludge at his enemies with it

4. Two, two, two weapons in one!

What is the name of Squall Leonheart's weapon from *Final Fantasy VIII*?

- Boomer Knife
- Shootstabber
- Gunblade
- Sling Blade

5. Living gods

Which of these characters is NOT named after a god?

- Ashura-O
- Kamui Shirō
- Athena Asamiya
- Sailor Pluto

1. How do you say Montezuma's Revenge in Japanese?

■ **Hello Kitty**. And one line from that infamous comic, "I have no mouth but I want to scream," is probably the most memorable lines in that or any comic book in a long while.

• **Pikachu**. Pikachu meets the Warner Brothers? That's already been done on the WB.

• **Astro Boy**. "I will succeed!" in getting you to get to the right answer!

• **Totoro**. Even though Totoro is a kids' anime, isn't he actually quite scary looking?

2. Canon ball

• *Ranma 1/2*. And how could you not love the sex-changing premise and twisted romances in *Ranma 1/2* that makes it one of the most well-known series today.

• *Sailor Moon*. What rock have you crawled under not to know *Sailor Moon*?

■ **CLAMP School**. Correct. No one needs to know anything about CLAMP school before he or she can call himself an "anime fan." Although it would be rather pathetic if they knew nothing about CLAMP.

• *Tenchi Muyō*. For a little geek, he is quite well-known in anime fandom.

3. Spoon!

• **He tries to scoop out the eyes of his opponents**. Ewwww . . .

• **He likes to eat while fighting**. Hey, if fighting makes you hungry, then why not? The answer is still wrong, though.

■ **He uses it to show he is psychic**. So what do spoons have to do with being psychic? A famous psychic claimed that he can bend spoons using only the power of this mind, and that is the association that the spoons have with psychic ability. And he can still scoop out eyes if it does not work.

• **He can fling sludge at his enemies with it**. Nope. Not unless he produces his own sludge (I wouldn't want to know how he does it, though.)

4. Two, two, two weapons in one!

• **Boomer Knife**. Nope, that's not what Squall calls his weapon (in public).

• **Shootstabber**. Nope. That's not the given name of the weapon either.

■ **Gunblade**. If you did not get this, then you obviously did not play the game. Go play it! The story is good! The art is great! Squall is a hunk and Rinoa's a babe! What's stopping you?

• **Sling Blade**. Um-hmm. Um-hmm. Uh-uh. Nope.

5. Living gods

• **Ashura-O**. Sorry. Ashura is a famous god that has six arms. Hmmm . . . or is that Vishna that has six arms? Or was I drunk when I saw those statues?

■ **Kamui Shirō**. His name may have something to do with "god," but no god's name is actually in it.

• **Athena Asamiya**. Athena is the goddess of wisdom. If you were as smart as her, you wouldn't have picked this answer, would you?

• **Sailor Pluto**. All the planets are named after Roman gods so that answer is incorrect.

The "Pokemon" Incident

On December 16, 1997, about 700 people in Japan, mostly young children, were afflicted by seizures. The seizures, called "photosensitive epilepsy," were triggered by a five-second shot of Pikachu with flashing red eyes. Most adults instinctively blinked during this scene, but some children did not. Since then, warnings have been placed on all episodes of the anime in Japan. When *Pokemon* was brought to the U.S., care was taken to prevent similar outbreaks. Flashes of light were notably dimmed, and repeating patterns of light or strobing were edited so that they slowed down or appeared still. The original offending episode will not be aired in the U.S.

After the *Pokemon* Incident, anime was attacked for its graphic violence and sexual content (although *Pokemon* has neither of these). All this negativity meant, however, that when *Pokemon* was picked up for U.S. broadcast, the announcement made the news. With the popularity in the United States at that time of both the digital pet Tamagotchi and the cute and collectable

1. Show us some leg!

Which of these girls do not fight in a skirt?

- Jun (*Gatchaman*)
- Fūko (*Flame of Recca*)
- Kaoru (*Rurōni Kenshin*)
- Makoto (*Sailor Moon*)

2. School daze

In the American version of *Sailor Moon*, what is the name of Serena's junior high school?

- Crisscross Junior High
- Crossroads Junior High
- Crossstick Junior High
- Crossfire Junior High

3. Is that your car? How impressive .

In *You're Under Arrest*, What is the name of Miyuki's famed mini-patrol car?

- NRA Turbo
- GSX Turbo
- Mini Patrol 4
- Today

4. Dynamite duos

Which of these pairs are NOT twin siblings?

- Tatsuya and Kazuya
- Mitsuru and Shinobu
- Kurumi and Minami
- Subaru and Hokuto

5. Before there was CLAMP School

Before the series known as *CLAMP School* was picked up by Animevillage, what did many fans and fansubbers call it?

- ANSWER: CLAMP _____

Beanie Babies, *Pokemon* had great timing. Add in the interesting concept of "Beanie Babies meets Street Fighter," and it's no wonder that *Pokemon* has become such a megahit.

Regardless of translation, there is one thing that is always a welcome import: cuteness. If Pikachu had looked like a rabid bulldog, would *Pokemon* ever have done so well?

Here's a simple quiz to test if you know your *Pokemon*. What do each of these Pokemon evolve into?

A. Bulbasaur	G. Ponyta
B. Charmander	H. Pikachu
C. Jigglypuff	I. Machop
D. Caterpie	J. Magikarp
E. Ekans	K. Kakuna
F. Staryu	L. Hitmonchan

Think that was easy? Now give the American name for these Japanese Pokemon:

A. Parasu	G. Purin
B. Staamii	H. Hitokage
C. Zubatto	I. Rokon
D. Aabokku	J. Zenigane
E. Kyatapii	K. Pippi
F. Doudou	L. Wanrikii

ANSWERS

A: Evolved Pokemon. B: Ivysaur. C: Charmeleon. D: Wigglytuff. E: Metapod. F: Arbok. G: Stamie. H: Rapidash. I: Raichu. J: Machoke. K: Gyrados. L: Beedrill. M: Trick question! Hitmonchan does not evolve.

JAPANESE POKEMON:
A: Paras. B: Starmie. C: Zubat. D: Arbok. E: Caterpie. F: Doudo. G: Jigglypuff. H: Charmander. I: Vulpix. J: Squirtle. K: Clefairy. L: Machop.

1. Show us some leg!

- **Jun (*Gatchaman*)**. Hey, in sentai groups, sometimes that is the ONLY way to tell who is a girl!

- **Fūko (*Flame of Recca*)**. Nope. Luckily, her skirt is flame retardant; otherwise Recca will have a hard time in a fight!

- ■ **Kaoru (*Rurōni Kenshin*)**. Of all these women, Kaoru is the only one who does not fight in a skirt. Which means that she can kick high and feel safe in her chastity.

- **Makoto (*Sailor Moon*)**. Sailor Senshi fighting in something other than a skirt? Watch the fanboys protest loudly!

2. School daze

- **Crisscross Junior High**. Nope, that is incorrect.

- ■ **Crossroads Junior High**. Correct. "Crossroads" implies that Serena has a decision to make in life. Andrew or Tuxedo Mask?

- **Crossstick Junior High**. Nope, that is also wrong.

- **Crossfire Junior High**. A junior high taught by Pat Buchanan? Perish the thought....

3. Is that your car? How impressive . . . and illegally parked

- **NRA Turbo**. Watch as this entire car turns into a big friggin' gun!

- **GSX Turbo**. Nope. Not this car.

- **Mini Patrol 4**. I guess this the car that is close enough to the ground where you are able to see up women's mini skirts . . .

- ■ **Today**. Perfect name, isn't it? If you bailed out on work in the company car and someone asked you if you went to work, all you have to do is say, "I rode in Today . . . "

4. Dynamite duos

- **Tatsuya and Kazuya**. Nope, these two are twin brothers in the anime *Touch*.

- ■ **Mitsuru and Shinobu**. Correct. These two are just roommates, or at least that's what they want us to think.

- **Kurumi and Minami**. Nope. These are Kyōsuke's younger twin sisters. Also Espers.

- **Subaru and Hokuto**. Well, these are twin siblings and they look quite alike. If you haven't read *Tokyo Babylon*, the closest thing is *Shakespeare's Twelfth Night*.

5. Before there was CLAMP School

■ **CLAMP Campus Detectives**

Why not THIS title? It sounds better, it's a more accurate translation, and to top it all off, it's what the Anime Web Turnpike still calls it! (That is if it has not changed by now).

1. No no Goto

Which of the following anime series has Kenji Goto NOT done the character designs for?

- *Martian Successor Nadesico*
- *Sorcerer Hunters*
- *Hyper Police*
- *Haunted Junction*

2. A city in Florida

In which of these anime series is the word "Jupiter" not mentioned (as a significant word)?

- *Sailor Moon*
- *One Pound Gospel*
- *Martian Successor Nadesico*
- *Ai no Kusabi*

3. Things on pointy sticks

What does Arale-chan in *Dr. Slump* like to run around and play with?

- A chocolate-covered banana
- A roasted marshmallow
- A severed doll's head
- Poop

4. Anime rehab

What is the best way to describe *Kodomo no Omocha* (Child's Toy) to an anime junkie who's never heard of it before?

- *Ranma 1/2* on crack
- *Evangelion* on depressants
- *Tenchi Muyō* on LSD
- *Marmalade Boy* on speed

5. The otaku in *Otaku no Video*

You would have to be a rather dedicated otaku to get this one ... Who is the first anime character quoted in the elevator scene of *Otaku no Video*?

- Char
- Harlock
- Doraemon
- Astro Boy

Here is a cute pic of young Subaru Sumeragi from *Tokyo Babylon*. What is the name of the outfit he is wearing?

(a) Shikifuku (b) Gomi (c) Kitana (d) "Murray"

1. No no Goto

- *Martian Successor Nadesico*. "You get to burning" yourself for getting this wrong!

- *Sorcerer Hunters*. A little bit of Tira Misu in my life, a little bit of Chocolate by my side . . . Yup, Goto did do the designs here; therefore, you've got to be wrong.

- *Hyper Police Catgirl*. Police with too much caffeine, on the next Oprah! Uh-uh.

- ■ *Haunted Junction*. I guess the concept was too scary for him to tackle . . .

2. A city in Florida

- *Sailor Moon*. Hello! Sailor Jupiter! Duh!

- ■ *One Pound Gospel*. Correct. The name "Jupiter" is not significant here.

- *Martian Successor Nadesico*. You'll find out soon enough how the planet Jupiter is involved with this story.

- *Ai no Kusabi*. In here, the name of the god-like computer is "Jupiter."

3. Things on pointy sticks

- **A chocolate covered banana**. Need something long and hard to stick in your mouth? Try these! They're delicious!

- **A roasted marshmallow**. Roasted marshmallows can only stay on a stick for so long because they get icky.

- **A severed doll's head**. How disturbing. How incorrect.

- ■ **Poop**. Arale-chan from *Dr. Slump* has a habit of playing with poop. How will they get THAT past the censors? Howdy-ho!

4. Anime rehab

- *Ranma 1/2* **on crack**. *Ranma 1/2* is already on crack! What are you talking about?

- *Evangelion* **on depressants**. More depressing than Eva? Do you have a death wish?

- *Tenchi Muyō* **on LSD**. Let's not freak out people too much here . . .

- ■ *Marmalade Boy* **on Speed**. Correct. Sana (who is supposed to be Miki's equivalent) is so full of energy and goes so fast that she just needs to be tested for drugs or sanity. And Akito looks a lot like Yū, so there you go.

5. The Otaku in *Otaku no Video*

- ■ **Char**.
- **Harlock**
- **Doraemon**.
- **Astro Boy**.

Gilles told me this. I have to trust him <^.^>

---

1. Darwin theory in light speed

In *Digimon*, which of these Digimon ulitmately transforms into Angemon at its highest transformation?

- Agumon
- Gabumon
- Patamon
- Gekomon

2. The sound of music

Madoka from *Kimagure Orange Road,* Miki Kaoru from *Revolutionary Girl Utena,* and Kei from *Marmalade Boy* all play what instrument?

- ANSWER: _____

3. I say "Whip it! Whip it good!"

Who does not use a whip on a regular basis?

- Sofia of *Battle Arena Toshinden*
- Akazukin Cha-Cha's teacher
- Tiramisu from *Sorcerer Hunters*
- Mousse from *Ranma 1/2*

4. Anthropomorphs

In the anime *Kenji's Spring,* all the characters take the form of humanlike what?

- Cats
- Dogs
- Monkeys
- Birds

5. Who're you gonna call? Gunbusters!

Which of the following anime characters have the same Japanese voice actors as Noriko and Kazumi of *Aim for the Top Gunbuster*?

- Akane and Shampoo of *Ranma 1/2*
- Kiki and Jiji from *Kiki's Delivery Service*
- Jean and Nadia from *Nadia Secret of Blue Water*
- Chacha and Shiine-chan from *Akazukin Chacha*

Here in *Utena,* Miki is offering you a white rose. What does this act symbolize?

(a) He challenges you to a duel (b) He wants to be your boyfriend (c) He is apologizing to you (d) He is just offering you a rose

1. Darwin theory in light speed

- **Agumon.** Nope. Whenever this dinosaur Digimon evolves, he never manages to get rid of that construction-work cone color.

- **Gabumon.** Regardless of what people think of the dub on this anime, the writers are totally right; he DOES look like a Saint Bernard with a horn on his head. Although they omitted "while on acid."

- ■ **Patamon.** Correct. And the proof? There's a transforming Digimon toy that transforms from Patamon to Angemon! It's one of the coolest things I've ever seen!

- **Gekomon.** Nope, not this one either.

2. The sound of music

- ■ **The piano**

The piano is a wonderful instrument that many people, whose playing genius is limited to the chord or melody of "Heart and Soul," feel they are masters of.

3. I say "Whip it! Whip it good!"

- **Sofia of *Battle Arena Toshinden*.** Sofia without a whip is like milk without cookies! If you can't get milk, what good are the cookies?

- **Akazukin Cha-Cha's teacher.** Hey, bullwhips keep students in line, don't they?

- **Tiramisu from *Sorcerer Hunters*.** Tiramisu, the queen without a whip? It's like milk without cookies . . . uh, hold on, I already used that analogy. It's like peanut butter without jelly; if

it's too sticky, you're not using enough jelly. Hmm . . . that's not right either. Oh, I give up.

- ■ **Mousse from *Ranma 1/2*.** Okay, so he doesn't use a whip on a regular basis. Let's move on. I got a headache trying to make a joke in the lines above.

4. Anthropomorphs

- ■ **Cats.** Ugh! Ranma's nightmare come to life! Well, this is the correct answer.

- **Dogs.** Nope. Sorry.

- **Monkeys.** Monkeys are humanlike to begin with. There's not going to be much of a change.

- **Birds.** And have them all make Superman look like an ordinary person? Wait till you hear from Superman's agent!

5. Who're you gonna call? Gunbusters!

- ■ **Akane and Shampoo of *Ranma 1/2*.** Correct! Wow, you have really good ears! How much bigger do they have to be because you can fly?

- **Kiki and Jiji from *Kiki's Delivery Service*.** Nope.

- **Jean and Nadia from *Nadia Secret of Blue Water*.** Uh-uh.

- **Chacha and Shiine-chan from *Akazukin Chacha*.** Sorry.

The voice actors for those roles are Noriko Hidaka and Rei Sakuma. Give them a hand folks! I'm not talking about applause; get them to come to anime conventions!

■ **Answer to picture puzzle:** (d) He is just offering you a rose. Don't read too much into it! Besides, there's only so much one can do with a two-dimensional character..

The Four Immigrants Anime

Anime has not been an overnight sensation, but some peak booms—four broad waves of immigration—along the way have definitely helped its popularity in the United States. These are:

FIRST WAVE
The "Astro Boy/Speed Racer" wave (1963) Even though anime came to the United States as early as the 1910s, the first impact of anime was felt when *Tetsuwan Atom* was released as *Astro Boy* in 1963. The popularity of *Astro Boy* helped bring other anime to U.S. shores, most notably *Mach Go-Go-Go*, known in the U.S. as *Speed Racer*.

1. Do not pass gas, do not collect $200

In the second episode of *Memories*, what causes the main character to produce lethal gas from his body?

- Nervousness
- Horniness
- Sexual excitedness
- Beans, the magical fruit

2. Basara, a name that can be licensed anywhere

The name "Basara" has been used in many different ways. But in which case has it NOT been used?

- In a fighting game
- In the *Final Fantasy* series
- For a character in the *Macross* series
- In the title of a manga

3. For my beloved . . .

In *Memories*, what is the name of Eva Friedel's beloved?

- Carlo
- Miguel
- Santiago
- Bubba

4. All access

In *Kaitō Saint Tail* (Magical Thief St. Tail), the mayor awards Asuka Jr. a medal that gives him what?

- Access to inspect the entire city
- Access to the mayor's confidential files
- Access to a secret police room
- Access to adult bars and strip joints, despite his age

5. So, how would you know this?

"Ossan Harem" is a Japanese Web site dedicated to the erotic pictures of which *Final Fantasy VII* character?

- Cloud
- Barret
- Sephiroth
- Cid

SECOND WAVE

The "Starblazers/Robotech" wave (1979) In 1979, *Starblazers* was first seen on U.S. televisions, ushering in a style of science fiction more dramatic than had been seen in previous anime. *Robotech*, a conglomeration of *Macross* anime, appeared in the U.S. in 1985; also notable was *G-Force*, known as *Gatchaman* in Japan. As a result, anime fandom discovered crossovers with other sci-fi fandoms such as those for *Star Trek* and *Star Wars*.

THIRD WAVE

The "Nintendo/Sega" wave (1983). Although technically not anime, video game characters drawn in the anime art style had and continue influence the acceptance of anime in America. The more people who play fighting games like *Street Fighter II* and *Fatal Fury* and role-playing games like the long-running *Final Fantasy* series, the more exposure anime gets.

FOURTH WAVE

The "Sailor Moon/Pokemon" wave (1995). *Sailor Moon*, the first anime feature specifically targeted to young girls in the United States, brought many new female fans into existence. Around the same time came *Dragonball Z*, targeted to young boys. Then in 1998, *Pokemon* took the U.S. by storm, bringing in many younger viewers. Notable about these more recent arrivals is how highly merchandisable they are, with *Pokemon* games and *Sailor Moon* dolls.

1. Do not pass gas, do not collect $200

- ■ **Nervousness**. Which makes him a perfect candidate to escape a tax audit!

- • **Horniness**. If the average man is supposed to think about sex once every three minutes, then no one is going to be safe!

- • **Sexual excitedness**. Ummm . . . isn't this the same as horniness? Pretty much. Consider this question a freebie!

- • **Beans, the magical fruit**. Ladies and gentlemen, the one-man orchestra! Nope.

2. Basara, a name that can be licensed any-where

- • **In a fighting game**. In *Samurai Shodown*, the man with a chain and a three tiered blade at the end is the dreaded Basara.

- ■ **In the *Final Fantasy* series**. Nope, there is no Basara mentioned in the *Final Fantasy* series.

- • **For a character in the *Macross* series**. Basara is the guitarist in the anime *Macross 7*.

- • **In the title of a manga**. Basara is the title of an anime series wherein a young girl disguises herself as a young man to fulfill a prophecy.

3. For my beloved . . .

- ■ **Carlo**. Correct. Carlo is the love of Eva's life.

- • **Miguel**. Nope. Miguel is the man mistaken for Carlo by Eva.

- • **Santiago**. Nope. No such person exists in that anime.

- • **Bubba**. I think he's an Italian lover from Southern Italy . . .

4. All access

- ■ **Access to inspect the entire city**. Yup. The badge serves as a kind of key to everywhere in the city. So, where are the women's locker rooms in the city?

- • **Access to the mayor's confidential files**. Well this answer is incorrect. And those scandalous pictures of the mayor and a goat at the petting zoo are going to stay there!

- • **Access to a secret police room**. Yes, it's the place where they store all the donuts in times of crisis! Nope.

- • **Access to adult bars and strip joints, despite his age**. That's like saying you can get into an adult movie house at children's prices! I don't think so.

5. So, how would you know this?

- • **Cloud**. Only in an erotic world can Cloud's spiky hair have other talents than poking someone's eyes out . . . (Go ahead, use your imagination).

- • **Barret**. A macho man like him is not so likely to explore his feminine side out on the web.

- • **Sephiroth**. Probably your first guess, right? Too much attention has been given to him, so let someone else get the spotlight!

- ■ **Cid**. Correct. And Cid likes it rough, just like his shave. And according to this web site, it's Vincent that often can do that for him.

Random B

Random A seemed like such a convenient category, I decided to do a Random B! Any objections? I thought not.

1. Monsters you can save on to a disk

In *Monster Rancher*, what was the name of Holly's first monster she ever created using a disk?

- Suezo
- Tiger
- Mochi
- Porygon

2. Only in your dreams

In *Tenchi Muyō* TV, when the characters create their own worlds, which person doesn't have Tenchi as a love interest in her world?

- Ayeka
- Sasami
- Mihoshi
- Kiyone

3. Well, my current job is hard to list on a resume . . .

What was *Crying Freeman*'s occupation before he became an assassin?

- Construction worker
- Casino card dealer
- Pottery maker
- Porn star

4. Six out of seven ain't bad

In *Revolutionary Girl Utena*, what is the name of the first battle that Utena lost (according to episode 13?)

- Self
- Conviction
- Adoration
- Fear

5. Look out Miss Universe!

Who won the swimsuit competition in the *Tenchi Muyō* TV series?

- Ryoko
- Ayeka
- Mihoshi
- Nagi

Yūsuke from *Yū Yū Hakusho* (Poltergeist Report) is blaming you for that smell. He is about to shoot you with his finger, so what is the best way to protect yourself?

(a) With an iron shield (b) With a mirror (c) With sunglasses (d) With airbags

1. Monsters you can save on to a disk

- ■ **Suezo**. With that much of Suezo's body taken up by an eye, there isn't much room for a brain, now is there?

- **Tiger**. Tiger, tiger, burning bright . . . more like burned up for getting this answer wrong!

- **Mochi**. Doesn't he look more like bubblegum to you? Nope.

- **Porygon**. That's a Pokemon, you lame-brain!

2. Only in your dreams

- **Ayeka**. If Ayeka did not have Tenchi as a love interest, there is something clearly wrong with that picture.

- **Sasami**. Sasami has a crush on Tenchi in her dream world. It's also when she turns into Pretty Sammy and fires a Cupid-like arrow through Ayeka and Ryoko with pretty interesting results.

- **Mihoshi**. Mihoshi imagines herself married to Tenchi. She also imagined Sasami being her child. Is there something that Mihoshi is not telling us about?

- ■ **Kiyone**. Correct. Kiyone's dream world was simply to live in a world without Mihoshi.

3. Well, my current job is hard to list on a resume . . .

- **Construction worker**. Nope. It makes sense, but it's not the right answer.

- **Casino card dealer**. Nope. His past is not in those cards.

- ■ **Pottery maker**. Correct. And if pottery making gives you a body like that, then let me at that clay!

- **Porn star**. Although he certainly has the body, assassins shouldn't be so conspicuous that underwear size becomes a vital statistic. Among other stats, of course.

4. Six out of seven ain't bad

- **Self**. Nope. This is the first duel that Utena fought.

- ■ **Conviction**. Correct. In this duel, Utena lost to Tōya because he played upon her weakness. (And to tell you that would spoil the plot!)

- **Adoration**. Uh-uh. This is the battle that Nanami fought in order to win her brother's love. Love should conquer all, but incest is still kind of strange . . .

- **Fear**. There is no sword battle named "Fear" in the first seven battles in Utena.

5. Look out Miss Universe!

- **Ryoko**. Nope. Her two-piece red outfit was cute, but not cute enough to sway the judges.

- **Ayeka**. She may have been pretty, but lacked the grace of a "real" princess. Which pissed her off royally.

- **Mihoshi**. Mihoshi and high heels don't mix.

- ■ **Nagi**. A last-minute entry in the competition, she DOES have the best swimsuit in the contest.

■ *Answer to picture puzzle:* (b) With a mirror. The beam that comes from his finger will be reflected like a beam of light.

1. How to forget

In *Marmalade Boy*, what does Arimi do to forget about Yū when she and Yū have finally broken up?

- Writes poetry
- Runs track
- Goes on a vacation
- Uses electroshock therapy

2. Love juice

In *Kodomo no Omocha* (Child's Toy), what juice does Sana accidentally spill on Hayama before he suddenly does the dirty deed (I mean kissing her! Get your mind out of the gutter!)?

- Grape juice
- Orange juice
- Apple juice
- Lemonade

3. His and her affections

In *Kareshi to Kanojo no Jijō* (His and Her Circumstances), when do Yukino Miyazawa and Sōichirō Arima become an official couple?

- When they accidentally drink out of the same shake using the same straw
- When they hold each other's hand at a school meeting under the table
- When Arima kisses Yukino at the top of the ferris wheel
- After both of them feel hangovers and toss their cookies in the same bowl

4. Opening to fire

Who sings the opening theme song to *Flame of Recca*?

- Oystars
- Blue Heavenly
- Boys Be Lovely
- Van Gogo

5. Sentai vs. the mustard girl?

In the *Marmalade Boy* movie, a group known as Gastaman battles what enemy played by Miki?

- The Towel Monster
- The Tennis Ball of Doom
- The Lowfat Gelatinous Sorbet
- The Witch Queen

What does Kintarō Ōe from *Goldenboy* do with this piece of clothing?

(a) Uses it as a slingshot for two stones (b) Uses it to scoop two cups of water (c) Blindfolds someone with it (d) Wears it

1. How to forget

- **Writes poetry**. Roses are red, I wish you were dead, you left me broken-hearted, you gave me gas until I . . . nope. Next!

- ■ **Runs track**. Yes! Distract the pain in your heart with pain in your legs!

- **Goes on a vacation**. Nope. Not the right answer.

- **Uses electroshock therapy**. Buzz! Wrong!

2. Love juice

- ■ **Grape juice**. Correct. What more can I say here? Grape juice is essentially unfermented wine and this was Sana's way of getting Hayama drunk? I doubt it.

- **Orange juice**. Nope. It wasn't the type of juice that you should never drink after immediately brushing your teeth.

- **Apple juice**. You mean recycle juice (The stuff that looks the same going in as it comes out)? Uh-uh.

- **Lemonade**. Is that the same lemonade on Shinji's hand in *End of Evangelion*? Nope, I seriously doubt that, and this answer is wrong.

3. His and her affections

- **When they accidentally drink out of the same shake using the same straw**. Ooh, how lovely! Swapping germs!

- ■ **When they hold each other's hand at a school meeting under the table**. It was quite a dramatic moment when they held hands. That is the single moment that determined their realtionship.

- **When Arima kisses Yukino at the top of the ferris wheel**. Ooh! Entrapment!

- **After both of them feel hangovers and toss their cookies in the same bowl**. Ugh. I imagine that can't be too lovely. . . .

4. Opening to Fire

- ■ **Oystars**. What is an "Oystar" anyway? A shellfish with an idol complex?

- **Blue Heavenly**. Hmm . . . isn't that the name of a lingerie shop? Or is it a dessert?

- **Boys Be Lovely**. Wow, that's pretty bad. You fell for the broken-English name.

- **Van Gogh**. Hmm . . . with only one ear, I don't think he can hear well enough to do music.

5. Sentai vs. the mustard girl?

- ■ **The Towel Monster**. Correct. Who knew that a towel could be so evil?

- **The Tennis Ball of Doom**. Fear the tennis ball! Bow down to it! Hail it! Love it! Serve the tennis ball! Hmmm . . . uh-uh.

- **The Lowfat Gelatinous Sorbet**. It might be disgusting, but it has half of the calories of the "Fat Gelatinous Sorbet!"

- **The Witch Queen**. Sorry. Wrong answer here.

■ *Answer to picture puzzle:* (d) Wears it. Sometimes in order to understand women, you have to become one.

1. I don't want a man whose name sounds like caca!

A certain character that is thought to be dead comes back to try to marry Miaka in *Fushigi Yūgi*. What is his new name?

- Keika
- Kaika
- Kekka
- Kafka

2. I want TWO separate presents!

Which of these *Battle Arena Toshinden* characters was born on Christmas Eve?

- Eiji
- Kayin
- Sofia
- Ellis

3. It's rather obvious why she's not interested in him

In *One Pound Gospel*, Kosaku has a romantic interest in a woman even though she is:

- Married
- A nun
- "Does not swing his way"
- Dead

4. Guess who's coming to dinner?

Ryōga from *Ranma 1/2* comes to your house for a dinner party. What hors d'oeuvres should you keep away from him?

- Rumaki
- Baklava
- Ritz crackers with stale cheese
- Ladyfingers

5. If I smashed your finger, will you finally get mad?

Which of these characters NEVER got mad during the entire anime series?

- Marron from *Sorcerer Hunters*
- Quatre from *Gundam Wing*
- Rei from *Neon Genesis Evangelion*
- Fū from *Magic Knight Rayearth*

1. I don't want a man whose name sounds like caca!

- Keika
- ■ Kaika
- Kekka
- Kafka

Personally, I would not want to marry a man whose name sounds like "caca," either. Come to think of it, I have no desire to marry a man; I'd rather just play the field.

2. I Want TWO separate presents!

- Eiji
- ■ Kayin
- Sofia
- Ellis

If you did happen to be born very close to Christmas and you only get one present for both, you definitely have cheap parents. So cheap in fact, that they planned to have you on Christmas for that purpose! Yes, it is a conspiracy against you! Ha ha ha ha ha ha ha ha . . .

3. It's rather obvious why she's not interested in him

- **Married**. Nope. Sister Angela has no ring around her finger, but he is "married" in a way.
- ■ **A nun**. Correct. And if you wondered about that woman's love activity, the name says it.
- **"Does not swing his way."** Without a swing set around, that would certainly be hard to prove, won't it?

- **Dead**. Okay, necrophilia is just beyond me! What is this, "Last Dance with Mary Jane?"

4. Guess who's coming to dinner?

- ■ **Rumaki**. Correct. This is an appetizer with bacon and liver. In fact, I think I'll stay away from those myself.
- **Baklava**. Nope. This Greek treat is very sweet and flaky. Like Ranma on a good day.
- **Ritz crackers with stale cheese**. This isn't a good idea to serve but it works in a pinch when company comes over unexpectedly and is hungry and you have nothing in the fridge except some cheese you accidentally opened and some crackers that you incidentally had for two months. Can you tell that this has happened before?
- **Ladyfingers**. What a cannibalisitc sounding dessert. But they're delicious!

5. If I smashed your finger, will you finally get mad?

- **Marron from *Sorcerer Hunters***. Marron gets mad whenever it concerns Carrot's safety. So I guess he won't be too pleased if I took his brother, blindfolded him, and dumped him into a vat full of alligators.
- **Quatre from *Gundam Wing***. Quatre can get angry. But he's cute when he's angry! Let's go irritate him some more!
- ■ **Rei from *Neon Genesis Evangelion***. Nope, she just doesn't get mad and has as much personality as a blow-up doll sometimes.
- **Fū from *Magic Knight Rayearth***. Nope. Fū can get mad if she is really passionate about something.

The Fandom Menace: The Otakudom (Fandom) in America

A lot of music stars and actors are in the habit of thanking their fans for getting them to where they are now. Anime is no different; without the anime otaku fandom that exists in America, anime would not be as diverse and as widespread as we know it here on this side of the Pacific.

Without fansubs, anime fans couldn't appreciate the diversity of anime that is available in Japan. In fact, some anime would never have been commercialized in the United States had fansubs of that anime not appeared beforehand. A perfect example of this is *Fushigi Yūgi*; long before its commercial release it had been popular among anime fans and had webpages dedicated to it because of the existence of fansub tapes.

The Internet has helped expand the anime fanbase by bringing disparate and widespread communities of anime people together through discussion groups and chats. With fan pages come fan fiction, fan art, and dou-

1. Just as censor happy as we are

In the Philippine version of *Yū Yū Hakusho* (Poltergeist Report), which changes did they make?

- They covered up Hiei's third eye
- They edited all the death references so it looked like Yūsuke was unconscious
- They took out the scene where Yūsuke and Kuwabara kiss, even if that was censored
- They renamed Kurama "Denise"

2. Personal presents

In the *Maison Ikkoku* anime, what is the only present that Sōichirō gave to his wife, Kyōko?

- His journal
- A piyu-piyu apron
- A dog
- A rock with animal fossils

3. War is heck. And if done right here, tasty!

In *Princess Mononoke*, before the boars go to war with the humans, what do they do to prepare themselves?

- They gather in prayer to the nature god
- They use mud as war paint on themselves
- They kill one of their own as a sacrifice to the boar clan
- They mate to ensure continuation of the boar clan

4. Pointless love confessions

In Mahō *Tsukai Tai*, Nanaka confesses her love to Aburatsubo-senpai despite the fact that:

- He is already in love with another girl
- He is already in love with another guy
- She already has a boyfriend
- They are in the middle of battle

5. Keywords

In *Please Save My Earth*, what is Haruhiko's keyword to the database on the moon, according to the English dubbed version?

- ANSWER: _____

jinshi (fan manga). Webrings link pages together and create common anime communities, like a CLAMP webring or an Anime Music webring. And every anime fan knows about the Anime Web Turnpike (**www. anipike.com**), a directory with several organized lists of anime and manga links.

The first U.S. anime convention was held in 1991, and since then anime conventions have proliferated in North America. At conventions you find cos-play (people dressed as anime characters), a dealers' room filled with anime merchandise, hours of anime programming, and other featured events and activities.

Having such an established anime fandom base in America meant that, when the *Pokemon* seizure incident occurred in Japan and people began to attack anime in America, there was enough anime advocacy to respond and fight back. Without such efforts, anime(and possibly other forms of expression) might have been subjected to censorship and never gained a secure foothold in America.

1. Just as censor happy as we are

- **They covered up Hiei's third eye**. And why would they want to cover that up? Because they're afraid that the third eye is actually a hypnotizing device to buy *Yū Yū Hakusho* products? Nah.

- **They edited all the death references so it looked like Yūsuke was unconscious**. Oh yes, edit the first five episodes and get everyone lost. Good idea …

- **They took out the scene where Yūsuke and Kuwabara kiss, even if that was censored**. I doubt that they were THAT paranoid about it.

- ■ **They renamed Kurama "Denise."** Yes, just like in the U.S., sex changes can easily take place with a stroke of a pen! Less painful than a knife.

2. Personal presents

- **His journal**. Why give Kyōko a chance to say, "I've read your diary. Now who's Natsumi?"

- **A piyu-piyu apron**. What kind of a present is that? That's like getting your wife a vacuum cleaner!

- **A dog**. Nope. The dog that bears the name of Kyōko's dead husband is not a present from him.

- ■ **A rock with animal fossils**. Correct. I would have thought of flowers, candy, and perfume, but if that's what turns Kyōko on …

3. War is heck. And if done right here, tasty!

- **They gather in prayer to the nature god**. Uh-uh. Sorry.

- ■ **They use mud as war paint on themselves**. Correct. You have to motivate each other somehow and mud war paint seemed to do the trick.

- **They kill one of their own as a sacrifice to the boar clan**. Interesting idea, but not true.

- **They mate to ensure continuation of the boar clan**. Hee hee. I'd like to see Disney try to censor that if that were true!

4. Pointless love confessions

- **He is already in love with another girl**. Wrong. And if you saw the anime, you would know why.

- ■ **He is already in love with another guy**. Yes he is. And he does not attempt to hide it. And Nanaka does not attempt to hide it either, and when she reveals her love, it's rather touching.

- **She already has a boyfriend**. Nope. Nanaka's no skank.

- **They are in the middle of battle**. Surprisingly this happens a lot in anime. But just not with Nanaka and her senpai.

5. Keywords

- ■ **Seeking Paradise in a Dream**

I never have to seek paradise in a dream. Las Vegas is only 12 hours away from San Francisco if you drive really fast!

1. What a drag!

In *Ping Pong Club*, Maeno and Izawa force Kinoshita to dress in drag. However, once they ARE finished with him, Kinoshita turns out to be a very pretty girl, and Kinoshita starts to act like a woman. So much like a female that what does he want Maeno and Izawa to call him?

- Kino-chan
- Ojōsama
- Kitty
- Queen

2. Things you can do with an explorer

In *Eat Man*, Anina, who owns the Promise Hotel, cannot inherit the rest of her fortune until she

- Becomes an explorer
- Marries an explorer
- Kills an explorer
- Has an explorer "explore her"

3. Room with a view

In *The Four Immigrants Manga*, Henry walked into the bathroom when the lady of the house was taking a bath. What was the first thing he said?

- Wow! Why are you covered in bubbles?
- Wow! Your hair are two different colors!
- Wow! Those "melons" are huge!
- Wow! White folks really *are* white!

4. The end is near!

In *Martian Successor Nadesico*, why can't Akito Tenkawa watch the last episode of *Gekiganger 3*?

- The tape with the last episode has a bomb in it
- It reminds him too much of his dead friend, Jirō Yamada
- His girlfriend threatened to dump him if he did
- He doesn't want *Gekiganger* to end in his heart

5. Last question

Who wrote *The Anime Companion*?

- ANSWER: _____

© GAINAX/Project Eva • TV Tokyo

"When a person like me, Shinji Ikari from *Neon Genesis Evangelion*, needs a boost, nothing beats a can of UCC before I pilot my Eva! It's much better than _____."
(Fill in the blank with an appropriate brand.)

(a) Starbucks (b) 7UP (c) Minute Maid (d) Cats

1. What a drag!

- **Kino-chan**. Nope. Too familiar sounding.

- **Ojōsama**. Nope. He's not the spoiled daughter of a rich father.

- **Kitty**. Nope. He's not a Sanrio character.

- ■ **Queen**. Correct. What's even more disturbing is that he does that Queen laugh (you know, laughing like Naga from *Slayers* or Kodachi from *Ranma 1/2)*. And he does it TOO well.

2. Things you can do with an explorer

- **Becomes an explorer**. Nope. She's way too busy running the hotel.

- ■ **Marries an explorer**. Correct. Her father was saved by an explorer so he stipulated this for his daughter.

- **Kills an explorer**. What is this? An "announce your evil plan to the enitre world before you get away with it" plan? This ain't *Scooby Doo*, you know.

- **Has an explorer "explore her."** No, but I imagine Bolt Crank had fun trying when they woke up in bed together.

3. Room with a view

- **Wow! Why are you covered in bubbles?** Because she's taking a bubble bath … duh …

- **Wow! Your hair are two different colors!** Whoa. What exactly does he see in the bathtub anyway?

- **Wow! Those "melons" are huge!** And Henry is fired for making that statement.

- ■ **Wow! White folks really *are* white!** Correct! I guess it was just a surprise to him when he saw a white woman's bare skin, or he thought that she must have scrubbed really hard to become that white.

4. The end is near!

- **The tape with the last episode has a bomb in it**. But a true fan would watch it anyway!

- **It reminds him too much of his dead friend, Jirō Yamada**. But a true fan would watch it anyway!

- **His girlfriend threatened to dump him if he did.** But a true fan would watch it anyway!

- ■ **He doesn't want Gekiganger to end in his heart**. But a true fan would … oh yeah, this does sound like fanboy sentiment. . . .

5. Last Question

- ■ Gilles Poitras.

Thanks, Gilles! ::deep bow::

■ ***Answer to picture puzzle:*** (a) Starbucks. UCC is a Japanese brand of canned coffee.

Speed Rounds

The speed round instructions are pretty simple. There are twenty-five questions in each round, and all of the answers for each round begin with the letter indicated. How many can you get right?

Speed Round: K

a _____ of Ramune (Lamune)
b _____, the White Lion
c The young robot that needs 30,000 friends to become human
d _____ Delivery Service
e Hello Kitty's frog friend
f Here Is Greenwood's _____ Hasukawa
g _____ no Omocha
h The girl in Yū Yū Hakusho (Poltergeist Report) who cried the most when Yūsuke died
i Blue Seed's Mamoru _____
j In Pokemon, Misty's name in Japanese
k Eldest of the Tendō sisters in Ranma 1/2
l Girl who claimed to be a Tendō sister to take over the Tendō dojo
m Son of a Buddhist monk in Haunted Junction
n Dragonball bald fighter with six dots on his forehead
o Guy in Poltergiest Report who is easily mistaken for a girl
p Apartment manager in Maison Ikkoku
q Mihoshi's partner from the Galaxy Police in Tenchi Muyō
r In X, the dragon who works in the red-light district
s The psychic boy in Kimagure Orange Road
t A sex manual that is also a name of an anime by Gō Nagai
u Ryu's longtime sparring companion in Street Fighter
v First U.S. commercially released yaoi anime
w In X, the fate of the world is in his hands
x Guardian of the Clow cards in Card Captor Sakura
y Nadia's pet lion

Speed Round: R

a Sex-changing martial artist
b Rat pokemon
c Carl Macek's version of Macross
d Creator of Urusei Yatsura,
e Name of Miki's mom in Marmalade Boy
f Final Fantasy VIII's _____ Heartlily
g In Please Save My Earth, he was Shion in a past life
h Street Fighter's main character
i Final Fantasy III (or VI?) esper that can be used as an esper or a sword
j Bakabaka girl in Nadesico
k Sakuragi's rival teammate in Slam Dunk
l _____Girl Utena
m Go, Speed _____, go!
n _____ Hunter in Robotech
o In Gundam Wing, Quatre _____ Winner
p Elf Princess _____
q Parappa the _____
r _____ Kenshin
s Boy who turns into a puppy-wolf in Akazukin Cha-Cha
t Kimagure Orange _____
u Magic Knight _____
v Tenchi Muyō's cabbit that turns into a spaceship
w The American name of Yoroiden Samurai Troopers
x In Gundam Wing, _____ Peacecraft
y The fighting merman in the game Darkstalkers

Speed Round: K

a _____ of Ramune (Lamune): **Knights**

b _____, the White Lion: **Kimba**

c The young robot that needs 30,000 friends to become human: **Key**

d _____ Delivery Service: **Kiki's**

e Hello Kitty's frog friend: **(Kerokero) Keroppi**

f Here Is Greenwood's _____ Hasukawa: **Kazuya**

g _____ no Omocha: **Kodomo**

h The girl in Yū Yū Hakusho (Poltergeist Report) who cried the most when Yūsuke died: **Keiko**

i Blue Seed's Mamoru _____: **Kusanagi**

j In Pokemon, Misty's name in Japanese: **Kasumi**

k Eldest of the Tendō sisters in Ranma 1/2: (also) **Kasumi**

l Girl who claimed to be a Tendō sister to take over the Tendō dojo: **Kurumi**

m Son of a Buddhist monk in Haunted Junction: **Kazuo**

n Dragonball bald fighter with six dots on his forehead: **Krillin**

o Guy in Poltergiest Report who is easily mistaken for a girl: **Kurama**

p Apartment manager in Maison Ikkoku: **Kyōko Otonashi**

q Mihoshi's partner from the Galaxy Police in Tenchi Muyō: **Kiyone**

r In X, the dragon who works in the red-light district: **Karen**

s The psychic boy in Kimagure Orange Road: **Kyōsuke Kasuga**

t A sex manual that is also a name of an anime by Gō Nagai: **Kama Sutra**

u Ryu's longtime sparring companion in Street Fighter: **Ken**

v First U.S. commercially released yaoi anime: **Kizuna**

w In X, the fate of the world is in his hands: **Kamui**

x Guardian of the Clow cards in Card Captor Sakura: **Kero-chan**

y Nadia's pet lion: **King**

Speed Round: R

a Sex-changing martial artist: **Ranma**

b Rat pokemon: **Rattata**

c Carl Macek's version of Macross: **Robotech**

d Creator of Urusei Yatsura: **Rumiko Takahashi**

e Name of Miki's mom in Marmalade Boy: **Rumi**

f Final Fantasy VIII's _____ Heartlily: **Rinoa**

g In Please Save My Earth, he was Shion in a past life: **Rin Kobayashi**

h Street Fighter's main character: **Ryu**

i Final Fantasy III (or VI?) esper that can be used as an esper or a sword: **Ragnarok**

j "Bakabaka" girl in Nadesico: **Ruri**

k Sakuragi's rival teammate in Slam Dunk: **(Kaede) Rukawa**

l _____ Girl Utena: **Revolutionary**

m Go, Speed _____, go!: **Racer**

n _____ Hunter in Robotech: **Rick**

o In Gundam Wing, Quatre _____ Winner: **Rareba**

p Elf Princess _____: **Rane**

q Parappa the _____: **Rapper**

r _____ Kenshin: **Rurōni**

s Boy who turns into a puppy-wolf in Akazukin Cha-Cha: **Riiya-kun**

t Kimagure Orange _____: **Road**

u Magic Knight _____: **Rayearth**

v Tenchi Muyō's cabbit that turns into a spaceship: **Ryo-Ohki**

w The American name of Yoroiden Samurai Troopers: **Ronin Warriors**

x In Gundam Wing, _____ Peacecraft: **Relena**

y The fighting merman in the game Darkstalkers: **Rikuo**

Speed Round: S

a *Sailor Moon*'s Usagi's English name
b *Final Fantasy VIII* main character
c Basketball anime
d Combat force or units headed by Col. Treize of *Gundam Wing*
e *Final Fantasy VII*'s evil yet handsome man
f 14-year-old protagonist in *Grave of the Fireflies*
g The young *onmyōjitsu* of *Tokyo Bablyon*
h That *onmyōjitsu*'s lover/mortal enemy
i Captain Tsubasa's team plays this kind of sport
j *Mahō Tsukai Tai*'s witch in red
k Young boy who has a crush on Cha-Cha in *Akazukin Cha-Cha*
l Practitioner of Martial Arts Tea Ceremony in *Ranma 1/2*
m *Bastard!!* main character, Dark _____
n *Fatal Fury*: Mai _____
o *Card Captor* _____
p Miaka in *Fushigi Yūgi* is the _____ no Miko
q In *Pokemon*, Ash's name in Japanese
r In *Pokemon*, Gary's name in Japanese
s Father and son team in *Dragonball Z*
t Ayeka's sister in *Tenchi Muyō*
u The name of Noa Izumi's division in *Patlabor*
v In *Utena*, green-tressed VP of the student council
w Title for addressing an upperclassman
x Sailor who carries the Silence Gliave
y In *Rurōni Kenshin*, the type of sword Kenshin carries around with him

Speed Round: T

a Ryoko and Ayeka always fight over him
b In *Pokemon*, Brock's name in Japanese
c Pompous swordsman in *Ranma 1/2*: _____ Kunō
d Miaka's love interest in *Fushigi Yūgi*
e That person's teammate who is deathly afraid of water
f A Koopa Troopa is this kind of animal
g In *Sorcerer Hunters*, the sister without the whip that likes Carrot
h Baseball anime
i Cursed monster in *Princess Mononoke*
j _____ *Babylon*
k _____ *Who Hunt Elves*
l Utena's last name
m Playstation game where you act as a stealthy assassin
n Ryōga achieved super strength when he had this on his abs
o _____ Bogard from *Fatal Fury*
p *Ushio and* _____
q *My Neighbor* _____
r In *Maison Ikkoku*, Coach Mitaka teaches this sport
s Boy dressed in yellow in *Bushido Blade*
t In *Card Captor Sakura*, Sakura's best friend
u And her older brother
v *Gundam* series where the Gundams look like they have moustaches
w From *Fushigi Yūgi*, Hotohori's seiyū: _____ *Koyasu*
x *Hana Yori Dango*'s _____ Dōmyōji
y *Kaitō* (Magical Thief) *St.* _____

Speed Round: S

a *Sailor Moon*'s Usagi's English name: **Serena**

b *Final Fantasy VIII* main character: **Squall Leonhart**

c Basketball anime: *Slam Dunk*

d Combat force or units headed by Col. Treize of *Gundam Wing*: **Specials**

e *Final Fantasy VII*'s evil yet handsome man: **Sephiroth**

f 14-year-old protagonist in *Grave of the Fireflies*: **Seita**

g The young *onmyōjitsu* of *Tokyo Bablyon*: **Subaru Sumeragi**

h That *onmyōjitsu*'s lover/mortal enemy: **Seishirō** Sakurazuka

i Captain Tsubasa's team plays this kind of sport: **soccer**

j *Mahō Tsukai Tai*'s witch in red: **Sae Sawanoguchi**

k Young boy who has a crush on Cha-Cha in *Akazukin Cha-Cha*: **Shiine-Chan**

l Practitioner of Martial Arts Tea Ceremony in *Ranma 1/2*: **Sentarou**

m *Bastard!!* main character, Dark _____: **Schneider**

n *Fatal Fury*: Mai _____: **Shiranui**

o *Card Captor* _____: **Sakura**

p Miaka in *Fushigi Yūgi* is the _____ no Miko: **Suzaku**

q In *Pokemon*, Ash's name in Japanese: **Satoshi**

r In *Pokemon,* Gary's name in Japanese: **Shigeru**

s Father and son team in *Dragonball Z*: **Son Goku and Son Gohan**

t Ayeka's sister in *Tenchi Muyō*: **Sasami**

u The name of Noa Izumi's division in *Patlabor*: **Section 2**

v In *Utena*, green-tressed VP of the student council: **Saionji**

w Title for addressing an upperclassman: **Senpai**

x Sailor who carries the Silence Gliave: **Sailor Saturn**

y In *Rurōni Kenshin*, the type of sword Kenshin carries around with him: **Sakaba**

Speed Round: T

a Ryoko and Ayeka always fight over him: **Tenchi**

b In *Pokemon*, Brock's name in Japanese: **Takeshi**

c Pompous swordsman in *Ranma 1/2*: _____ Kunō: **Tatewaki**

d Miaka's love interest in *Fushigi Yūgi*: **Tamahome**

e That person's teammate who is deathly afraid of water: **Tasuki**

f A Koopa Troopa is this kind of animal: **turtle**

g In *Sorcerer Hunters*, the sister without the whip that likes Carrot: **Tiramisu**

h Baseball anime: **Touch**

i Cursed monster in *Princess Mononoke*: **Tataragami**

j _____ *Babylon*: **Tokyo**

k _____ *Who Hunt Elves*: **Those**

l Utena's last name: **Tenjō**

m Playstation game where you act as a stealthy assassin: **Tenchū**

n Ryōga achieved super strength when he had this on his abs: **tattoo**

o _____ Bogard from *Fatal Fury*: **Terry**

p *Ushio and* _____: **Tora**

q *My Neighbor* _____: **Totoro**

r In *Maison Ikkoku*, Coach Mitaka teaches this sport: **tennis**

s Boy dressed in yellow in *Bushido Blade*: **Tatsumi**

t In *Card Captor Sakura*, Sakura's best friend: **Tomoyo**

u And her older brother: **Tōya**

v *Gundam* series where the Gundams look like they have moustaches: **Turn-A Gundam**

w From *Fushigi Yūgi*, Hotohori's seiyū: _____ Koyasu: **Takehito**

x *Hana Yori Dango*'s _____ Dōmyōji: **Tsukasa**

y *Kaitō* (Magical Thief) *St.* _____: **Tail**

The Anime Trivia Rating Scale

You probably started out this book with some idea of where you stood on the anime continuum. Does your score confirm your (or your friends') suspicions? As you work through the various rounds and categories, mark each correct answer on the chart below. You can copy these pages as often as needed so each participant can track his or her own progress.

0–100 questions correct: You have a lot more to worry about than not doing well on this quizbook! I've designed the questions so that no one can get everything right, but it's not my fault that *you are statistically unlucky*. You should get about 100 questions correct just by guessing. So listen, don't go to Vegas. I mean it.

101–200 questions correct: Well, well, well . . . at least *you are an anime fan*. So you probably haven't seen a whole bunch of anime. There's no reason to blame you for having a life, you know. Either this, or you are one lucky guesser. Technically, you're an amateur. At least you shower.

201–300 questions correct: Well all right! *You are quite a big anime fan*. Not big meaning you wear a shirt size with more X's than a dirty movie. I mean you definitely know your anime more than the average person. You

have the makings of an otaku, but you're not quite there yet. You still have 10 or 20 pounds to go.

301–400 questions correct: Yes, *you are an otaku in full bloom* (just don't bloom in my direction without warning me first <^.^>). You have got more than a few fansubs in your tape collection, and probably know some Japanese (or you think you can fake it really well). You have the toys, the music, the posters, the wall scrolls, and you preach anime to the masses. And you could have bought yourself a church and pulpit with all the money you've spent on your love of anime.

401–500 questions correct: First of all, are you sure you didn't make the mistake of reading this quiz book from right to left as you would a Japanese manga? You probably did. But if you didn't, then I am truly impressed! You have a high capacity for useless information, and instead of becoming a millionaire, you became an anime otaku! Congratulations! *You are immersed in the hobby you love*, and I'm sure that within the next few years you will find a way to develop physical contact with your favorite animated catgirl/catboy. Until then, I hope there's someone who can challenge you better than than I can! *Ja mata*!

page 10	TOTAL	page 16	TOTAL	page 22	TOTAL	page 28	TOTAL	page 34	TOTAL	page 40	TOTAL
1. ___		1. ___		1. ___		1. ___		1. ___		1. ___	
2. ___		2. ___		2. ___		2. ___		2. ___		2. ___	
3. ___	___	3. ___	___	3. ___	___	3. ___	___	3. ___	___	3. ___	___
4. ___		4. ___		4. ___		4. ___		4. ___		4. ___	
5. ___		5. ___		5. ___		5. ___		5. ___		5. ___	

page 12	TOTAL	page 18	TOTAL	page 24	TOTAL	page 30	TOTAL	page 36	TOTAL	page 42	TOTAL
1. ___		1. ___		1. ___		1. ___		1. ___		1. ___	
2. ___		2. ___		2. ___		2. ___		2. ___		2. ___	
3. ___	___	3. ___	___	3. ___	___	3. ___	___	3. ___	___	3. ___	___
4. ___		4. ___		4. ___		4. ___		4. ___		4. ___	
5. ___		5. ___		5. ___		5. ___		5. ___		5. ___	

page 14	TOTAL	page 20	TOTAL	page 26	TOTAL	page 32	TOTAL	page 38	TOTAL	page 44	TOTAL
1. ___		1. ___		1. ___		1. ___		1. ___		1. ___	
2. ___		2. ___		2. ___		2. ___		2. ___		2. ___	
3. ___	___	3. ___	___	3. ___	___	3. ___	___	3. ___	___	3. ___	___
4. ___		4. ___		4. ___		4. ___		4. ___		4. ___	
5. ___		5. ___		5. ___		5. ___		5. ___		5. ___	

Column Total ___   Column Total ___   Column Total ___   Column Total ___   Column Total ___   Column Total ___

page 46	TOTAL	page 62	TOTAL	page 78	TOTAL	page 94	TOTAL	page 110	TOTAL	page 126	TOTAL
1. ___		1. ___		1. ___		1. ___		1. ___		1. ___	
2. ___		2. ___		2. ___		2. ___		2. ___		2. ___	
3. ___	___	3. ___	___	3. ___	___	3. ___	___	3. ___	___	3. ___	___
4. ___		4. ___		4. ___		4. ___		4. ___		4. ___	
5. ___		5. ___		5. ___		5. ___		5. ___		5. ___	

page 48	TOTAL	page 64	TOTAL	page 80	TOTAL	page 96	TOTAL	page 112	TOTAL	page 128	TOTAL
1. ___		1. ___		1. ___		1. ___		1. ___		1. ___	
2. ___		2. ___		2. ___		2. ___		2. ___		2. ___	
3. ___	___	3. ___	___	3. ___	___	3. ___	___	3. ___	___	3. ___	___
4. ___		4. ___		4. ___		4. ___		4. ___		4. ___	
5. ___		5. ___		5. ___		5. ___		5. ___		5. ___	

page 50	TOTAL	page 66	TOTAL	page 82	TOTAL	page 98	TOTAL	page 114	TOTAL	page 130	TOTAL
1. ___		1. ___		1. ___		1. ___		1. ___		1. ___	
2. ___		2. ___		2. ___		2. ___		2. ___		2. ___	
3. ___	___	3. ___	___	3. ___	___	3. ___	___	3. ___	___	3. ___	___
4. ___		4. ___		4. ___		4. ___		4. ___		4. ___	
5. ___		5. ___		5. ___		5. ___		5. ___		5. ___	

page 52	TOTAL	page 68	TOTAL	page 84	TOTAL	page 100	TOTAL	page 116	TOTAL	page 132	TOTAL
1. ___		1. ___		1. ___		1. ___		1. ___		1. ___	
2. ___		2. ___		2. ___		2. ___		2. ___		2. ___	
3. ___	___	3. ___	___	3. ___	___	3. ___	___	3. ___	___	3. ___	___
4. ___		4. ___		4. ___		4. ___		4. ___		4. ___	
5. ___		5. ___		5. ___		5. ___		5. ___		5. ___	

page 54	TOTAL	page 70	TOTAL	page 86	TOTAL	page 102	TOTAL	page 118	TOTAL	page 134	TOTAL
1. ___		1. ___		1. ___		1. ___		1. ___		1. ___	
2. ___		2. ___		2. ___		2. ___		2. ___		2. ___	
3. ___	___	3. ___	___	3. ___	___	3. ___	___	3. ___	___	3. ___	___
4. ___		4. ___		4. ___		4. ___		4. ___		4. ___	
5. ___		5. ___		5. ___		5. ___		5. ___		5. ___	

page 56	TOTAL	page 72	TOTAL	page 88	TOTAL	page 104	TOTAL	page 120	TOTAL	page 136	TOTAL
1. ___		1. ___		1. ___		1. ___		1. ___		1. ___	
2. ___		2. ___		2. ___		2. ___		2. ___		2. ___	
3. ___	___	3. ___	___	3. ___	___	3. ___	___	3. ___	___	3. ___	___
4. ___		4. ___		4. ___		4. ___		4. ___		4. ___	
5. ___		5. ___		5. ___		5. ___		5. ___		5. ___	

page 58	TOTAL	page 74	TOTAL	page 90	TOTAL	page 106	TOTAL	page 122	TOTAL	page 138	TOTAL
1. ___		1. ___		1. ___		1. ___		1. ___		1. ___	
2. ___		2. ___		2. ___		2. ___		2. ___		2. ___	
3. ___	___	3. ___	___	3. ___	___	3. ___	___	3. ___	___	3. ___	___
4. ___		4. ___		4. ___		4. ___		4. ___		4. ___	
5. ___		5. ___		5. ___		5. ___		5. ___		5. ___	

page 60	TOTAL	page 76	TOTAL	page 92	TOTAL	page 108	TOTAL	page 124	TOTAL	page 140	TOTAL
1. ___		1. ___		1. ___		1. ___		1. ___		1. ___	
2. ___		2. ___		2. ___		2. ___		2. ___		2. ___	
3. ___	___	3. ___	___	3. ___	___	3. ___	___	3. ___	___	3. ___	___
4. ___		4. ___		4. ___		4. ___		4. ___		4. ___	
5. ___		5. ___		5. ___		5. ___		5. ___		5. ___	

Column Total ___   Column Total ___   Column Total ___   Column Total ___   Column Total ___   Column Total ___

page 142	TOTAL	*page 152*	TOTAL	*page 162*	TOTAL
1. ___		1. ___		1. ___	
2. ___		2. ___		2. ___	
3. ___	___	3. ___	___	3. ___	___
4. ___		4. ___		4. ___	
5. ___		5. ___		5. ___	

page 144	TOTAL	*page 154*	TOTAL	*page 164*	TOTAL
1. ___		1. ___		1. ___	
2. ___		2. ___		2. ___	
3. ___	___	3. ___	___	3. ___	___
4. ___		4. ___		4. ___	
5. ___		5. ___		5. ___	

page 146	TOTAL	*page 156*	TOTAL	*page 166*	TOTAL
1. ___		1. ___		1. ___	
2. ___		2. ___		2. ___	
3. ___	___	3. ___	___	3. ___	___
4. ___		4. ___		4. ___	
5. ___		5. ___		5. ___	

page 148	TOTAL	*page 158*	TOTAL	*page 168*	TOTAL
1. ___		1. ___		1. ___	
2. ___		2. ___		2. ___	
3. ___	___	3. ___	___	3. ___	___
4. ___		4. ___		4. ___	
5. ___		5. ___		5. ___	

page 150	TOTAL	*page 160*	TOTAL
1. ___		1. ___	
2. ___		2. ___	
3. ___	___	3. ___	___
4. ___		4. ___	
5. ___		5. ___	

page 170

SPEED ROUND K

a. ___
b. ___
c. ___
d. ___
e. ___

f. ___
g. ___
h. ___
i. ___
j. ___
k. ___
l. ___
m. ___
n. ___
o. ___
p. ___
q. ___
r. ___
s. ___
t. ___
u. ___
v. ___
w. ___
x. ___
y. ___

SPEED ROUND R

a. ___
b. ___
c. ___
d. ___
e. ___
f. ___
g. ___
h. ___
i. ___
j. ___
k. ___
l. ___

m. ___
n. ___
o. ___
p. ___
q. ___
r. ___
s. ___
t. ___
u. ___
v. ___
w. ___
x. ___
y. ___

PAGE 172

SPEED ROUND S

a. ___
b. ___
c. ___
d. ___
e. ___
f. ___
g. ___
h. ___
i. ___
j. ___
k. ___
l. ___
m. ___
n. ___
o. ___
p. ___
q. ___
r. ___

s. ___
t. ___
u. ___
v. ___
w. ___
x. ___
y. ___

SPEED ROUND T

a. ___
b. ___
c. ___
d. ___
e. ___
f. ___
g. ___
h. ___
i. ___
j. ___
k. ___
l. ___
m. ___
n. ___
o. ___
p. ___
q. ___
r. ___
s. ___
t. ___
u. ___
v. ___
w. ___
x. ___
y. ___

Column Total ___	Column Total ___	Column Total ___	Column Total ___	Column Total ___	Column Total ___

Total correct answers: _____

Anime Index